GROWING UP GODLESS

Growing Up Godless

NON-RELIGIOUS CHILDHOODS
IN CONTEMPORARY ENGLAND

ANNA STRHAN &
RACHAEL SHILLITOE

PRINCETON UNIVERSITY PRESS
PRINCETON & OXFORD

Published by Princeton University Press
41 William Street, Princeton, New Jersey 08540
99 Banbury Road, Oxford OX2 6JX

press.princeton.edu

Library of Congress Cataloging-in-Publication Data

Names: Strhan, Anna, author. | Shillitoe, Rachael, 1989– author.
Title: Growing up godless : non-religious childhoods in contemporary England / Anna Strhan and Rachael Shillitoe.
Description: Princeton : Princeton University Press, [2025] | Includes bibliographical references and index.
Identifiers: LCCN 2024040965 (print) | LCCN 2024040966 (ebook) | ISBN 9780691247250 (pbk.) | ISBN 9780691247267 | ISBN 9780691247243 (ebook)
Subjects: LCSH: Skepticism. | Agnosticism—Study and teaching. | BISAC: SOCIAL SCIENCE / Sociology of Religion | RELIGION / General
Classification: LCC B837 .S86 2025 (print) | LCC B837 (ebook) | DDC 211/.72—dc3/ eng/20241015
LC record available at https://lccn.loc.gov/2024040965
LC ebook record available at https://lccn.loc.gov/2024040966

British Library Cataloging-in-Publication Data is available

Editorial: Fred Appel and James Collier
Production Editorial: Ali Parrington
Jacket/Cover Design: Felix Summ
Production: Lauren Reese
Publicity: William Pagdatoon and Charlotte Coyne
Copyeditor: Tash Siddiqui

Jacket Image: Mathias Reding / Unsplash

This book has been composed in Arno

Printed in the United States of America

10 9 8 7 6 5 4 3 2 1

CONTENTS

ACKNOWLEDGEMENTS

MANY PEOPLE have contributed to the completion of this book. Our greatest debt is to the children, parents, and staff at the schools who took part in this study and shared their experiences, ideas, thoughts, beliefs, and time with us. We learnt so much from you all. The research for this book was funded by grants from the John Templeton Foundation (Grant ID #60624) managed by the University of Kent and by the Queen's University of Belfast (Grant ID #61928), and the Leverhulme Trust (Grant ID ECF-2021-212). Special thanks to our collaborator Lois Lee, who initially encouraged us to pursue this research by suggesting that scholars of non-religion would be interested in a study focusing on children, and who subsequently, as collaborator on the 'Becoming Non-Believers' project, provided an invaluable contribution to our analysis and helped sharpen our arguments and the direction of the book. Lois has been a generous interlocutor and supporter of our research throughout all its stages and we are incredibly grateful. The research also benefitted significantly from the feedback and suggestions of the Advisory Board members of our 'Nonreligious Childhood' and 'Becoming Non-Believers' projects: Gordon Lynch, Abby Day, Ellie Lee, Colin Campbell, Valerie van Mulukom, and Hugh Turpin. We are also grateful for administrative support at the Department of Sociology at the University of York, the School of European Languages and Cultures at the University of Kent, and to Kat Osborne for research assistance.

Material in this book has previously appeared in earlier journal publications. Sections of chapters 2 and 3, some data excerpts in chapter 1, as well as discussion of our methods and research questions, can be found in 'The Stickiness of Non-Religion? Intergenerational Transmission and the Formation of Non-Religious Identities in Childhood', *Sociology* 53(6): 1094–110 (2019). Some of the material about Religious Education in chapter 3 was published in 'The Experiences of Non-Religious Children in Religious Education', *Journal of Religious Education* 70: 261–72 (2022), and some data extracts in this chapter were published in '"Just Leave It Blank": Non-Religious Children and their Negotiation of Prayer in School', *Religion* 50(4): 615–35 (2020). The identification and discussion of humanism interwoven in the book was developed in 'Becoming Humanist: Worldview Formation and the Emergence of Atheist Britain', *Sociology of Religion* (2024), co-authored with Lois Lee, and material from that article features in sections of chapters 1–3 and 5, as well as in the Introduction and Conclusion. We are grateful to the publishers of these journals for granting us permission to reprint this material here, and to the anonymous reviewers and editors of those journals for their helpful comments.

The book has benefitted from the opportunity to present papers at conferences, seminars, and symposia. These have included: the Nonreligion and Secularity Research Network conference (2018, 2021); the British Sociological Association Sociology of Religion Study Group annual conference (2018); the British Association for the Study of Religion conference (2018); the University of Leeds Centre for Religion and Public Life research seminar (2018); the European Association for Research on Learning and Instruction SIG 19 conference (2020); King's College London INFORM seminar (2021); the European Sociological Association Sociology of Religion Research Network biannual conference (2022); the American Sociological Association annual meeting (2022, 2023); the Association for the Sociology of Religion annual meeting (2022, 2023); the Association of University Lecturers in Religion and Education annual conference (2022); the Society for the Scientific Study of Religion annual conference (2022); Nonreligion in a Complex Future: Meet the Author seminar series (2022); and Régimes de Vérité International Colloquium, Groupe Sociétés Religions Laïcités, CNRS, EPHE (2023). We had the good fortune to be invited to organize a 'manuscript-meets-critics' session at the Association for the Sociology of Religion annual meeting in Philadelphia in 2023, and are enormously grateful to our critics—Joe Blankholm, Rebecca Catto, and Anna Hickey-Moody—who provided invaluable comments and insightful feedback on draft chapters, which helped spur us on to get the manuscript finished. Ruth Sheldon, Lois Lee, and Jeff Guhin also read and offered helpful feedback on early drafts of specific chapters which helped clarify what ended up in the book. Martin Block read drafts of every chapter at least once and provided encouragement, support, and insightful suggestions throughout. The book is immeasurably better as a result of all of their contributions. Finally, we would like to thank our editor Fred Appel, the insightful anonymous reviewers he found, James Collier, Ali Parrington, everyone in the production team at Princeton University Press, and copy-editor Tash Siddiqui, who have all greatly contributed to the development of the volume.

Beyond the academic world, our heartfelt thanks, as ever, to our families and friends for their encouragement and support, in innumerable ways.

GROWING UP GODLESS

Introduction

SHAUN AND AVA were nine-year-old pupils at Sunnybank Community Primary School. As they sat at a table drawing pictures of the things that they saw as important in their lives, Rachael asked them, 'I was wondering if you could tell me about what you believe in.' Shaun replied, 'I believe in chocolate', and Ava said, 'I just believe that unicorns are real and Pegasus. Pegasus and unicorns.' Shaun went on, 'I believe that chemicals in the universe created Earth and that we evolved from fish to monkeys and then to humans. I believe in evolution . . . I don't believe that God made the earth and made humans. . . . Because if you really look into it, it just isn't true, and I really know it.'

Rachael asked Shaun if he'd always not believed in God. He replied that he 'used to think God was real', but when he was six years old, he'd asked his mum whether she believed in God, and she'd replied that she didn't, because she didn't believe God created the earth. Shaun carried on:

> SHAUN: So then I started thinking, and I just thought God really doesn't exist. I think my mum is talking the truth.
> AVA: Nobody can have superpowers; it's just nonsense.
> SHAUN: I asked my dad as well, and . . . well, his religion because he's part-Pakistani—he said that people believe in . . . Allah, that Allah is another way of saying God—that's what he told me—and that Jesus was just a helper of God, he wasn't his son . . . I was thinking of ways to think if he was real, if he wasn't. But then I thought, I don't think he really is. So then I just thought he's not real.

Shaun said that he then asked his mum:

> SHAUN: 'What are you if you're not a Christian? Are you just a nonbeliever?' Mum said, 'if you don't believe in God or you don't believe

in Allah then you're . . . atheist'. So when I was about seven, I started
calling myself an atheist.

AVA: I don't believe in God really, but until my parents tell me or until I
get christened, then I'll be an atheist too.

As non-religious nine-year-olds, Shaun and Ava are not unusual for their generation. Indeed, Britain and many parts of Europe and North America have seen
sharp rises in those saying they have 'no religion' in surveys alongside declining
institutional Christian belief and belonging. This has been especially pronounced amongst younger generations. In the US, for instance, the General
Social Survey of 2018 reported that a third of those aged eighteen to twenty-nine
cited 'no religion' as their own 'religious preference'.[1] This rise of 'no religion' in
many western societies is taking place at the same time as increasing religious
plurality also feeds into rapidly shifting religious landscapes (Beaman 2022). Yet
despite growing public and academic interest in 'non-religion', we know little
about the beliefs, concerns, and experiences of this new generation of children
for whom being non-religious is the 'new normal' (Woodhead 2016) or about
how their non-religion and non-belief are being formed in everyday life.

Drawing on interviews and ethnographic fieldwork conducted with
children, their parents, and teachers in different parts of England, this book
addresses this gap through examining how children are growing up non-
religious, and what this means—both for the children themselves and for how
we think about the nature of 'non-religion' and 'non-belief' in landscapes of
growing religious diversification. Moreover, looking beyond the negative aspects of *non*-religiosity or *non*-belief, the book examines the positive, substantive dimensions of what these children believed in and cared about, and how
their ways of knowing the world were created and sustained through particular
spaces, places, and relations with others.

Approaching the Formation of Non-Religion
and Non-Belief

The rise of those identifying as 'non-religious' in many former liberal Christian
democracies has been rapid, accompanied by declining institutional religious
belief and belonging (Woodhead 2017). In Britain, 'no religion' has overtaken

1. As Stephen Bullivant notes, the figures are even higher for the 2021 General Social Survey,
with 44% of 18- to 29-year-olds identifying as nones, but the pandemic conditions of 2021 mean
that the very sharp rise between 2018 and 2021 should be treated with caution (2022: 8).

Christianity as the majority identity, while only around half the overall population now express 'some sort of belief in some sort of God' (Voas and Bruce 2019: 27). This growth of 'non-religious' identification reflects changes taking place in many countries around the world, although the pace and form of these shifts vary (Lee et al. 2023). In the US, around a quarter of adults now say they have no religion, but this growth of the US 'nones' has been relatively recent (Bullivant 2022), while Sweden, for instance, secularized historically early compared with many other societies (Kasselstrand et al. 2023). Belief in God(s) is also waning in most places with rising populations of the 'nones', with this decline tending to follow on from falling religious identification as part of a 'secular transition' (Voas 2007; Lee et al. 2023). This decline in belief in God is evident in a wide variety of countries, with the European Values Survey and World Values Survey (1981–2020) revealing a number of countries having a decrease of more than 20 percentage points over the years measured by the surveys, including Britain, Belgium, Spain, Australia, the United States, Iceland, South Korea, Norway, and New Zealand (Kasselstrand et al. 2023: 66). And some of these decreases have been dramatic, as Isabella Kasselstrand and her colleagues note: in Britain, belief in God declined from 82 to 48 per cent between 1982 and 2018, while in Sweden, it declined from 60 per cent in 1982 to 36 per cent in 2017.

The decline of religion is hardly a new story in sociology. Indeed, secularization theory—situating the declining significance of religion as a consequence of modernization—can be traced back to the early nineteenth-century writings of Henri Saint-Simon and Auguste Comte. However, the recent rapid growth of non-religious populations in many parts of the world has fuelled renewed scholarly and popular interest in the reasons for this change. Within this literature, it is now widely accepted that the rise of non-religion is due to a 'generational effect' (Gärtner and Hennig 2022). More people are self-identifying as 'non-religious' not because adults are losing their religion, but because each new generation is less religious than the previous one, with older generations of Christians gradually being replaced by those raised with no religious affiliation (Voas and Bruce 2019; Stolz et al. 2023; Kasselstrand et al. 2023). Moreover, this population of the 'nones' looks set to increase further over the coming years, as they have children and pass on their non-religion to the next generation (Woodhead 2017). This suggests that the growth in non-religious identification is increasingly 'driven by what happens to people *before* they reach adulthood, not after it' (Tervo-Niemelä 2021: 444), which begs the question: what is happening before adulthood that drives these changes?

Much of what we currently know about the growth of the 'nones' across generations has emerged from studies which have tended to frame these processes in terms of the 'success' or 'failure' of religious transmission. Existing studies have demonstrated that waning religion and belief in North America and Europe is linked to both a decline in parents seeking to bring their children up as religious and an increase in parents giving their children choice in relation to religion, which leads them to disaffiliate as teenagers (Stolz et al. 2016; Thiessen and Wilkins-Laflamme 2017; Tervo-Niemelä 2021). A large-scale mixed-methods study exploring the transmission of religion across three generations in Germany, Hungary, Italy, Canada, and Finland, led by Christel Gärtner, has revealed the relative absence of religion in family life in East Germany (Müller and Porada 2022) and has examined how a non-religious habitus develops over three generations in a German family context (Gärtner 2022). Focusing on the United States and Canada, Joel Thiessen and Sarah Wilkins-Laflamme (2017) demonstrate that feeding into the rise of the 'nones' is an increase in 'irreligious socialization', while Christel Manning's (2015) qualitative study of how unaffiliated parents in the US are raising their children underscored the imperative of 'personal worldview choice' for these parents, and how their parenting often incorporates aspects of religion in ways that challenge binary categorizations of their practices as *either* religious *or* secular.

Examining the generational effect of declining religiosity through an analysis of churchgoing in West Germany, Jörg Stolz and colleagues (2023) assessed the relative significance of different factors often presented as key predictors of religious decline: family disruption or divorce, parents' liberal values, secular leisure activities competing with religious attendance, urbanism, pluralism, and the secularity of the broader environment in which children are growing up. They found—aside from modest effects for family disruption and secular context—no *one* specific predictor is mainly responsible for religious decline, and therefore suggest that 'perhaps religious socialization fails because of a *general and societal* change in attitudes to both socialization and religion' (2023: 18). For instance, seeing religion as a matter of personal choice is part of a broader cultural valuing of autonomy, which as they note, is 'almost universally shared in western societies' rather than associated with particular kinds of family attributes. They conclude that perhaps what matters most in determining (non)religiosity is not so much the families' characteristics but rather 'the dominant worldview' of the broader social context in which socialization takes place 'and the perceived social significance of religion' (2023: 19). As well as parents' impact, previous studies have also identified education as contributing to declining religiosity, as educational practices increasingly afford children autonomy to question parental religious beliefs (Stolz 2020; Klingenberg and Sjö 2019).[2] Yet we know little about *how* children engage with the aspects of religion they encounter in schools or the role this plays in shaping their non-religiosity.

Taken together, these studies indicate that what happens during childhood is crucial to understanding the rise and formation of non-religious and non-believing worldviews. However, we currently lack crucial investigations based on data from non-religious children themselves about their own experiences and perspectives. The literature to date has largely drawn from retrospective narratives from adults reflecting on their own childhoods or describing their current child-rearing practices, or has examined teenagers' experiences, and it has primarily focused on family contexts. The historic marginalization of children's perspectives in the sociology of religion means there has been little qualitative research exploring the formation of non-religion and atheism with children, especially children within 'middle childhood' (aged seven to eleven)—the period during which children are becoming conscious of their non-religious identities and worldviews, as Shaun's comments suggest. Moreover, we know little about children's experiences in schools or about the interplay of processes in homes, schools, and other spaces which create, sustain, or strengthen their non-religiosity. If, as Stolz and colleagues (2023) argue, what really matters is 'the dominant worldview' in which children are growing up, then what *is* the dominant worldview that children are encountering and what are its overarching values? When and where, in practical terms, do they encounter it, and how does it feed into their non-religion and non-belief and changing locations of the sacred and spiritual in contemporary social life? And how do they contribute to shaping its textures?

Addressing these questions, this book is in conversation with a burgeoning interdisciplinary literature examining non-religion, atheism, irreligion, and other forms of 'religion's others' (Smith and Cragun 2019). This literature seeks to move beyond how previously dominant sociological lenses were shaped by secularization theories that viewed non-religion through the lens of 'subtraction' and

2. A number of studies have indicated that education in broad terms, such as length of compulsory schooling, can have a negative impact on religious and paranormal beliefs (e.g., Mocan and Pogorelova 2014). National education policies regulating the place of religion within schooling may also play a role. In contexts such as England, where children in state-funded schools receive Religious Education and schools are legally mandated to provide acts of collective worship, primary schools represent a key site in which many children first encounter ideas related to belief in God(s) (Strhan and Shillitoe 2019).

portrayed non-religiosity and secularity in terms of the 'absence' of religion (Taylor 2007). While secularization accounts, as Lois Lee puts it, were 'preoccupied with how far people and societies have moved away from their supposed religious pasts', this work on non-religion 'shifts attention to the ways in which people and societies may move towards non-religious presents' (Lee 2015: 14). Seeking to explore the 'substantive' nature of non-religion (Lee 2015), this literature is deepening understanding of non-religious, secular and non-believing identities, imaginaries, and practices, and their place 'in the formation of subjectivities and societies' (Lee 2019a: 45). The term 'non-religion' in this literature is generally taken, following Lee's definition, to refer to 'any phenomenon— position, perspective, or practice—that is primarily understood in relation to religion but which is not itself considered to be religious. Alternatively expressed, non-religion is a phenomenon understood in contradistinction to religion' (Lee 2015: 32). In North America, this 'non-religiosity' often tends to be termed 'secularism' or 'secularity', and the non-religious as 'secular'.[3] Within this field, the terms 'unbelief', 'non-belief' and 'non-believing' refer to a lack of belief in traditionally religious phenomena, such as belief in God, rather than the idea of having no beliefs (Lee et al. 2017; Blankholm 2022). In what follows, we follow these established uses of non-religion and non-belief, and when using 'secular' and 'secularity' analytically, we refer specifically to 'the subordination of religious authorities and concerns to other ones' (Lee 2015: 190).

The fast-growing literature on the non-religious includes an emerging body of work exploring non-religion and atheism amongst teenagers and young adults.[4] Yet although children's involvement or non-involvement in religion is often the subject of highly politicized debates, their voices are generally absent within these. Thus, in providing insight into children's perspectives on the place of (non)religion in their lives, school worlds, and wider society, this book aims to enrich understanding not only of the formation of non-religion and atheism but also—and perhaps more importantly—of how non-religious children are growing up and making their way in the world, and to learn from them about their values, priorities, and experiences in relation to religion.

---

3. Lee (2015: 190) notes that the term 'secular' is used in such a variety of ways—including the absence of religion, antipathy to religion, religious pluralism—as to often be confusing, and argues that distinguishing between non-religion and secularity enables examination of both phenomena with greater clarity.

4. See, for example, Catto and Eccles (2013); Hemming and Madge (2017); Singleton et al. (2021); Nynäs et al. (2022).

While non-religion and non-belief are 'troublesome words', in a sense 'pulling us back to what they are trying to get away from' (Engelke 2017: 135), the book demonstrates how what is at stake in the act of negating these—also troublesome—contested terms (God, gods, belief, religion) is deeply revealing of what does and does not matter to children, as well as of the changing place of religion in contemporary social life.

Studying Non-Religious Childhoods

This book presents the findings of multi-sited ethnographic research which set out to explore how, when, where, and with whom children are growing up non-religious and non-believing in three contrasting areas of England, and how they live their lives in relation to religion. As well as understanding the factors contributing to the children's turning away from religion or theism such as the absence of religion in their upbringing, we also wanted to explore the relations between the children's non-belief and substantive other-than-religious worldviews, such as the humanist, agnostic, subjectivist, or anti-existential worldviews that Lois Lee (2015) identified in her study of the non-religious in south-east England, or the indifferent or the spiritual-but-not-religious worldviews that Andrew Singleton and colleagues (2021) found amongst non-religious teenagers in Australia.

Addressing these questions required spending time with children and observing how they engage with aspects of religion and asking them about their beliefs, experiences, and the presence (or not) of particular elements of religion in their lives. Moreover, gaining deeper insight into the place of religion in their homes and schools and how children's views relate to their family and school contexts required talking to their parents and teachers as well. Grant funding from the 'Understanding Unbelief' research programme enabled us to carry out ethnographic fieldwork and interviews with children, their parents, and teachers in three state-funded primary schools,[5] involving six–seven weeks' participant observation in each school in 2017–2018. A detailed description of the research methods, sample, and interviews is included in the appendix. Institutional ethical approval was obtained and ethical issues were taken seriously throughout the research. Both child and parental consent were obtained for child participants, and all respondents and schools have been anonymized and names replaced with pseudonyms.

5. Primary schooling in England is for children aged 4–11.

To explore how the children's experiences were shaped by particular contexts, the research was conducted in schools located in contrasting geographical 'microclimates' of (non)religion in England (Voas and McAndrew 2012). The first school, St Peter's, was a Church of England Academy[6] located in an urban area in southern England, with a diverse pupil population in terms of race, ethnicity and religion. Although the school did not have faith-based admissions criteria,[7] its religious character was tangibly present: wall displays, school mottos, school letters' headers and footers, strong links with the local church, and the presence of prayers, hymns and Christian teachings in assemblies all clearly communicated the Christian character of the school. There was also a strong focus on diversity and inclusion in the school ethos—including religious diversity—and the children interviewed made it clear that you did not have to be Christian to attend. Religious Education lessons were taught weekly here.

Waterside Primary Academy was located in a largely middle-class suburban setting in northern England, chosen to enable insight into suburban cultures of non-belief beyond stereotypes of 'godless suburbs'. Formerly a community primary school, it had joined a multi-academy trust which included both faith and non-faith schools. Religion was much less visible here than at St Peter's or Sunnybank, with a small cupboard and a wall display area for Religious Education down one corridor. Other curriculum subjects often took precedence over Religious Education, and while the school held regular assemblies, these were sometimes weekly rather than daily occurrences, and did not typically feature references to religion. Songs in assemblies tended to be pop songs or songs from films rather than hymns. There had recently been tensions at the school with some non-religious parents due to a local evangelical group having come into the school to lead some assemblies. The local vicar occasionally led assemblies but this was limited to festivals such as Easter and Christmas.

Our final fieldsite, Sunnybank Community Primary School, was located in a predominantly rural setting in north-west England, in a largely working-class area where a relatively low proportion of the population identified as non-religious. While not a faith school, there were aspects of Christian material culture around the school, such as crucifixes or plaques referring to angels. The school had links with the local church, which pupils often visited for Religious

6. Academies are state-funded independent schools which are run free from local authority control, often operating as part of academy trusts. Many are run by faith groups.

7. This was due to its former status prior to becoming an academy as a voluntary-controlled school. See chapter 3.

Education. Assemblies took place most days and these included prayers. The region the school was located in was divided in terms of race and ethnicity, and local tensions, racism, and hate crime had led the local authority to establish various initiatives to promote social cohesion. The local schools in the area largely mirrored residential divisions in terms of their pupil intake, with the student population at Sunnybank mainly white British, while other nearby schools were mainly South Asian and British South Asian.

Ethnographic methods are effective ways of working with children and allowed us to observe how aspects of religion were interwoven in the children's school worlds both within the formal school curriculum and through more implicit occasions, such as registration and play times. Shillitoe[8] spent most of her time during participant observation with Key Stage 2 children (aged seven to eleven), acting as a teaching assistant, and observing daily school life, with a particular focus on Religious Education (RE), Personal, Social, Health and Economic Education (PSHE), and collective worship or assemblies. Alongside participant observation, paired interviews with children (aged seven to ten) in each school (115 children in total) enabled us to ask about their experiences in relation to religion and belief across different spaces, as well as observing how they interacted with each other in discussing religion. During the interviews, the children had drawing materials and craft materials to hand and as we asked them about things that were important to them in their lives, they often drew images or made Play-Doh objects to represent these things. To gain further insight into their experiences at school, we also asked the children to take photographs of things and places that were important to them in their schools.

We sampled children using a worksheet activity in which they were asked about their (non)belief in God. Prior to the activity, Shillitoe had spent a fortnight in each fieldsite informing the children about the study and answering any questions they had. For instance, at St Peter's, when walking to lunch with Fatima, a Muslim child from Year 5, Fatima asked her, 'for your project, when you say, "God", do you mean our God, Allah, or your God?' Such interactions helped inform how we presented the study to the children. A child-friendly presentation about the research was given to each class, in which it was explained that no particular definition or religious understanding of God was being used, and there were no right or wrong answers. Following this, worksheets were distributed, and children who gave the answer 'no' or 'not sure' to the question, 'do you believe in God?' were invited to participate. In describing the children as

---

8. Referred to as Rachael in interview excerpts.

'atheist' in this book, we are therefore referring to a de facto 'negative' atheism in the sense of an absence of belief in God(s), rather than a self-conscious atheist identity. Indeed, relatively few children self-identified as 'atheist'.

Interviews were also conducted with the parents/carers of thirteen to fifteen children in each school (55 parents/carers in total). Depending on the parents' availability, these were sometimes conducted with the children present, and explored parents' beliefs, values, and the place of religion in their own upbringing and how these related to their children's upbringing. While the children were all atheist in the negative sense of atheism outlined above, their parents had diverse religious and non-religious identities (including Christian, Jewish, Muslim, humanist, and agnostic) and theist, atheist, and agnostic beliefs. However, like the children, the parents often articulated a sense that typical religious identification labels used in surveys did not accurately convey their stances. For instance, when asked how she would identify, Monica, a St Peter's parent, said:

> I would say 'atheist', but it always sounds such a horribly harsh word. . . . I appreciate nature and amazing wonders . . . but I can't really put it into any box, if that makes sense. I guess I'm a free thinker. I think, if anything, that would be it. I expect to be treated the way I would treat someone else. This is something my dad's always said: 'Treat others how you expect to be treated.' In other words, just be nice to people and live a moral life.

We also conducted interviews with four teaching staff in each school (12 teaching staff in total), exploring how religion and belief were located in the school.

During the ethnographic phase of data collection, we analysed data thematically, identifying and reflecting on emerging patterns. Following data collection, the data were reviewed and re-analysed according to the kinds of socialization the children were experiencing in relation to theism, atheism, religion, and worldviews, and the interplay of factors across different spaces and relationships shaping their non-belief. This latter phase of analysis was also further developed through the 'Becoming Non-Believers: Explaining Atheism in Childhood' project, funded by the Explaining Atheism research programme, working with Lois Lee. This project drew on Lee's earlier proposal that recognizing new ways of life amongst the non-religious implies that 'the change societies have experienced is one of cultural transformation rather than cultural decline' (2015: 182). This contributed to the distinction we make between 'push' factors that encourage children away from religion and belief in God (e.g. the absence of religious socialization, negative perceptions of religion) and 'pull' factors that draw them towards other-than-religious world-views, and to the identification of and conceptual approach to humanism in the argument we present in this book.

The form that non-religious worldviews take is an emerging area of research,[9] with initial studies revealing some diversity in the outlooks of those identifying as having no religion or no belief in God, or both (Strhan et al. 2024: 9). In her research with the non-religious in south-east England, Lee identifies five worldviews she found amongst her participants: (i) humanism, which understands humanity to be special and 'a repository of existential, in-cluding moral knowledge' and which emphasizes the knowability of the world and valorizes scientific methods (2015: 162); (ii) agnosticism, which like hu-manism legitimizes scientific methods as a way of knowing the world, but which, in contrast, considers 'that this knowledge of the world is profoundly limited' and valorizes unknowability (2015: 163); (iii) theism, which views 'the origins and outcome of life in terms of a centralized, autonomous being' (2015: 166); (iv) subjectivism, which posits individual experience as a central way of knowing the world; and (v) the anti-existential, which involves 'the rejection of existential philosophies and cultures in general' and emphasizes instead 'the immediate—everyday needs, responsibilities, and pleasures' (2015: 169). These worldviews, as Lee notes, are not necessarily expressed in clear, devel-oped propositions: rather worldviews tend 'to emerge through fragments of articulated belief and also in accounts of real-world encounters of various sorts'; moreover, aspects of different existential modes and traditions— including both religious and non-religious—can be 'combined in creative and self-contradictory ways' (2015: 172). We anticipated that this research would explore the variety of worldviews children hold alongside their non-belief and the role these play in shaping their non-religion and atheism. Instead, as we spent time reflecting on the children's accounts of their non-belief and of what was important to them in their lives, we found a pervasive humanism, much more consistent with Callum Brown's (2017) argument that a humanist 'moral cosmos' has displaced—or is displacing—Christianity in many western societies (Strhan et al. 2024). This book, therefore, aims to bring to light what that pervasive humanism looks like in children's lives, how it is formed, and how it is expressed in ways that do not necessarily correspond with established humanist discourses.

9. See, for instance, Baker and Smith (2015); LeDrew (2015); Lee (2015); Taves (2019); Van Mulukom et al. (2023); Singleton et al. (2021); Watts (2022).

Overview of the Volume

This book tells the story of how and why children in England are growing up non-religious and non-believing, and what this means to them. In doing so, it reveals that their non-religiosity and non-belief take shape and are expressed in relation to their being drawn towards a humanist form of life. This humanism centres the agency, significance, and achievements of humans, rational thought and the scientific method, and moral principles of equality and respect (Lee 2015). The book reveals how the children 'figure out' (Irvine et al. 2019) their non-religion and humanism through relationships with their parents, peers, school contexts, and wider cultural forms, and opens up the ethical dimensions interwoven in their forms of life, especially the centrality of values of 'respect' and 'equality' (Beaman 2017a).

We begin in chapter 1 by centring the children's reflections on what it means to them to be non-believing and non-religious, and the relative salience of these matters in their lives. This chapter engages with the Christian—and broadly Protestant—'genealogies of belief' (Day 2011) that have shaped sociological portraits of non-belief and non-religion, before moving on to explore the children's narratives of their non-belief, and how their non-belief in God is bound up with their valorization of science, empiricism, rationalism, and other human-centred ways of knowing, and is also held alongside a range of other beliefs, including beliefs about life after death and in supernatural and magical figures. We argue that their different modes of belief challenge narratives that equate non-religion or secularity with disenchantment, and situate the different contours of their belief as broadly located within a lived, 'lower-case humanism' (Strhan et al. 2024). Chapter 2 focuses on the parents' perspectives, hopes, concerns, and practices in relation to (non)religion and beliefs in their family contexts. We demonstrate the relative lack of discussion about religion or belief amongst parents and children in most of our families—even where the parents were religiously affiliated and attended church—combined with a variety of stances towards religion, belief, and spirituality. Underlying the different positions taken by the parents was a shared sense that as parents, it was not for them to decide their child's (non)religious identity or belief, but rather to support their children in working out for themselves who they are and their place in the world.

Chapter 3 turns to explore the significance of schools in shaping how children were growing up non-religious. While religion continues to feature prominently in education frameworks in England, we argue that schools are nevertheless making a humanist form of life available to children, which feeds into how the children think about what it means to be non-religious and non-believing. This chapter explores how central aspects of a humanist worldview—principles of autonomy, and the valorization of science, rationality, and empiricism—were interwoven in school life, and also considers how children were responding to the forms of religion they encountered in school. We argue that the prevalence of this humanist worldview is not because of Humanist or Secularist organizations' intentional influence over schools, but rather because these values cohere with wider educational frameworks. These values also cohere with the parents' values and how they were seeking to raise their children, meaning that the children were—across home and school—being provided with resources to 'figure out' their own humanism and atheism (Irvine et al. 2019).

Chapter 4 builds on a growing literature exploring non-religious and atheist embodiment, which has challenged stereotypes of atheism and non-religion as primarily intellectual. This chapter approaches the children's non-belief through the lens of 'aesthetics', understood not in the sense of the beautiful in relation to the arts, but rather an Aristotelian notion of *aesthesis*—a means of organizing our sensory experience of the world (Meyer 2012). We explore the aesthetics of the children's non-religiosity, atheism and humanism and the interrelations between these through focusing on the sensations, affective registers, media and materiality implicated in its formation. We examine the feelings through which the children—and some of their parents—situate themselves as other-than-religious, for instance, indifference to religion or boredom, but also sometimes stronger emotional registers, such as disgust or disturbance. We then examine the 'substantive' aesthetic formation of key contours of the children's humanism, including their enjoyment of science and nature, and modes of magical belief, and highlight the importance to the children of these immanent attachments and affective registers of enjoyment.

The final chapter examines the ethics and values bound up in the children's non-religion, and draws together the ways in which an ethics of authenticity, respect, and individual autonomy in relation to religion is privileged by children, parents and school staff. Through comparing how the children and parents talk about 'choice', 'respect' and 'equality', we demonstrate that liberal humanist ethical sensibilities in relation to religion are shifting somewhat amongst the non-religious in England, as moral critiques of religion expressed by parents are giving way amongst their children to an ethic that is primarily articulated in terms of respect for religious—and other kinds of—difference, within a wider social context of growing religious plurality. We conclude by suggesting that we may be seeing a 'new humanism' emerge amongst these children, which while expressing concern for human freedom and flourishing also seeks to challenge racism and other forms of dehumanization, and acknowledges a sense of responsibility to and interconnectedness with non-human beings (Gilroy 2000, 2005; Pinn 2015; Blencowe 2016). Finally, the conclusion reflects on the book's key contributions and the questions following on from this, especially in relation to how we approach humanism empirically and conceptually, and the importance of further mapping the lived textures, contours, and social impacts of humanism and other forms of religion's others.

1

What Does it Mean to Children to Grow up Godless?

ZOE AND LOUISE were sparky, confident nine-year-olds at St Peter's. At the start of their interview, as they drew pictures of things that were important to them in their lives, they described what they were drawing and spoke about teddy bears, family members, pet goldfish and kittens, spaces that were special to them—such as their bedrooms—and dragons, which, Louise said, 'can fly and they can breathe fire. . . . They're magical.' Rachael complimented them on their drawings and asked if they could say something about what they believe in. Louise went first:

> LOUISE: Well, it's kind of difficult to explain. I don't believe in God . . . I don't know how to explain it. . . . Basically, I would say I believe in science and the Big Bang theory. The problem is that my mum told me science is just a word for the evidence that comes from a theory or an experiment. I thought, well, how can you believe in that, or do you trust it? I wasn't entirely sure which one to use.
>
> RACHAEL: As in belief or trust?
>
> LOUISE: Yes, like *trust* the evidence is right, or do I *believe* that the evidence is right?

Rachael said this was a good question, and Zoe then articulated her non-belief in God:

> ZOE: I don't think I believe in God, because it's funny because he's meant to create people, but if he was a person and he created people, how

could he have been created? So, it's all really confusing . . . because I'm not sure how a person like God could have just made himself.

LOUISE: What I don't understand is, I ask people who do believe in God . . . 'well, if God created all this stuff, then where did he come from?' People say he didn't come from anywhere, he was just there always. Then I think, well, if he came from nowhere, everything has to come from somewhere. I know it sounds weird because it would never happen, but imagine if a pencil appeared in front of me out of the blue. It would still have to come *from* something. . . . It would still have to come from somewhere, whereas if God comes from nowhere then how can he exist? . . .

RACHAEL: So . . . Louise . . . you believe or trust in the Big Bang or the science theory, but you don't believe in God . . . I think it's really interesting, this idea of belief and trust. What makes you trust something and what makes you believe something?

LOUISE: Well, sometimes I think it makes me trust something if I can actually know why the person I'm trusting thinks it, or something like that.

Both girls said they would identify as 'no religion'. Zoe explained that to her this meant 'that you have a free way in doing things, but things that you know are right. . . . So if you want to celebrate Christmas, you can celebrate Christmas, but if you're religious, like Muslim, then you can't celebrate Christmas, which to me would be really, really sad because I really like Christmas.' Louise replied:

LOUISE: So do I. I think 'no religion' to me means you don't ask for help from somebody who is in the sky.

ZOE: And who you can't actually see.

LOUISE: Who you can't actually see and who is everywhere. . . . You might need help, but you don't pray or spend time of your own time, like Christians go to church every Sunday. That's wasting a bit of their Sunday to go and do that, but you wouldn't sacrifice that.

ZOE: I'm not really sure I'd put 'no beliefs' because—do believing in Santa and things like that count?

RACHAEL: Yes . . . there are no limitations here in terms of what we're thinking about and discussing . . .

ZOE: I think if I had a survey, if there was one [option] that's 'no religion', then I'd put that because 'no beliefs' isn't exactly true, because I believe in things like Santa and the tooth fairy.

Louise then dropped a bombshell:

LOUISE: I don't believe in Santa or the tooth fairy, because—
ZOE: What? You don't?

Louise diplomatically said that she thought the 'tooth fairy is probably more likely than Santa', which prompted discussion about the feasibility of Santa's annual mission. Rachael asked whether they'd always thought of themselves as having 'no religion'. Zoe replied:

ZOE: I've always thought of myself as having no religion but believing in some things that most people believe in.
RACHAEL: Such as?
ZOE: Like Easter Bunny and things like that. And Santa.
RACHAEL: So you always thought of yourself as having no religion, but still believing in things that other people do.
ZOE: Yes, and that seem true to me.

This exchange opens up several interwoven threads of what 'belief' means for young non-believers. When asked about belief, the first thing Zoe and Louise articulate is their non-belief in God, which they immediately link with their 'belief' or 'trust' in science and their perception of belief in a creator God as just plain illogical. After all, how could something come from nothing, as Louise, like many philosophers before her, questions? Louise's comments demonstrate her awareness of 'belief' and 'trust' being two different concepts as well as her sense of the relational dimensions of trusting *in* a person, combined with her rationalist sensibilities as she notes that she would want to know the reasons *why* someone would hold a particular view. Both girls link their identifying as 'non-religious' to their non-belief in God, as well as not having to engage in religious practices, such as attending church. Yet at the same time, Zoe emphasizes that she is nevertheless a believer, albeit not in God. Moreover, in describing herself as believing in some things that 'most people believe in', Zoe underscores her sense of belief as a shared, social condition, while also articulating a link between belief and truth, and, through her phrase 'that seem true to me', an implicit sense that what counts as true is related to perception and context.

Discussions about 'belief' in Euro-American societies, especially in relation to younger generations, tend to tell a story articulated using the language of religious decline and the loss of belief: the 'long, melancholy, withdrawing roar' which the Victorian poet Matthew Arnold heard from the 'sea of faith' as it retreated. This narrative of loss emerges in part from the great extent to which sociology—as well as wider public debates about religion—has been shaped by secularization theories which situate secular forms of life through the lens of 'subtraction' (Taylor 2007: 26–7) and focus on recording the 'absence' of religious belief rather than the presence of alternative, other-than-religious forms of life (Lee 2015). Indeed, the terms we use to describe these phenomena—nonreligious, non-believing—are informed by this sense of absence. Portraits of religious decline have also often been interwoven with narratives of disenchantment[1] such as that articulated by Charles Taylor, who writes, 'Everyone can agree that one of the big differences between us and our ancestors of 500 years ago is that they lived in an "enchanted" world and we do not' (2011: 38). Taylor portrays our contemporary 'secular age' as purged of magic and spiritual entities, with the modern, rational self bounded and 'buffered' rather than 'open and porous and vulnerable to a world of spirits and powers' (Taylor 2007: 27).

The quantitative research methods which have historically dominated sociological approaches to religion feed into this narrative framed in terms of the loss of belief, with surveys posing questions using traditionally religious frames of reference such as 'do you believe in God?' or 'do you believe in life after death?', with 'belief' or its lack assessed through ticking a box next to these questions. In these approaches, as Abby Day (2011) highlights, the nature and meaning of belief has generally been taken for granted, predicated on a conception of belief in terms of cognitive, private assent to Christian-associated teachings. Thus the extent to which secularization was taking place could be measured according to a decline or rise in survey responses to these questions recording belief, alongside measures of affiliation and attendance at religious institutions.

However, Zoe's comments indicate that this idea of belief centred on Christian-related categories does not necessarily represent how the non-religious reflect on what it means to them to believe. Zoe's misgivings mirror academic discontent with dominant understandings of belief, as over the past two decades, established sociological approaches to belief have come under sustained criticism. Influenced by feminist theories and methods, scholars within the 'lived religion' approach have drawn attention to how the historic sociological privileging of survey data on beliefs and institutional affiliation

---

1. The term 'disenchantment', used by Weber in his essay *Science as a Vocation*, became central to influential secularization theorists writing in the 1960s such as Peter Berger (1967) who portrayed rationalization, secularization, and disenchantment as part of the same process.

has perpetuated a particular Protestant notion of religion that effaces the importance of bodies, feelings, and the complexities and nuances of lifeworlds that cannot be 'stuffed into . . . [a] questionnaire's categories' (McGuire 2002: 196). Lived religion scholars have therefore highlighted the importance of attending to how individuals may engage a range of beliefs, practices, and identities in configurations that do not fit neat 'official' definitions of 'proper' religion (Ammerman 2021).[2]

Anthropologists have also explored how power and privilege have been implicated in conceptualizations of 'belief'. The Christian legacy that shaped anthropological use of 'belief' was highlighted by scholars such as Rodney Needham (1972), Malcolm Ruel (1997) and Talal Asad (1993), who developed an influential critique of Clifford Geertz's portrayal of belief as 'a modern, privatized Christian one because and to the extent that it emphasizes the priority of belief as a state of mind rather than a constituting activity in the world' (Asad 1993: 47).[3] Engaging with these debates, studies exploring belief have increasingly looked beyond the historic focus on propositional[4] beliefs to explore the different forms that belief can take in different times and places. This has included opening up the relational, material, spatial, and temporal dimensions of belief (Day 2011),[5] as well as attention to how the beliefs of the non-religious in Euro-American societies continue to be distinctively shaped by Christian grammars, even as individuals may seek to extricate themselves from hegemonic religious cultures (Blankholm 2022). This interdisciplinary body of work has challenged religious–secular binaries that shape popular understandings of the non-religious through revealing how non-religious people may at times

---

2. These scholars highlighted how power relations shaped dominant approaches to belief: it was the liberal modernist Christianity of elite, adult, male specialists—who constructed 'proper' religion as rational, privileging propositional belief—which was the standard focus of scholarly attention, with religiosities that did not fit this perceived as 'other' (McDannell 1995; Orsi 2005).

3. See Abby Day's insightful discussion of the 'genealogies of belief' within sociology and anthropology in *Believing in Belonging* (2011).

4. Joel Robbins, building on the earlier work of Ruel (1997), draws a helpful distinction between 'propositional' forms of belief, which express 'belief that' the proposition is true (e.g., I believe that God exists), and the idea of 'believing in', which implies a sense of trust and commitment. Robbins argues that while historically anthropologists tend to assume that propositional beliefs were the most important aspect of a culture, 'belief in' statements may be 'more fundamental than "belief that" ones in trying to identify what people are up to culturally' (2007: 15).

5. See, for example, Robbins (2007); Day (2011); Guest et al. (2013); Strhan (2013, 2015).

draw on religious or spiritual repertoires in fashioning their beliefs and identities, while at other moments in their lives, religious belief is of little salience (Day 2009, 2011; Manning 2015; Blankholm 2022).

However, despite this growing attention to different modalities of belief, we currently know little about the beliefs of non-religious children, or what it means to them to be non-religious or non-believing. This reflects the broader historical marginalization of children's experiences in studies of religion, combined with the broader historical lack of social research on non-religion and non-belief. Previous studies of belief in relation to childhood and youth have been dominated by large-scale North American studies which have tended to be based on largely Christian samples and have focused on teenagers or young adults (e.g., Smith and Denton 2005; Pearce and Denton 2011). These studies—like broader studies of belief—have largely charted the decline of religious identification and belief amongst such populations, but have also shown how young people today find their sources of meaning, happiness, and morality through their relations with friends and family rather than religious institutions and authorities.

Interwoven in these studies has often been a pessimistic note in which young people's beliefs are measured against older generations and found wanting. Abby Day notes, for example, that Christian Smith and Melinda Denton's landmark study of the religious and spiritual lives of US teenagers questions the legitimacy of teenage belief and portrays their young participants as living in a 'morally insignificant universe' (Smith and Denton 2005: 156–8), where their lives are not guided by larger moral frameworks or religious or philosophical sources (Day 2011: 91). Day's influential ethnographic study of belief and identity in a northern English town provides an important challenge to this narrative that younger generations' beliefs are insufficient or absent: she argues that their beliefs are rather *differently* grounded and fundamentally rooted in belonging. Her approach to belief has helped fuel an emerging literature exploring the beliefs and identities of non-religious teens and emerging adults[6] which has revealed that these younger generations are 'mostly secular, mostly liberal and mostly helpful' while also drawing attention to how distinctive sociocultural contexts shape how (non)religiosity is lived and resourced (Nynäs et al. 2022: 313).

6. See, for instance, Day (2009); Vincett and Collins-Mayo (2010); Catto and Eccles (2013); Hemming and Madge (2017); Katz et al. (2021); Singleton et al. (2021); Nynäs et al. (2022).

Building on these studies, we contend that children's perspectives[7] are also crucial to understanding both what it means to be non-religious and the contemporary formation of non-religious beliefs. How do children talk about what it means to believe—or not—at different points in their lives, and does belief mean the same thing to non-religious children as it does to teens and young adults? *Is* belief actually important to children, and to what extent is the way they talk about belief shaped by particular religious genealogies? Do their beliefs suggest that childhood is a time of enchantment and wonder, as often portrayed in popular culture, or do they inhabit a 'morally insignificant universe' marked by a loss of transcendent meaning and value, as some scholars have lamented?

Since sociologists have tended to pay scant attention to what children have to say about religion and belief on their own terms, in what follows, we centre the voices of children as they articulate their own narratives of belief and reflect on the place—and absence—of God(s), religion, and other supernatural beings in their lives. We begin by exploring how the children talk about what it means to them to be 'non-believing', and demonstrate that their non-belief in God is articulated using Christian 'propositional' grammars, interwoven with their sense of the implausibility or illogicality of Christian theistic beliefs. While some children expressed uncertainty about their non-belief, overall, the children saw this non-belief as *theirs*, and often fluid over time. We then examine how many children saw their non-belief in God and non-religiosity as interrelated, and how for them, questions of (non)religious identification were relational and bound up with family belonging. Challenging wider narratives that equate secularity with disenchantment, we turn to explore how the children's non-belief in God is bound up with their faith in science, empiricism, rationalism, and other human-centred ways of knowing, and is also held alongside a range of other beliefs, including beliefs about life after death and belief in supernatural and magical figures. We argue that these playful, subjunctive beliefs in the magical and supernatural are nevertheless intimately bound up with the children's relationships with their friends, family, and belonging. Reflecting on the children's desire for more 'substantive' understandings of their worldviews

7. Here, we also build on a growing ethnographic literature on children's engagements with religion and faith, including Ridgely Bales (2005); Orsi (2005); Fader (2009); Scourfield et al. (2013); Hemming (2015); Strhan (2019); Kitching (2020); Hickey-Moody (2023); Shillitoe (2023). For an overview of how a focus on religion and childhood has emerged across different disciplines, see Strhan et al. (2017).

beyond negative framings of 'non-religion' and 'non-belief', we conclude by suggesting that the different modalities of belief described in this chapter are interwoven within what we describe as a broadly humanist form of life.

Narratives of Non-Belief

At the start of their interviews, the children were invited to talk about and draw things that were important and special to them in their lives, and were then asked about what they believed in and did not believe in. Some children—as we will discuss below–launched into discussions of things they believed in, often referencing supernatural, magical, or fantasy entities. However, when asked about their beliefs, most children said that they did not believe in God, with some commenting that they were unsure. Here, much like adult non-believers in the US (Blankholm 2022), these children's non-belief in God demonstrated the ongoing cultural significance of Christianity in shaping their grammars of non-belief: they were either rejecting, or not giving assent to, the proposition that God is real, and this non-belief was largely articulated in reference to Christian doctrines, such as belief in God the Creator, or belief in the Resurrection.[8]

Lewis and Dan from Waterside spoke about how they believed in ghosts and Santa, but not God or Jesus. Expanding on his belief in Santa, Dan stated 'people have actually got proof, like videoing, because some people have actually caught Santa on video. So, like, there is proof.' Talking about their non-belief in God, the boys linked their non-belief in Jesus to the lack of proof. Dan said, 'I don't believe in Jesus. . . . There's no proof', and they discussed this in relation to Christian belief in the Resurrection:

> DAN: Because you can't come back alive as a person, because you're dead, so you can't really make yourself back alive . . .
> LEWIS: Yes, because there were all those stories about Jesus and stuff . . .
> it was way, way back in those times no one would have been able to . . .
> DAN: Actually write.

8. Matthew Engelke's study of the British Humanist Association (BHA, now Humanists UK) also demonstrated that for BHA members and affiliates, religion is understood in terms of 'propositional assents', which, he argues were perceived by his informants as irrational, stupid, delusional, or illogical (2014: 300). Whilst the children perceived religion in terms of propositional belief, they would not have used terms such as 'stupid' or 'delusional' to describe religious belief.

LEWIS: They probably wouldn't be able to read and write. So they wouldn't be able to write down the stories, and it's not . . . like one of your great, great, great, great grand-dads were there. So . . . it's not like their ancestors would have passed it right down to your era without forgetting it.

Hayden from Sunnybank said he didn't believe in God 'because there's no proof of him. You can't just be like some person who created everything because who created him?' He added, 'I also think there's a bit of a hole in the Bible because Adam and Eve have children and then they marry . . . then their children get married. Where did the other women come from? I don't get that.' When Rachael asked when he had started to reflect on this, Hayden said that when he was in Year 1 or 2, he had asked his Nan if he could buy a children's Bible from a local shop, and when reading it, had noticed 'holes' in the creation and other stories: 'How did the whole earth just flood? Where did the water come from? . . . Noah's Ark, where did he get the instructions from? . . . How can you build it that big?'

Many children felt the idea of God was just plain implausible, and they articulated this in terms that expressed their perception of non-belief as self-evident. Coco from St Peter's said, 'I'm not religious in any way. I don't really think that there is a God in the sky, because that is just a weird thing to believe in, I think.' Steve and Craig, also from St Peter's, said:

STEVE: I don't believe in God because I think it's just a huge myth that's been going around.
CRAIG: Like, it's insanely impossible.
STEVE: Yes. It's like there's this really weird religion, I think it's called Pastafarian, and they just believe there's a huge Spaghetti Monster. That's what I've been told by Dad.
CRAIG: It's like this, this is what I think God's like, if people believe in God, it's like they're believing in a giant tomato guy.
STEVE: Spaghetti Monster [laughter]. I think I'm having a bit too much fun here.

Some children perceived a social desirability effect in play here, which meant the taken-for-grantedness of non-belief tilted against expressing theistic perspectives. Nicole from Sunnybank said she thought sometimes people say they don't believe in God 'just to fit in with other people. . . . Because people don't like God and they don't know whether someone [would] want to be their friend if they believe in it.' A handful also expressed a sense that the God they did not believe in—conceptualized in Christian terms—did not fit with their values. Claudia from Waterside speculated that God was 'claiming, "I'm the owner of this world"', and said, 'I wouldn't believe a guy who says, "I own this world."'. She compared this idea of God 'owning' the world with the idea of individuals 'owning' playground games: 'It's like when I'm out in the playground and I ask people, "Can I play with you?" And they say, "Ask whoever, they're the owner of this game." Because I think, "But you're all playing it, so why don't you *all* just own it, because you're the ones playing it."' A few children also commented that the suffering of humans and animals made it hard to believe in God.

While overall most children said—usually with little hesitation—that they did not believe in God, some were unsure, and they sometimes shifted between uncertainty and non-belief as they articulated their ideas in the interview. Carl from Sunnybank shifted between uncertainty and unbelief as he articulated how experiences of inequality undermined belief in God, stating, 'I don't really know if God exists. Because God usually makes lives even. So, like everyone has friends, poor or rich, but I don't really feel like that because a lot of the time, well, usually, I don't have many friends. So, it feels like God doesn't exist for me.' When asked what she believed in, Pearl from Waterside said that she was unsure whether she believed in God and elaborated:

> I'm not sure. Not really. I, kind of, do believe in the more scientific version of . . . the Big Bang and stuff like that. Earth was formed of dust . . . and it all came together. That just sounds way more realistic . . . Christians say that he [God] made the earth. . . . Well, scientists have discovered stuff that sounds way more realistic, and they've just discovered more things that they actually found out there themselves, instead of people saying that God made the world but they have no proof whatsoever. I don't want to offend anyone, but Christians, the person who said that God made the world, they don't have any proof whatsoever if Jesus was actually real, if God made the world, or about anything else either. . . . But scientists actually have *proof*. So yes, I'm just going with the scientific one.

While Pearl began her answer from a stance of uncertainty, as she spoke, she appeared to be figuring out her thoughts, pausing initially at the start of her answer, and then coming to a worked-out position of non-belief as she articulated her ideas.

Children seemed comfortable expressing their uncertainties with each other. Callie from Sunnybank expressed her non-belief, saying 'I don't believe in a God and I just believe that the world came to make itself. I don't believe that a God made it.' Her friend Zara responded by describing her uncertainty:

> My dad said that the world was created with nature . . . so I'm not really sure how the world came: by nature or God? I'm thinking it might be nature, because how can we make the trees? How can we make the clouds? How can we make the seeds? And I'm thinking it's because of nature because the trees are nature, the birds are nature and the sea is a kind of nature. That's how I think of it. I don't believe in God. I don't know if I believe in God because I don't know if he's real or not and I'm just not sure at all.

Sam from Sunnybank articulated his uncertainty in relation to the different beliefs within his own family:

> I don't know if I actually do [believe in God] cus my mum doesn't believe in anything but . . . my nan believes in evolution and then granddad believes in God, so I don't know what my beliefs are supposed to be. I weren't christened from church. I was born in a hospital. Nothing special happened to me in a church. So, I don't actually know what my beliefs are. I can't say what I should believe in.

However, later in the interview, Sam expressed a stronger sense of non-belief. In response to his friend Callum saying that he might believe in Christianity when he's older, Sam replied, 'I don't think I'll believe in Christianity when I grow up . . . because I don't actually believe God created the earth, when he put two people down and he gave them the dust. I don't fully believe that happened—that just sounds weird.'

While many children expressed some sense of uncertainty, this was slightly more widespread amongst children at Waterside than at Sunnybank or St Peter's. Although as a qualitative sample we would not generalize from this, this difference might reflect the fact that religion was more present within the schools and local communities at Sunnybank and St Peter's than at Waterside, affording the children more opportunities to reflect on their own positions in relation to the religious beliefs and identities they were encountering at school. Amongst the children who were uncertain, none expressed a strong stance of agnosticism in the sense of it being impossible to know whether or not God is real (Lee 2015). Rather, their expressions of uncertainty involved weighing up different aspects of evidence for and against the existence of God, or expressing a faith that as humanity's collective knowledge advances, we will gain progressively better understanding. Henry from Waterside, for instance, said 'in the future' scientists might develop an understanding of what had happened at the start of the universe, 'but now, we're not 100 per cent sure'. His friend Louis concurred, stating that scientists 'might not have found this new material, and then in the future they did. Then it would just be like a whole different world.' In contrast with standard portrayals of uncertainty as a source of discomfort, these children seemed comfortable in their uncertainty, resonating with Jacqui Frost's (2019) study of non-religious adults in the US which found that uncertainty in relation to religion was not a cause of anxiety or discomfort.

This sense of uncertainty or expressing positions that shifted over the course of the interview is, we would suggest, related to the fact that for many of these children, the question of whether they believed in God was not an issue of much salience in their lives. While it was something that they were encouraged to think about in Religious Education lessons, for most of them, it was not a subject they reflected on much otherwise in their everyday lives. As Louis from Waterside put it, he 'never really think[s] about God and stuff'. This lack of salience was more pronounced at Waterside than at Sunnybank and St Peter's, where religion was more present in everyday school life than at Waterside. Lewis and Dan from Waterside, for example, both picked 'no religion' when asked how they would identify in relation to religion, and said that this is because they don't believe in a god. Reflecting on this, Lewis said, 'I don't believe in a God and I'm not really—I'm not too bothered. . . . If someone said, "You have to believe in a God", I'd be like, "Okay, that's fine", because I don't really mind if I believe in a God or not.' Thus while Lewis's non-belief in God informed his non-religious identification, it was an issue he saw as of marginal salience in his life.

Despite this lack of salience, the children were keen to underscore that their (non)beliefs belonged to *them*. Lewis, whose mother was Christian and believed in God, said, 'if your mum and dad believe in a god, they shouldn't force you to believe in a god . . . they shouldn't force you to be a Christian. They should let you make your own decisions.' Demonstrating his sense of his own agency in these matters, he said, 'I think my mum and dad said that I was christened, but I don't really want to be a Christian, because I don't believe in anything.' While emphasizing that they themselves had chosen their beliefs, many children also acknowledged the influence of their family in shaping their beliefs. Craig, for instance, said:

CRAIG: I've never believed in God.
RACHAEL: Have your beliefs changed?

CRAIG: I think I believe that God isn't real stronger than my mum and
   dad, because they don't believe in God. That makes me not want to
   believe in God.

RACHAEL: So they don't believe in God?

CRAIG: No, my parents don't believe in God, no. . . . So, that's why I think
   I more strongly believe that God isn't real, because my parents don't
   believe. So, I didn't anyway, but then because my parents don't believe
   he's real, that makes me believe *more strongly* that he's not real.

Some children saw their parents as shaping their religious identities, as we will
discuss below, but on the question of belief, children saw their own autonomy
as central. Ava from Sunnybank, for instance, as noted in the Introduction, said
that she didn't believe in God, and added, 'until my parents tell me or until I
get christened, then I'll be an atheist'. Rachael asked if she thought it was up
to her parents what she believed, and Ava—underscoring her sense of
agency—replied: 'No. I just think it's up to me really because I think we all
have choices in our beliefs and disbeliefs.'

Many children were conscious of the temporal dimensions of their agency,
and as they reflected on 'choice' in their lives, they 'zigzag backwards and
forwards across time', drawing reflections together reflections about their
past, younger selves with anticipations of their futures as adults (Hickey-
Moody 2013: 277). Louise expressed these temporal conjunctures as she
reflected, 'when you're young, you always seem to follow what your parents
do. But when you grow up, you have more of a choice. But I've chosen to be
the same as my parents because that's what I believe. I could have chosen
something else.' Other children emphasized that the emergence of their non-
belief over time was shaped by their growing understanding of belief. Charlie
from St Peter's said:

I've never really believed in God. Yes. I've not generally been a believer in
God for quite a long time. When I was in the nursery,[9] I didn't know what
anything was. I didn't know what beliefs were. I didn't know, but when I
moved into here, into Reception,[10] I kind of got to know what stuff was.
Then I kind of decided what was what.

9. 'Nursery' is the term used in the UK for a daycare centre for children aged 2–4.
10. Reception Year in English schools is for children aged 4–5.

Fran from Waterside also zig-zagged backwards as she reflected on her present non-belief and herself as a much younger child, commenting that the way that she 'processed' her beliefs had changed with time:

> Since I've been in about Year 2 or 3,[11] when I've actually been able to process it, yes. I've never believed in God. Well, I used to believe in him; I used to believe that my dad was God. . . . When I was about one or two. I used to say, 'So, God, Daddy', because . . . he's, like, 6ft 5in, so he's really tall, so I always used to think that God was really tall. . . . So, I was a bit crazy when I was younger.

Hailey and Connor from St Peter's framed the emergence of their non-belief across time in terms of shifting from an idea that God created the world to this being challenged as they learnt about science at school:

> HAILEY: When I was younger, I think I believed in God because I didn't know the Big Bang even existed.
> CONNOR: Yes, the same as me. All I knew was that there was a thing called the Big Bang. . . . I just thought God was the thing that made sense, an immortal human, basically. Now that just doesn't make any sense to me.
> HAILEY: Now I've heard of the Big Bang, now I'm starting to think the Big Bang might be true. I didn't really know about the Big Bang when I was younger. Now, maybe I'm starting to lean away from God and lean up to the Big Bang. I'm starting to believe in the Big Bang.

These children's reflections on their (non)belief across time moves against the grain of how much of childhood studies since the early 1990s had a presentist temporal emphasis, situating children as 'beings not becomings' (Qvortrup et al. 1994: 2). This focus on children as 'beings' emerged as a reaction against how developmental psychology situated children as 'pre-adult becomings' through focusing on age-bound developmental stages which positioned the child developing into an adult in terms of 'a progression from simplicity to complexity of thought, from irrational to rational behaviour' (Prout and James 1997: 10). Recent work in childhood studies has reacted against this, drawing attention to how focusing on children only as 'beings' 'cultivates an analytical blindspot' and 'encodes . . . a kind of denaturalized child which exists in a here-and-now' (Spyrou et al. 2019: 4). This body of work has argued that children, like adults, might be better understood in terms

11. The age range of Years 2–3 is 6–8.

of ongoing processes of 'becoming' and 'intra-action', which acknowledge how we are shaped by our ongoing capacity to be affected by others. In this sense, children are always both 'being' *and* 'becoming', as the children's words express. Bronwyn Davies articulates this idea of children as becoming:

> My emphasis on openness to becoming different in one's encounters does not run against or deny the very specificity of the person, or the longing each one of us has to be recognized in that specificity. Rather, I am suggesting the very specificity of the individual is *mobile* and *intra-active*; in each encounter we are affected by the other (Lenz Taguchi 2010). Our capacity to enter into encounters, to recompose ourselves, to be affected, enhances our specificity and expands our capacity for thought and action (Davies 2014: 1).[12]

The children's descriptions of the temporalities of their (non)belief reveal how they themselves recognise this process of 'becoming', while at the same time, their emphasis that their beliefs are *theirs*—and also influenced by their parents—reflects their desire to be recognized in their singularity.

Karl Kitching argues that rather than judgemental, teleological notions of children growing 'up' from 'blank innocence to all-knowingness', we might instead think of their engagement with plurality as a form of 'growing sideways'[13] as they find 'creative ways of negotiating their own differences, knowns and unknowns within generational stages and adults' religious/secular representations of the world' (2020: 31). The children's descriptions of their changing non-belief illuminate how they find their own ways of negotiating knowns and unknowns in relation to their generational stages. At the same time, it also gestures towards how they are influenced by wider cultural discourses of 'development', which infuse educational practices and encourage children—and adults—to think of their internal states in terms of development (Oswell 2013: 271). Thus, while the children themselves often speak of 'growing up', we might acknowledge that this growing up is 'never very final', as children, like adults, are in a process of both being and becoming in the world (Hickey-Moody 2013: 284).

---

12. This idea is discussed in relation to religious becomings through encounters with plurality in Kitching's *Childhood, Religion and School Injustice* (2020: 18).

13. Kitching draws here on Kathryn Bond Stockton's conceptualization of 'growing sideways' in *The Queer Child, or Growing Sideways in the Twentieth Century* (2009). See also Henry (2022).

The Question of (Non)religious Identity

For the children, non-belief and non-religion were often intertwined. When we asked whether they belonged to a religion and showed them a list of possible religious and non-religious identities they might choose from, the most common answer was 'no religion', followed by 'not sure', while a number—at Sunnybank especially—chose 'Christian'. For those who chose 'no religion', when talking about what this meant to them, many explained this in terms of their non-belief, although several also referenced not engaging in religious practices. Benjamin and Theo from St Peter's articulated how for them 'no religion' was about both non-belief and non-practice, as well as religion's lack of significance for them:

> BENJAMIN: It [no religion] means that I don't believe in anything.
> THEO: Yes.
> BENJAMIN: Well, to me I don't really care about any of that.
> THEO: Yes, like you're no religion, so you don't believe in anything, and you don't follow any of those rules.
> BENJAMIN: Or you don't do any of those recitals or anything.

Both commented that they still celebrated Christmas, but Benjamin positioned it as more bound up with national culture than religion, commenting, 'sometimes religious things can be pretty dull. Christmas, it's actually a national thing.'

Some children were somewhat unsure about whether they belonged to a religion. This uncertainty is in part, we would argue, because the children perceived their religious belonging as to a certain extent ascribed and determined by their parents through practices such as christening, while at the same time also feeling that they should have agency in determining their identities. While the theistic beliefs the children were rejecting were perceived as located within the individual, being 'religious' or 'non-religious' was more bound up with ideas about collective belonging and relationships (Day 2011). This sense of relationality was revealed as the children spoke about whether or not they belonged to a religion and referenced their family members' identities and beliefs or the presence—or absence—of rites of passage as potential markers of their belonging. For those who identified as Christian, this identification was often linked solely to having been christened, which they saw as ascribing a Christian identity (Day 2011). Frank from Sunnybank said he was 'Christian' because he had been christened, and expanded: 'technically it's my mum's decision and my dad's decision to say what religion I am'. He added that he would not himself have chosen to be christened, stating, 'it should be my choice, but you can't do anything about it when you're little. It could be a law not to be christened until you know what it means.'

Sophia and Annie from Waterside both said that they were 'not sure' when asked whether they belonged to a religion, and Sophia's reply shows how she deferred to her parents on this, while at the same time, suggesting the question's lack of salience for her:

SOPHIA: . . . if you got asked this question, you'd definitely have to go home . . . ask the question because you're like, 'I've never asked this question to my parents', because it's just one of those odd questions where you go, 'Wait, when have I ever asked this question?' It's just one of the odd questions that you never ask.

RACHAEL: So this is a question you've never been asked before?

SOPHIA: No, or you never ask.

RACHAEL: . . . It's a question that doesn't come up very often?

SOPHIA: Yes.

ANNIE: I once asked it . . .

RACHAEL: When did you ask it?

ANNIE: I asked it to my mum and said, 'Oh, are you part of a religion?' And she said 'no, I don't think so'. But I think she said that my granddad has a religion. I can't remember . . .

SOPHIA: If your mums don't know, maybe their mums might know. But if their mums don't know, their mum might know. . . . Probably like people in India or Africa maybe ask that question quite a lot because something is special to them that we might not know.

Sophia's comment about needing to ask grandmothers and great-grandmothers about whether their family belonged to a religion suggests her sense of religiosity as located in the past rather than the present. Her comment about India and Africa also reveals her sense that, despite growing religious diversity in England associated with accelerating migratory flows and movements of postcolonial and decolonial bodies across Europe, religion matters 'elsewhere'.[14] She further articulated this idea, stating that in India and Africa

14. This resonates with Céline Benoit's (2021) study of religion in primary schools in the West Midlands of England, and Strhan et al. (2023), a study of religion and citizenship in schools across different parts of England, Wales and Scotland. Both reveal how many children implicitly construct religious communities as 'foreign'.

'more people . . . have a religious type of thing. And we're the people that we're not quite sure.' Yet at the same time, as well as implying a sense of 'we' in England as implicitly non-religious in 'our' uncertainty, Sophia, like a handful of other children, also implied a perception of England as 'Christian'. She stated that she thought that her parents might be likely to identify as Christian because of their being 'English', gesturing towards how broader contexts of British colonization have fed into the othering of forms of religion which were not historically English or British (Hickey-Moody 2023: 156). As we will explore in chapter 5, many children sought to challenge these forms of othering, and Annie emphatically challenged Sophia's linking of religion with national identity, stating, 'You can be born in this country and have that religion or that religion or that religion', pointing to different religious identities on a piece of paper. Further emphasizing her sense that religious identity was not tied to ethnic or national identity, Annie stated, 'You're allowed to have whatever religion you want, and it doesn't matter about what colour skin you have, what you look like, or what country you live in. It doesn't matter.'

The following day, further demonstrating her sense of religious identity as shaped by her parents, Sophia wanted to correct her previous statement that she was 'not sure', stating that she now wanted to choose 'no religion'. She explained that she had discussed this with her father the previous evening and said, 'he didn't know either, so we . . . said, "no religion", because . . . I think one day I will change to a religion. . . . So just put "no religion".' The way Sophia spoke about her (non)religious identification reveals both how, as for most of the children, she had a sense that her religious identity was shaped by her family and she therefore wanted to ask her father about this, and at the same time, reveals how she sees her (non)religious identity as potentially shifting over time.

This idea of (non)religious identification as fluid relates to how children experience themselves as inhabiting a period in their lives that is marked by transitions as they grow older. Annie said, 'until I'm older, I'm not going to choose', and commented that her mother had told her that children *could* choose their religious identity, but did not have to choose until they were older. At the same time as stating that she had not herself yet chosen, Annie emphasized that children should be able to choose their religion, noting, 'if your mum and dad have a religion that you didn't want to be, then you wouldn't follow them, would you?' Ruby from St Peter's also expressed this idea that she was too young to decide: 'It's a difficult thing to decide if you're religious or not when you're eight years old, especially when you don't have a religious family. So, I'm not really sure, because my dad's not religious, my mum's not.'

Lucas from Sunnybank also expressed a sense of uncertainty about his (non) religious identity, describing himself as 'in the middle of being a humanist and a Christian'. Like Sophia, he articulated how being non-religious was in his eyes 'normal', while at the same time, he saw himself as closer to Christianity than other religions. Discussing Christianity, he said, 'I'm not a big fan of it, but at least it's something to be religious for. And then again, because I'm not a big fan of Christianity, I'm not really very big on it, like going to church and things like that.' When asked what the term 'humanist' meant to him, he replied:

> It means to me it feels like to be normal, to feel like you're actually part of the world. Because when I'm like with Christians, or if I felt like if I was a Muslim or a Christian, I would feel like I'd be in heaven, because that's basically where everything is, like God, the angels, everything like that is in heaven. And it . . . just makes me think, well, I'd like to be down to earth, but I'm stuck up here in heaven. So it just makes me feel very far away from where I'm actually at.

Lucas's words indicate his sense of religion as associated with the transcendent and other-worldly which is at odds with his sense of humanism as 'normal' and concerned with everyday immanent realities.

Many children expressed a more confident articulation that they were non-religious. Shaun from Sunnybank said that he was 'no religion', and when asked what 'no religion' meant to him, replied matter-of-factly: 'You don't have a religion. None of them. I don't really support a religion. . . . If I go to a church, I only go for weddings, funerals and christenings.' Yet at the same time, Shaun, like several other pupils, expressed a sense that he was not *entirely* happy with being defined in the negative sense of an absence of religion or belief. As noted in the Introduction, Shaun mentioned that he had discussed his non-belief in God with his parents and had asked his mother what you were if you're not a Christian, 'Are you just a non-believer?' And when she replied 'atheist', he then began calling himself atheist. Other children also expressed this sense of wanting a substantive rather than a negative identification. Callie said:

> when I became the age of seven, we were all talking about God and I didn't believe there was a God, I just thought it was made up like a myth. I didn't believe it and then I said to my mum, 'Is there a religion that I can have, because I don't want to be nothing.' That felt to me like I'm not special. . . . My mum said there's a humanist, so I became a humanist when I was eight or nine.

As we will explore in chapter 3, the children at Sunnybank did have some—albeit limited—opportunities to learn about Humanism at school, and found this meaningful. However, for the most part, children did not necessarily know or identify with 'positive' atheist or non-religious identities such as 'humanist' or 'atheist', and we will consider, in the following chapters, how this is because they were not being given the language to do so. At the same time, for some children, their uncertainty about whether they belonged to a religion stemmed from the fact that they did not recognise themselves in the 'official' descriptions of religion that they were being presented with at school, as they incorporated some—but not other—aspects of religious practice or belief in their lives. As Annie put it, 'I'm not a Christian but I still sort of believe in Jesus and I still celebrate Christian celebrations.'

Epistemologies of Non-Belief: Empiricism, Rationalism, and Science

When asked to talk about their non-belief in God and what that meant to them, a few children said they did not know. Sophia said 'I just don't believe in God for a reason but I don't know that reason.' Some linked their non-belief, like their non-religion, to their not engaging in religious practices. However, most children linked their non-belief to the idea that there was no evidence for God, or the idea of God just not fitting with their understanding of what is real or possible. This points towards the significance for the children of their valorization of empiricism, rationalism, and science. Mason and his friend Kevin from Sunnybank exemplified this as they spoke about their non-belief in God:

KEVIN: . . . if they've got no evidence, then how do you know it's real?
MASON: Yes, and if God created the whole of the world, then who created God? I think the Big Bang is more scientific and logical.

When asked what they believed in, both boys said that they believed in 'the scientific theories', and further articulated their empiricist sensibilities:

MASON: . . . you can't just say that, 'Oh God created everything', without . . .
KEVIN: Without any scientific evidence.
MASON: Yes, without any evidence. They're saying that Jesus was that, but then it could be someone just making a story up, and then it got

improvised throughout, and then it's come to now, and now there's a whole faith of Christians who've come along about 200 years ago, or something like that.

Fran and Hannah from Waterside expressed their sense that belief in God does not make sense when set against scientific theories:

FRAN: If scientists have already proved that dinosaurs were the first, like, living creature thing on Earth, if God, he would have to have been a living creature. If he made the Earth, then scientists would have found out, but because they haven't or because they already know that dinosaurs were the first living thing, then God couldn't have made the Earth. Otherwise, the dinosaurs wouldn't have been living on the Earth.

HANNAH: Yes, and apparently, people that believe in God, like Christians, they think that Adam and Eve were the first people and first things . . . but scientists have proved that dinosaurs were, so how could Adam and Eve been?

This empiricist sensibility was the most prominent thread in how the children spoke about what it meant to them *not* to believe in God, and some children—all of whom were pupils at Sunnybank—named this stance as 'humanist'. Hayden said, 'I feel like I'm a humanist because I like science, and . . . I always like to back up my answer.' He described how the reason he didn't believe in God 'is because I really like science, and because I like science, I always want something to back up my answer, so that's why I don't believe in God'. He expressed his faith in the authority of human knowledge, stating that he would 'always trust an encyclopaedia'. Other children demonstrated how their empiricism informed their non-belief in God with reference to their own experiences. Annie said, 'some people say God is just in the air, always. But I think that is totally not true, because if you pray to him it doesn't ever work, so that sort of proves he's not actually real.'

This empiricism sometimes had a psychologizing dimension, as children described how they saw belief in God as filling some sort of psychological or existential need in others' lives, which for them was met in other ways. Zoe said, 'I always thought maybe somebody made up God so people could have a thing to believe in about how things were created. Because that story has been around for quite a long time, people think that maybe it's true.' Theo said he did not believe in God because 'sometimes you don't need to worship someone because you've [already] got someone to look up to', and explained he looked up to his 'brother, or a famous rap artist, or famous American football players'. Annie commented that rather than praying to God, 'when I'm upset or something has upset me at home, I don't pray to God. What I go and do is I go and sit in one of my lambs' stables and just cuddle with them. It just makes me feel more comfort.' Here we see how some children's empiricism was interlinked with a pragmatist sensibility: belief in God did not 'work' for them in the way that it did for others. What others might find through God was for them located instead in science and their relations with family, animals, and celebrities.

Children's perceptions of atheism as interlinked with empiricism and science were being resourced by some parents and also by their schools, as we will explore in the following chapters. Their empiricism and valorization of science were not however merely matters of cognitive knowledge: many children also expressed their enjoyment of science and maths. When asked who they found inspiring, Milo and Oscar from St Peter's said:

MILO: Einstein, probably. . . . The theory of relativity. I don't understand it but I know about it.
RACHAEL: Why does Einstein inspire you?
MILO: I just really enjoy science and maths and I like things like that.
OSCAR: Probably David Attenborough, he inspired me about all the underwater world and the abyss, the tropics.

Louise also said that she found 'the great scientists' inspiring, adding, 'I'd like to be a scientist when I grow up. I'd really like to find out something new that has never been found out before. That might be quite difficult seeing as I don't actually know everything about science at the moment . . . but for those people who discovered these new things, they're very intelligent and they inspire me.' This enjoyment of science and maths gestures towards how the material and physical world and scientific principles were of more interest and relevance to the children than God and the 'mistiness of metaphysics', which for them—as for the pragmatist William James—was 'detached from consequences and oblivious to evidence' (Schaefer 2022: 166). For many children, theological speculation was simply uninteresting compared with science and learning about the physical world.

Religious studies scholar Donovan Schaefer notes that histories of nonreligion tend to reinforce stereotypes of atheist scientists or philosophers deploying detached rationality to 'grind down' irrational, emotional religion (2022: 22). Through a historical analysis of the place of feeling in the work of scientists and philosophers, Schaefer demonstrates how the pursuit of knowledge through reason and science is interwoven with emotional registers which ground 'both our felt sense of pleasure in things clicking together and our sense of dissonance, frustration, and discomfort when information grates or jars with what we think we know. Yes, we believe what we want to believe. But *one of the things* we want to believe is the way things actually are' (2022: 18). While we will explore further the children's enjoyment of science in chapter 4, it was clear that for them, belief in God does not 'click', and they perceive this as due to it not fitting with their rationalist and empiricist epistemologies. This dissonance emerges in part from how 'the stunning success, reach, and prestige of the programmatic reconstruction of human knowledge achieved by science have totally rebuilt the backdrop of belief' (2022: 23), making religious belief one option among many—one which for the children does not fit with how they have come to know and experience the world.

Subjunctive Belief

Alongside their non-belief in God, some children told us they did not believe in other supernatural, magical, or fantasy figures. However, for many children, their empiricist epistemology did not exclude belief in supernatural, mythical, and fantasy figures, or belief in life after death. Lewis and Dan said that they believed in ghosts and Santa and speculated that there might be some form of life after death, noting that your spirit might 'stay somewhere', and discussing the possibility that, as Dan put it, 'you can have a second life as a different thing, because . . . you could be reborn with the same spirit'. Jonathan, Henry, and Louis from Waterside evoked how imagination and senses of magical possibility were interlinked as they described how Henry used to have a fabric tunnel in his bedroom and, as Louis said, 'we always used to say if you went through it, it took you to Legoland somehow. . . . And we wished.' When asked what they believed in, the boys launched into an involved discussion about ghosts and aliens:

> RACHAEL: So, what do you all believe in?
> LOUIS: I believe in ghosts.
> JONATHAN: Yes, ghosts. Me and my friend across the road, Milan, and my other friend, Aidan, we set up this ghost club because at my mate's house all the time—he lives in the attic and there are four doors—
> LOUIS: It's well creepy.

JONATHAN: Yes, in the night, the doors are opening and shutting and stuff. . . . Also, Aidan said that he heard this knock on his side door and there was apparently this dummy in it.

LOUIS: Some of the knocking, I bet it was just the floorboard expanding and stuff. . . . Like some of the doors opening and closing, it was generally the environment outside.

JONATHAN: I always have doors slamming in my house . . .

LOUIS: I believe in ghosts because my grandma said that her friend's son went into the loft and apparently there was this little girl riding a bike upstairs. . . . My grandma . . . never really jokes about stuff.

Jonathan and Louis expanded at length on their belief in ghosts, then Henry commented he was not sure he did believe in ghosts, 'but I like alien kind of stuff'. Louis replied:

LOUIS: I don't really believe in aliens.

HENRY: I don't believe in it not necessarily. . . . You can always find out about it and I do it because it's fun to talk about it. It's something to get a conversation started.

JONATHAN: I do believe there's kind of like something out there.

LOUIS: I don't really believe in aliens, because whereas ghosts are more likely to be on earth, it's easier to see them. . . . They've so far not really found any life of aliens. They've found bacteria and stuff [on other planets], but not really aliens. . . .

RACHAEL: You were saying that it's not necessarily whether you believe in aliens, but it's to get a conversation started?

HENRY: Yes, I'm happy to believe it. I don't see why not.

LOUIS: I want to believe it, but every time I've heard someone say, 'Oh, I've seen an alien', it's always been fake.

In these boys' exchanges, we see how for Jonathan, belief in ghosts is interwoven with his friendships and social belonging (Day 2011), and for Louis, it is also about trusting his grandmother. While discussing ghosts, the boys hold on to their empiricist sensibilities as they speculate on possible naturalistic explanations for the doors slamming, and Louis expresses how there is more likely to be evidence for ghosts than for aliens. Henry also reflectively articulates that these forms of belief play a role in their everyday social relationships, prompting fun conversations with friends. As the boys discussed their non-belief in God over time, they also expressed a sense of these kinds of supernatural beliefs as both playful and especially associated with younger childhood:

LOUIS: . . . In Early Years[15] I didn't really have much common sense and stuff. Whatever I heard someone say, I'd be like, 'Oh yes, that's really true.' Whereas now I know what I'm doing.

JONATHAN: At first I think because I had such a big imagination, I was thinking it [belief in God] was all true . . .

HENRY: It's the same with aliens. It's fun to believe. Especially when you're young. . . .

JONATHAN: When you're little, you have all these dreams. Then when you grow up, you start realising that reality is a bit different. . . .

LOUIS: It's like you just believe it because it's really cool and stuff. You would say, 'Monsters are really cool', and stuff. You'd start drawing them and you'd compare them: 'oh look, mine only has one eye' and stuff.

JONATHAN: It's like, it's nice to believe. But in reality it—

HENRY: Yes, I've still got that thing in my mind saying, 'It's not true', but if someone wanted to talk about it, I'm okay with that.

The ways in which these boys talk about belief here has a distinctive texture, as they articulate holding together a developing rationalist sensibility that these beliefs did not represent 'reality' with the sense that it was 'fun' to hold these beliefs (Lee et al. 2023).

Many children spoke in detail and enthusiastically about their magical and supernatural beliefs. This is because discussing, drawing, and playing out these beliefs were part of their friendships and belonging with each other, as they co-created these beliefs intersubjectively through their interactions. At the same time, they also often laughed as they spoke about these beliefs and indicated that they did not take them *entirely* seriously, or reflected—like Henry— that their 'belief' in such phenomena was qualitatively different from when they were younger. We would describe these playful beliefs as a form of subjunctive belief, with an 'as-if' quality that expresses 'a shared "could be" that constructs individuals in relation to others' (Seligman and Weller 2012: 93). For example, Jasmine and Ella from St Peter's excitedly discussed their beliefs in unicorns as they drew pictures of them together, and Jasmine said, 'I believe they're magical and . . . I just believe in them. My wish is to see a unicorn. I really want to see one.' She positioned believing in these magical entities in

15. Early Years in education in England refers to the years from birth to 5 years old (including nursery, pre-school, and Reception years).

relation to her friend, and contrasted this magical belief with her non-belief in religion, stating, 'I don't really believe in the religious part of stuff. I believe in stuff like, same as Ella, unicorns, the tooth fairies, Santa, and stuff like that.'

While many children detailed their beliefs in unicorns, fairies, dragons, Santa, the Tooth Fairy, and the Easter Bunny, they often at the same time—like Jonathan, Henry, and Louis—expressed a consciousness of younger childhood as a period of their lives that was *especially* infused with this sub-junctive mood of belief, which they were in the process of moving away from, and often commented on their younger siblings' beliefs in these phenomena. Dan commented that his younger brother believed in the Easter Bunny, and Lewis replied, 'Yes, when I was like, four or five, I believed in everything.' Ariana and Joe also expressed a sense of moving on from some of these beliefs over time, although for them, as for some other children, a belief in ghosts lingered on longer, perhaps reflecting relatively widespread belief in ghosts among the wider adult population in Britain:[16]

> ARIANA: . . . Three and five year olds . . . they always believe in fairies and stuff.
> JOE: Yes. But I believe in ghosts. Because ghosts are real. Ghosts are real.
> ARIANA: Really. Ghosts are real. We are not kidding.

Much has been written within psychological literature about the role that belief in imaginary friends, angels, and supernatural beings plays in the development of children's imaginations in early childhood.[17] However, when thinking about sociological understandings of atheism, these subjunctive modes of belief challenge stereotypical understandings of atheist or non-religious cultures as disenchanted through showing the ongoing presence of magic and the supernatural in children's lives. They also illustrate children's own consciousness of childhood as a *particular* time of magic and enchantment, a construction of childhood which is co-created by parents and children (Lee et al. 2023). Discussing her son Tim's belief in Santa, Debbie, a parent at Waterside, said, 'it's like, "Tim, we all want to believe in the magic. If you want to carry on and believe in that magic . . . then that's great - you do so." And he's been quite happy with that.'

---

16. According to a YouGov poll in 2014, nearly 30 per cent of adults in the UK believe that ghosts or supernatural beings probably or definitely exist (N=1629), and nearly as many claim to have seen or felt the presence of a supernatural being (YouGov 2014).

17. J. Bradley Wigger provides a comprehensive overview of psychological studies in this field (2019: 217–19).

This subjunctive 'as-if' mode of belief was also evident in how some children spoke about life after death. Although many did not believe in life after death, many did, and speculated on what form it might take. Jonathan and Louis demonstrated the intersubjective nature of how children figured out their beliefs about this, echoing each other's phrasing and ideas, while Henry expressed his non-belief in life after death:

JONATHAN: They go to heaven. I generally believe.

LOUIS: I think they turn into just a new person.

JONATHAN: Well, either I believe they go to heaven . . . or reincarnate into a different body, like an animal or something.

RACHAEL: You said something similar. What did you say?

LOUIS: They turn into something else. I mean they turn into their favourite animal in their past life or something.

HENRY: I just think they're not—I don't think they can think anymore. They don't know that they're dead. Or they have a split second to realise, 'Right, I'm dead', and then . . .

JONATHAN: The thing that scares me is that we're just one tiny dot out of the entire galaxy, and it scares me because when you die there will just be like trillions of years keeping going on without you in it.

Other children saw belief in life after death as a comfort. Ryan said, 'I don't like thinking that there's nothing after death because that's just disturbing, but I don't believe in God, for sure. It's just, kind of, worrying to say . . . you don't believe in anything . . . after death. So, I'm, kind of, sure that you go to something like heaven or hell and stuff like that, but, you know, it's a bit complicated.' Pearl spoke about ideas of reincarnation, and said, 'I don't know what happens when you die . . . I'm just trying to look on the bright side, in a way, because I just don't know what happens.'

Tiffany and Claudia, pupils at Waterside, also reflected on beliefs in heaven and reincarnation. Claudia, whose mother was Buddhist, speculated on these ideas and the fact we don't have evidence for them, while rejecting ideas of hell as manipulative:

I'm not sure either one [heaven or reincarnation] is true or none of them are true or both of them are true, I just don't know. Because people who are in heaven can't come down and say, 'Heaven is true, I live in heaven.' Some people believe in ghosts and some people say that there is hell. And I don't really believe in that, because it's making people sound like they have to be good and if they're bad then they're going to go to hell. I wouldn't be bad anyway, but I just don't think you would go to hell. You might just die and then go and be an animal. I don't know.

As other children discussed these ideas together, they often drew on Christian teachings, or Hindu or Buddhist conceptions of reincarnation. Several also articulated their own playful narratives which incorporated aspects of religious repertoires. Lily from Sunnybank said she thought you would turn into 'an angel or a demon', while her friend Charlotte spoke about heaven and hell, and mentioned that her cat had gone to 'heaven because he was a really good boy'. Lily's beliefs about becoming an angel or demon however did not relate to any judgement about behaviour, but rather seemed in her eyes to be a matter of individual, personal choice:

LILY: . . . I need to decide if I want to be an angel or if I want to be a demon when I die. I think I—I don't know if I want to be an angel because they have really nice wings, angels.

CHARLOTTE: Angels are really pretty.

LILY: When I die, what if I could have, when I've died and I turn in— I wish I could have powers so I can go back to the world.

CHARLOTTE: I believe that when people die they go to Candyland, some people, if they have a sweet tooth or maybe—

LILY: I really want to go to Candyland when I die.

Many of the children speculatively expressed several differing ideas about life after death, sometimes shifting between belief and non-belief. We suggest that this reflects the fact that—in contrast with their beliefs in Santa, fairies, and ghosts—they had not given the question of life after death much thought before; as Juliet from St Peter's commented, 'I've never really thought about it.'

These subjunctive modes of belief were, we would suggest, easier for children to sustain than traditional religious beliefs because they do not come 'in packages with a variety of other beliefs and norms' that require significant commitment on the part of the believer (Lanman and Buhrmester 2017: 13). Miles, the father of Ella, explained why he was happy to encourage belief in Santa and the Tooth Fairy, but not in God, 'I guess it's because I associated that [belief in God] with a whole load of other baggage around churchgoing, duty, that kind of formalized religion. Whereas actually a relationship with a godlike or fantasy being could be . . . as exciting and as fun as the Tooth Fairy.'

The beliefs about life after death that some children expressed—while drawing on religious repertoires—also had 'minimal cultural baggage' (Lanman and Buhrmester 2017: 13). Moreover, the imaginaries required to sustain their beliefs in fairies, dragons, unicorns, and ghosts were richly resourced by contemporary media and culture, as we will explore in chapter 4, as well as their friendships.

These forms of belief challenge some historically dominant strands in childhood studies which have approached childhood through 'purging it of those genealogical markers such as "innocence", "incapacity", "dependence", "wonder"' (Davies 2014: 20) and have neglected 'collective wonder in childhood' (Kitching 2020: 16). At the same time, these subjunctive beliefs in the magical and supernatural are located within a human frame of meaning, as they are ultimately bound up for the children with their desire to create and maintain forms of social belonging. Thus their hermeneutic frameworks are located within their interactions with each other, family members, and the media and culture that resource these beliefs. This therefore aligns, as Abby Day argues in relation to supernatural beliefs amongst her participants, with the form of secularism 'proposed in the nineteenth century by G.J. Holyoake as a philosophy to "interpret and organise life without recourse to the supernatural"' (Day 2011: 202).

Faith in Friends and Family

When the children were asked about what was important to them in their lives, almost all spoke about their family, friends, and pets, and they often rooted special occasions, objects, places, or memories in these relationships. George and Jacob from Waterside discussed the importance of family, friends and pets in relation to objects, events, memories, and places:

> GEORGE: Well, I've got this picture in my room and it's a picture of a cat and its name's Chucky. It used to be my grandma's cat but then it passed away. Whenever I look at it, it makes me think of Chucky and it makes me feel really happy.
>
> JACOB: I have this picture and it's from a party [with friends]. It just makes me smile. . . . One of my favourite places is Australia because one of my aunties lives there.

The children spoke confidently—and often at length—about why these people, animals, and things mattered to them. This resonates strongly with other research which has shown how meaning, belief, and moral frameworks for young people in the UK, as well as in the US, are located in the 'immanent' realm of relationships with family and friends (Day 2011; Smith and Denton 2005; Savage et al. 2006). At the same time, it also reveals how these children are reflexive evaluators, able to recognize the value of their relationships with family, friends, and companion animals as 'relational goods' in their lives (Archer 2012: 99; Day 2011). Shaun from Sunnybank, for instance, spoke about how he suffered from 'a bit of depression', which he had spoken to his mother and doctor about, and said, 'when I see my friends, it just takes [the depression] away. I'm always happy when I'm with my friends.' He commented that his friends 'make my life so good. I just couldn't be without them.'

During fieldwork, we invited the children to take photographs of spaces and places at school that were special to them and to talk about the significance of these. One photograph was of school uniform ties attached to the school gate, which was a ritual Year 6 children performed each year on their final day of primary school before leaving for secondary school. Explaining what this meant to them, the children said that it showed that they were part of the 'school family' even after they had left. Another photo showed a wooden bench in the playground, and the children explained that this was where they would spend time with friends if they were sad, and they sometimes sat on the bench to indicate to their friends that something was wrong and they wanted to talk about it. The bench for this reason was often called 'the buddy bench'.

These examples illustrate how rituals and spaces at school encouraged the children to reflect on their friendships and belonging within the school community as significant. Furthermore, the ways the children interacted with each other revealed how their relationships are their most significant source of meaning and value, expressing how children's worlds are shaped by their 'longing to belong' (Pugh 2009). As the children described the importance of their friendships with each other, they demonstrated how their sense of self was relationally constituted through openness to an other. Molly and Rosie from St Peter's articulated this evocatively in terms that challenge the idea of the non-porous, 'buffered self' with which Taylor (2007) characterizes the human in 'the secular age', revealing their sense of porosity to each other:

RACHAEL: What about you, Molly, then, is there anybody that you find particularly inspiring, it could be real life?
MOLLY: Rosie.

RACHAEL: Oh Rosie. Why do you find Rosie inspiring?

MOLLY: Because she's been with me pretty much ever since I was born and she's been understanding of me and she's been knowing what I've been going through. I just think to have a best friend like Rosie nobody could be luckier.

RACHAEL: That's really lovely.

ROSIE: I also think that Molly inspired me because when we first—we became friends as soon as we saw each other, but she's helped me and inspired me to do stuff that I really like to do and she's helped me—I can't explain it. She's helped me become who I am. If she wasn't there I would be a completely different person.

MOLLY: Same, I wouldn't be me.

ROSIE: I wouldn't be like what I am.

MOLLY: I wouldn't be happier.

ROSIE: I might be happy but not in the same way as I am now . . .

MOLLY: Nobody's like Rosie.

ROSIE: I would never choose another best friend over Molly. . . . If she wasn't there I would be a different person, I'd still be happy but I would do different stuff in different ways. . . .

MOLLY: I wouldn't be me without Rosie.

While 'enchantment' may not be the right word to capture the richness of the friendships that these children have crafted and which form who they are, there is nevertheless a sense of *fullness* in how children experience these relationships. This challenges how Weber's 'disenchantment' narrative has often been taken to imply a sense of emotional emptiness or a lack of meaning (Schaefer 2022). While these modes of relationality are not unique to the non-religious and non-believing, they nevertheless challenge the idea of non-religious or atheist cultures as marked by lack or loss.

Conclusion

Attending to children's narratives of what it means to be non-believing opens up the different textures of their belief, from their propositional non-belief in a largely Christian God, to their belief in science and empiricist ways of knowing, their subjunctive beliefs in supernatural, magical entities, and life after death, and the significance of their everyday relationships with each other and their family. Studies of atheism in majority Christian contexts have often portrayed adolescence as a time marked by the loss of childhood belief, feeding into a perception of losing religion taking place as part of a coming-of-age process (Brown 2017). Many of the children we worked with never had a religious faith to lose, and their narratives reveal how children in 'middle childhood' experience childhood as a time of becoming, in which (non)belief is fluid. This is shaped in part through a wider social construction of childhood informed by developmental psychology in terms of the intentional 'staging' of learning which shapes schooling, as well as increasingly taking on empiricist and rationalist epistemologies. While many children positioned their own younger childhoods as a particular time of fantasy and magic, many still held onto subjunctive beliefs in the supernatural and magical, which they saw as enabling their social belonging, while at the same time knowing that they may not entirely reflect 'reality'.

These children's beliefs challenge widespread stereotypical narratives of 'non-religious modernity' as somehow disenchanted or shaped by the experience of the 'loss' of belief. In *The Myth of Disenchantment*, religious studies scholar Jason Josephson-Storm argues that not only does increasing atheism not correlate with a decline in enchantment, if anything, secularization 'seems to amplify enchantment' (2017: 32). Examining the place of magic in the history of the human sciences, he argues that belief in magic never really went away, and contends:

> The majority of people in the heartland of disenchantment believe in magic or spirits today, and it appears that they did so at the high point of modernity. Education does not directly result in disenchantment. Indeed, one might hazard the guess that education allows one to maintain more cognitive dissonance rather than less. Secularization and disenchantment are not correlated (Josephson-Storm 2017: 304).

We would agree that 'disenchantment' does not accurately represent the social realities of these children's worlds, and that many of them do—to a certain extent—believe in magic. However, we would suggest that the reason the disenchantment narrative does not convey these children's worlds is not—or, at least, not *only*—because they believe in magic, since not all did, and moreover the children tended to locate their subjunctive registers of belief as belonging distinctively to childhood and as something they will therefore move away from at some point. Rather, we would argue that narratives of disenchantment and the 'loss' of belief are wrong insofar as they evoke a sense of atheism as fundamentally a state of lack, emotional emptiness, or as part of an 'iron cage of modernity'.[18] Scholars such as Jane Bennett (2001) and George Levine (2011) have challenged the disenchantment narrative through showing how science and reason can be their own forms of enchantment, while Schaefer (2022) emphasizes how pursuits of truth through reason and scientific method can be intrinsically pleasurable and have their own distinctive affects. The ways in which many of the children expressed their enjoyment of science supports this idea that disenchantment—as stereotypically understood in terms of cold, rationalistic science pitted against irrational religion—is a myth, while at the same time, demonstrating the ongoing salience of the religion–science conflict narrative in shaping how the children articulated their non-belief in God.

Yet at a more fundamental level, narratives of atheism framed around disenchantment or the 'loss' of belief do not resonate with how these children experience their lives. Our analysis suggests that there *is* a shift towards what Charles Taylor calls 'the immanent frame': 'a "natural" order, to be contrasted to a "supernatural" one, an "immanent" world, over against a possible "transcendent" one' (2007: 542). However, as modes of value and meaning become anchored in this-worldly concerns, this should not be interpreted as a shrinking or contraction of horizons of significance, but rather reveals how the everyday and immanent is for these children the site of meaning, depth, and fullness. While Taylor notes that 'we can certainly go on experiencing fullness' in a secular society (2007: 26), his depiction of religious unbelief is nevertheless still characterized by 'the sense of an absence; it is the sense that all order, all

18. Josephson-Storm (2017) and Schaefer (2022) have each developed provocative and illuminating analyses of the concept of 'disenchantment', both arguing that Peter Berger's influential interpretation of Weber as developing a single 'rationalization–secularization–disenchantment' complex was wrong, based on an assumption that 'iron cage' and 'disenchantment' were synonyms for Weber. As Schaefer notes, the terms might 'sound the same in English, but *rationalization* (leading to "sensualists without spirit") and *intellectualization* (leading to "disenchantment") are different processes with different drivers and different outcomes' (Schaefer 2022: 87). In Josephson-Storm's analysis, the 'disenchanted modernity' narrative is wrong primarily because the ideas of 'disenchantment' and 'modernity' are both myths, and magic never went away. For Schaefer, the disenchantment narrative is not wrong, but has been misinterpreted. He argues that the pursuit of science as a calling that Weber identifies *does* bring disenchantment in the sense of *demagicification*, but that this has its own emotional resonances and affects, and is fully compatible with 'excitement, passion, and a kind of resolute dignity' (Schaefer 2022: 94). While our analysis supports Schaefer's argument, we would nevertheless be hesitant to use the term 'disenchantment' to describe these children's lives because it has become so synonymous with the 'iron cage' narrative.

meaning comes from us. We encounter no echo outside. . . . A race of humans has arisen which has managed to experience its world entirely as immanent. In some respects, we may judge this achievement as a victory for darkness' (2007: 376). Yet if we pay empirical attention to how these children live and perceive their place in the world, we see that their form of life is not some 'sad residue that is left over when the transcendent has been cast off' (Lee 2015: 167). It would therefore be more accurate to describe this shift towards human meaning and significance as a process of cultural transformation, rather than one of loss.

The children expressed little sense that they experienced their lives in terms of lack, loss, or absence. When asked whether they belonged to a religion, Oscar and Milo articulated how their life was already full without religion:

> MILO: I'm really interested in learning about other religions, but just not really being another religion, because I'm already part of a lot of things in my life.
>
> RACHAEL: Like what?
>
> MILO: I go to a childminders with my friend, Thomas, and I do Kung Fu every Monday and it's like a part of GB Fit, where we do loads of fun things. We go to Christmas parties and stuff like that together with Edward and Steve.
>
> OSCAR: I'm part of a . . . cookery club—which is really fun. . . . I'm also part Welsh because—
>
> RACHAEL: . . . So I got the idea that you're already part of some clubs, so you kind of feel like you've got—
>
> MILO: Enough.

On one level, their words could be taken merely as an indication that their lives are too busy for religion—which may be true.[19] Yet on another level, their comments suggest that these children see the needs which 'religion' might meet as amply fulfilled through their everyday, ordinary activities and relationships with others. Milo's 'enough' is resonant with a sense of not needing anything *more* in his life that religion might offer beyond these modes of connection and activity: he experiences life as *full*.

---

19. See, for example, Stolz et al. (2016), who present a theory of 'religious–secular competition', arguing that 'secular drift' is in part caused by the fact that religions in western European societies now need to compete against both secular and religious alternatives in a marketplace of leisure activities.

Moving beyond narratives of the loss or belief or decline of religion, shaped by the Christian 'genealogies of belief' which have formed sociological and anthropological imaginaries (Day 2011), the children's beliefs reveal a cosmology which centres the human and everyday human life as sources of meaning and significance. Seeking to honour the desire expressed by several children to be defined as what they *are* rather than what they are *not*, we would see 'humanist' as the most apt name for the form of life they are growing up within and themselves shaping. Although the majority of the children had not encountered and therefore did not identify using this term, we would nevertheless suggest that the broad contours of their beliefs can be situated in relation to key coordinates of humanism which other scholars have identified (Strhan et al. 2024).

'Humanism' is a term with many meanings, informed by its varied historical inheritances and lineages (Bullivant and Lee 2016; Blankholm 2017; Fassin 2019; Brown et al. 2023). In using the term here, we approach humanism as a form of life which centres the agency and significance of humans and broadly rejects the idea of supernatural or divine influences within the world in favour of 'taking up the mantle of reason, the tools of science, and the potentials of free thought' (Engelke 2015a: 72; Strhan et al. 2024). It *may*, as we have seen above, include some elements of supernatural or theistic belief, but overall, what is felt as *mattering* in this form of life is 'the lives and experiences of people here on Earth, rather than . . . institutions or doctrines, or the theology of the Beyond' (Bakewell 2023: 2). Humanism also has distinctive moral textures interwoven in everyday actions and interactions, as we will explore in chapter 5. Emphasizing individual human rights, freedoms, and equality, humanism is 'about respect for other people *qua* humans', as members of the same species (Lee 2015: 162). These ideas are broadly encapsulated by the British Humanist Harold Blackham's description that the humanist cause, 'in the vastest and vaguest of phrases, is "life and freedom", and on the enemy front are all those doctrines, institutions, practices and people hostile to life or freedom' (Blackham 1968: 159).

When we refer to humanists in the chapters that follow, we mean those whose form of life is humanist, whether they self-consciously identify as humanist or not. For clarity's sake, we distinguish between upper-case 'Humanism' and lower-case 'humanism' (Strhan et al. 2024). We use the former to refer to a self-conscious identification with Humanist histories and traditions and explicit Humanist discourses and organizations, such as Humanists UK and Ethical Culture, while the latter is an analytic category which identifies a form of life which does not necessarily include conscious association or identification with these organizations or histories, even if it continues to be shaped by their inheritance (Copson 2015: 4–5; Copson et al. 2023: 23). Just as lived religion scholars have emphasized how lived religious practices may draw on religious and spiritual repertoires in ways that do not align with the 'coherence' of 'official' institutional religious doctrines and creeds, so the children's humanist beliefs were rarely expressed in clear, developed creedal propositions. Rather, their humanism tended 'to emerge through fragments of articulated belief and also in accounts of real-world encounters of various sorts', as well as through embodied practices and interactions (Lee 2015: 172). Moreover, humanism and other non-religious worldviews are rarely mutually exclusive, and can be combined—including with aspects of religious world-views—in creative, seemingly self-contradictory ways in individuals' lives (ibid.). We will see in chapter 5, for example, how the children combine their humanism with expressions of equality extending to animals in terms that resonate with the 'emerging worldview' Lori Beaman identifies in her study of the worldviews of sea turtle rescue volunteers which 'recognizes interdependence, based on both scientific evidence and an ethic of respect that invokes a reformulated understanding of equality' (Beaman 2017b: 25–6).

While humanism's demise as a scholarly standpoint has been proclaimed in critical theory, philosophy, sociology and other disciplines due to its having been seen as inextricably entangled with human exceptionalism and racist, colonial histories,[20] important *empirical* questions remain about the contemporary contours of humanism and its interrelations with non-belief. As Claire Blencowe argues, drawing on Paul Gilroy (2015) and Sylvia Wynter (1995), in our desire 'to be done with the evils of colonial humanism', we should not 'dismiss all the counterhumanisms that have grown up through the experience of living with and contesting colonialism' (Blencowe 2016: 37). These other humanisms might include a 'magical humanism' which allows for different textures of enchantment and wonder (Blencowe 2016: 32), and a 'planetary humanism' which seeks to resist racism and other forms of dehumanization of the other (Gilroy 2000, 2005). Over the following chapters, we will explore the particular textures of the children's humanist form of life and how it was resourced by parents, school contexts, wider culture, and the children's relations with each other. First let us turn to the parents.

20. See, for example, discussions in Braidotti (2013); Asad (2015); Wentzer and Mattingly (2018); Mahmood (2018); Fassin (2019).

2

Raising Godless Children

GORDON WAS A MIDDLE-CLASS parent at St Peter's in his early fifties who worked as a civil servant. Rachael met Gordon after school when he came to collect Charlie, and they all walked home together, Charlie telling his Dad about what had happened at school that day, and Rachael briefly discussing our broader project. As they sat down in the living room, Charlie went upstairs to play his new guitar. At the start of the interview, Rachael asked Gordon how he would answer if he was completing a survey that asked about his religious position. He replied 'no religion' and explained that to him this meant, 'I don't have a belief in things that are magical or supernatural or things that, I guess, fit within a definition of superstition.' Gordon had identified as non-religious from early childhood and remembered coming home from Sunday School when he was about Charlie's age and telling his parents that the Christian teachings they were learning at Sunday School were 'stories and I wasn't really interested'. He described his parents as 'quite liberal' and his home growing up as 'a generalist C of E [Church of England] type household where there were some cultural links to the church in that sense of there being births, deaths, marriage links'. Gordon said he would identify as 'secular', 'rationalist', and 'humanist', and when asked what those terms meant to him, said:

> by 'secular' it's a hope, really, that society can move towards a place where people's spirituality or rationalism is not something that is used to divide people and consider people as others in another group. The 'rationalist' is something that I think is another hopeful thing, really—hoping to be quite positive and hopeful that, through dialogue and a more open society, people can take a more rationalist approach to problems.

He then explained what 'humanist' meant to him:

> I think there's generally, it seems to me, some good evidence that people
> can be really great to each other. One of the things we wanted to talk about
> was what things I get a sense of awe and wonder and delight from, and some
> of those things are really small things like kindnesses people do or extra
> steps people make. There was an ambulance driver on the TV . . . who had
> taken the trouble to learn Urdu so he could talk to people and communicate to
> those people who didn't have the facility of English or the older generation
> immigrants that he was visiting. . . . He took the trouble to do that and I
> thought that's great. That's really awesome. Other things like the wonder of
> the natural world. Looking at the moon glow last night or the night before,
> it was nearly a full moon and it was really bright. If you think that's just re-
> flecting light itself, it's not a glowing thing. Those sorts of things, I think,
> are what I feel are important to me.

Asked about his non-belief in God, Gordon said belief in God was 'a social
construct . . . I think it's something that has come from people, that has developed over time and the pathways are reinforced over time that have led to
sectarianism and consolidation of particularly strong ideas that defined some
groups against other groups, but all, I think, probably rooted in the need to
find answers or present answers.' He added that since becoming a father, he
had more insight into why 'people would want to present an answer to a child
as a reassurance that there's a reason for something or that something is
known and that's okay', but added that he felt that there was 'a positive in
saying we don't know, we're exploring it, and people are trying to find out and
understand'.

Reflecting on how he was raising his children, Gordon sought to encourage
his children's empirical sensibilities, to foster, as he put it,

> an interest in science and the scientific method and all that comes from
> that, really. That thing that you have ideas and you test them and you test
> them with other people and those ideas that no one can prove are wrong
> are the ones that stick around, and that's how you explore, whether it's
> materials or ideas of how society works.

Asked whether he sought to pass on a particular worldview to his children, he
said he hoped he was passing on 'a positive view of humanity and humanity's
capacity to develop good solutions to the problems that we're facing with an
increasing population and an industrial heritage and technologies and

inequality. . . . It's the idea of moving towards using the technology in a positive way for humanity.'

Although Gordon said that they didn't discuss religion much as a family, religion was not absent. At Christmas, his sons attended church nativity services with his mother-in-law, and Gordon commented that his children were aware of 'some interesting ideas that come from their grandma, like about where rainbows come from . . . something to do with God doing something'. Gordon commented that he had in the past wondered whether to challenge the Christian perspectives she was sharing, and decided he would not, 'because it would have been unkind, really, and difficult for the boys because I would have been challenging a strongly held belief of hers in front of them, which would have been not a positive thing'. He commented that Charlie was 'socially aware and sensitive' towards his grandma's faith, and was 'selective' in how he presented his non-belief depending on who he was with. Gordon emphasized the importance of allowing his children's freedom in relation to religion and said that this was part of 'the respect I think they're due'. While Christian rites of passage had been present in his own earlier life, Gordon and his wife had no rituals to mark their sons' births. Yet he positioned his atheist cosmology as contributing to his sense of wonder at their births, describing how he had felt 'delight and thankfulness and gratitude. . . . It was that feeling of being really fortunate and lucky to have . . . two healthy boys and stuff like that and it's all a wonderful thing. It is in the context of being in a deep, cold space on the planet that's whizzing around, which makes it more remarkable, but that's where I come from, I think.'

Gordon's positioning of himself in relation to religion and belief is revealing of a number of ideas and practices which were common amongst the parents. We can see a clear decline of religion across generations, as Gordon's parents' liberal Anglicanism was not something he sought to pass on to his sons, in a pattern that was present for many of our families. Yet, expanding beyond this 'decline' narrative, we can also see how Gordon's non-religious identification and atheism were two interrelated threads within a distinctively humanist form of life, which, as outlined in the previous chapter, centres the human within its cosmology and rejects ideas of supernatural or divine influences in the world in favour of empirical evidence and human capacities of reason and concern for human flourishing. Gordon's rejection of magical or supernatural influences is interwoven with his empiricism, valorization of science, and his belief that humanity and human knowledge are forces for good, stances which he sought to pass on to his children. These ways of knowing and experiencing the world locate meaning and significance within the 'immanent frame' but are not experienced in terms of disenchantment (Taylor 2007). Rather, they are imbued with textures of wonder at the 'natural world' and awe and delight in everyday acts of kindness, through which 'the good' is defined not in terms of a religious or metaphysical framework but rather through the affirmation of ordinary life.

While Gordon was not explicitly critical of or hostile towards religion, an implicit critique was evident in his positioning of secularity and rationalism as contributing to a more harmonious society, especially read alongside his view of religion as a 'social construct' which has led to 'sectarianism' and groups being defined 'against others'. This temporal and moral construction of progressive, rationalist secularity, in alignment with science, and contrasted with divisive, illusory, irrational religion, can be located within broader (post)Christian, humanist narratives of progress. What makes these temporal orientations humanist is not simply the modernist idea of progress 'but rather the association of progress with human knowledge' (Lee 2015: 163), which Gordon, like several other parents, articulated. Yet alongside his critique of religion, Gordon was at the same time sensitive to others' faith and mindful of the effects on his children of how he negotiated religious differences within their family.

These distinctive, interrelated elements of a humanist form of life were, as we will explore below, present to varying degrees amongst most parents we spoke with, shaping the intellectual, moral, and imaginative resources available to children as they figured out their beliefs. Parents are widely recognized as one of the most important influences on the religious or non-religious lives of their children, and this is not surprising: raising children means helping to shape what comes to matter to them and what they find interesting and meaningful—or boring and irrelevant. We can see this dynamic in play in how Charlie's explanation of his non-belief mirrors Gordon's interest in—and sense of the importance of—science:

> CHARLIE: I don't believe in God because of science, basically, because there are different regions of science which I'm interested in, such as chemistry and biology. I have quite a few science books at home. I kind of discover what is real and what isn't by reading quite a lot. Reading is also quite important to me.
> RACHAEL: That helps to sort of give you an idea of what to believe and what not to believe because science is really important to you?
> CHARLIE: Yes. Science is really important to me.

This resonance between how Charlie and Gordon articulated their atheist stances highlights the part played by parents in shaping the textures of non-believing forms of life, and invites attention to the question of *how* parents help shape children's non-belief: what—if anything—are these parents actually doing with their children in relation to religion or belief? What do they talk about when they're talking about religion, and when and how are they talking about it? How are parents rendering particular aspects of religious belief or practice present or absent in children's lives? Do parents give the impression that particular forms of religion are interesting, boring, important, dangerous, funny, exotic, or valuable, for instance? How do these aspects of raising children in relation to religion interrelate with and contribute to the children's humanist form of life that we explored in the previous chapter?

In addressing these questions, this chapter is in conversation with debates about religious socialization and transmission, in which parental upbringing is widely recognized as playing a leading role in shaping the religious or non-religious lives of their children.[1] The rise of the religious 'nones' across many countries has prompted growing attention to how changing socialization in relation to religion is fuelling this shift. Quantitative studies have shown that parental religious socialization is declining in Europe (e.g. Stolz et al. 2016; Tervo-Niemelä 2021), while studies focused on North America (e.g., Thiessen and Wilkins-Laflamme 2017; Bengtson et al. 2018) reveal that key catalysts for the growth of non-religion are both an increase in 'irreligious socialization' and religiously identifying parents increasingly giving their children choice in relation to religion, resulting in their disaffiliating when they reach adolescence. Feeding into this waning of religious socialization is its changing status, increasingly considered optional rather than a social duty (Stolz et al. 2016; Day 2022).

However, while these studies indicate that changing socialization in relation to religion is contributing to the growth of non-religion across generations, there has been little attention to the everyday micro-processes through which children are growing up non-religious and non-believing, or about the interplay of processes at home and in school through which children become non-religious. The 'neonatal' body of work in this area has demonstrated the importance of parents in the process of how non-religion develops across generations within families (Bengtson et al. 2013, 2018; Gärtner 2022; Müller

---

1. See, for example, Myers (1996); Crockett and Voas (2006); Petts (2009); Stolz (2009); Stolz et al. (2016); Voas and Storm (2012); Bengtson et al. (2009, 2013); Scourfield et al. (2013); Smith et al. (2020).

and Porada 2022). Christel Manning's study of how non-religious parents in the US are raising their children has provided important insight into the 'diverse range of their perspectives and behaviors that is not easily characterized as religious or secular', but underlying which is a commitment to the imperative of personal worldview choice (Manning 2015: 5). However, we know little about the experiences of parents whose children are growing up non-religious in contexts such as England where being non-religious is now a majority identity. How do their experiences compare with each other? Are parents in England seeking to impart a distinctive non-religious worldview? Or is what is going on better understood as a lack of religious practice and participation? Or both? Furthermore, we know little about whether and how parents are raising their children in relation to other-than-religious forms of life that scholars of non-religion have identified, including humanist, agnostic, or subjectivist (Lee 2015; LeDrew 2015; van Mulukom et al. 2023; Singleton et al. 2021).

Historian Callum Brown's study of how people living through the 1960s became atheist argues that a 'new moral cosmos' of humanism has become the dominant worldview in western societies (2017: 161). Brown notes that conventional histories of Humanism trace its development through philosophical lineages beginning in ancient Greece, via Christian Humanism, the European Enlightenment, to late modern secular moralists (2017: 161). Yet there has been little attention, as he notes, to the formation of humanism amongst those who did not get it from reading books or listening to Humanist thinkers, which invites the question: Where *are* they finding it? (2017: 162). In answering this question, Brown suggests that humanism was intuitively obvious to the people he spoke to, even before they came to identify as humanist: 'Humanism was neither a philosophy nor an ideology that they had learned or read about and then adopted. There was no act of conversion, no training or induction which turned them into humanists.' Instead, Brown traces the dominance of humanist values in western cultures to 1945 and the extension of rights to those who had previously been denied them and the legal frameworks regarding human rights emerging from the Second World War, which became central to the United Nations and European Law (Brown 2017: 168).[2] Yet Brown's argument that humanism appears intuitive to those who come to identify as humanist

2. Brown, Nash and Lynch's history of Humanist organizations in Britain (2023) demonstrates that the Humanist movement played a significant part in these shifts, through their vocabulary of human rights being taken up in wider politics and international relations.

raises further questions. Modern humanism does not express universal human values: as historian Alec Ryrie notes, its ethics of 'gender and racial equality, sexual freedom, a strong doctrine of individual human rights, a sharp distinction between the human and non-human realms—are, in a long historical perspective, very unusual indeed' (2019: 202). While these values might have appeared intuitive to Brown's participants, we need to ask *how* it is, in practical terms, that they become intuitive.

In this and subsequent chapters, we explore how the children's humanism was being formed in everyday life. In this chapter, we ask what was being passed on by their parents, and in what ways, as children came to think of themselves as non-believing and non-religious and to inhabit the broadly humanist form of life outlined in the previous chapter. We demonstrate the relative lack of discussion about religion or belief amongst parents and children in most of our families—even where parents were religiously affiliated—combined with a variety of stances towards religion, belief, and spirituality articulated by the parents. However, underlying the diversity of positions taken by the parents was a shared understanding that their role as parents was not to decide their child's religious or non-religious identity or faith, but rather to provide them with the resources to work out for themselves who they are and their place in the world, as part of what Margaret Archer (2012) describes as the 'reflexive imperative of late modernity'.

'It's Not a Thing': On Not Talking about Religion

In Manning's (2015) US-focused study, most parents intentionally incorporated a distinctive religious or secular worldview into how they were raising their children. For many, this involved taking their children back to the church or synagogue of their own childhood, while others sought out alternative non-religious communities or sought to impart a non-religious worldview without institutional support, drawing on advice from books such as *Parenting beyond Belief* (McGowen 2007). Manning notes that the least common[3] strategy was to take no action to transmit any particular worldview, religious or secular, to their children. The picture looks very different amongst our parents. When we

3. Manning notes that her sample is not representative and that because she was conducting a study exploring how None parents do or do not incorporate religion in their children's upbringing, parents for whom religion or secularity were matters of interest were more likely to participate (2015: 135–6).

asked whether they were intentionally seeking to incorporate religion, spirituality, or a particular secular worldview into their child's upbringing, many were unsure how to answer this, either saying they didn't know, or looking puzzled and asking for clarification, or commenting that they felt that it was the school's responsibility—not theirs—to educate their child in relation to religion. This is not to say that the parents were *not* imparting distinctive worldviews to their children, just that this was not something that the parents necessarily reflected on consciously in relation to *religion*.

This situation is because, for many of the parents, religion was positioned within the home as a matter of minimal significance. When we asked the children and their parents whether they discussed religion much at home, most said it was not something they discussed much, other than in relation to what the children had been learning about in Religious Education lessons. Lewis, who we met in the previous chapter, whose parents identified as Church of England, said that religion only came up in discussion at home if he or a sibling had learnt about it at school, and said, 'it's not like a normal subject that we talk about in our house'. This minimal place afforded to religion in everyday discussions was underscored by the fact that many children were unsure whether their parents were religious or believed in God. Edith and Amy, pupils at St Peter's, said they did not think their parents were religious, noting the lack of religious practice in their lives:

> EDITH: My mum, I don't really know about her because I think she's the same as me, she doesn't really know. . . . I think my dad, I'm not sure about him either because he might be really religious, but I don't know about it. I'm not really sure.
> AMY: If you don't know about it, I don't think he'd be really religious.
> RACHAEL: What makes you say that?
> AMY: Because then you'd be going to church every Sunday, wouldn't you, if he was really religious. You know what I mean, if he was really religious I think you'd probably know.
> EDITH: Yes, because he'd probably be like praying to God every night.
> AMY: Yes, he'd have a prayer mat and you could just hear someone every night, 'Hmmm', something like that.
> EDITH: Meditating.

Charlie, Gordon's son, said religion was never discussed and mentioned that it was only because of a discussion prompted by the letter to his parents about our study that he became aware of his parents' humanist identities.

Some parents were unaware of their children's religious beliefs or identities, for example, Cassandra and Liam, parents at Sunnybank:

CASSANDRA: As far as we're aware, they don't believe in it. We've never really . . .
LIAM: No, I don't really talk about it much.
RACHAEL: I was going to say, does it come up in conversation much?
CASSANDRA: No, it just doesn't. That's probably why they [the children] don't believe in it.

This relative lack of discussion about religion can be seen as an instance of what Phil Zuckerman (2008) terms 'bald secularity'.[4] In his research with non-religious populations in Denmark and Sweden, Zuckerman argues that his informants' reluctance to speak about religion arose from 'the simple fact that religion is such a marginal aspect of their culture, and such a minimal element in their daily lives' that they lack a 'narrative structure' when it comes to religion (2008: 103). While, as we will outline below, this was not the case with all parents, the *relatively* minimal place afforded to discussing religion in most children's everyday home lives fed into their perception of religion as an issue of marginal salience or value. Since people tend to talk about what matters to them—whether friendships, sport, music, or politics—when little is said about religion, 'the messages are subliminal, but their accumulated socialization effects are powerful' (Smith and Adamczyk 2021: 24).

Several parents mentioned that not talking about religion stemmed from their own lack of interest. Miles, the father of Ella from St Peter's, described moving away from the Christianity of his upbringing as an adult. He said he felt there was a change from his parents' generation 'to my generation where we moved to a more secular approach, and we didn't feel like a draw to the church. I think that sense of duty that I felt as a child, I didn't feel as an adult, so I haven't felt that or any sense of need to search for something that might provide a guide.' He described himself as non-religious and agnostic, adding, 'I'm like, take it or leave it, in a way, with religion. I don't have strong opinions of it now. I might have done when I was younger. I don't think it's such a significant thing in my life. I know it is in other contexts, but it's not a big thing in my life.' Miles reflected on how religion's lack of significance for him was

---

4. It is worth noting that lack of discussion of religion does not necessarily indicate 'bald secularity' (although it does in this case). If a community is completely immersed within a religion which is thus largely taken for granted, they may not also spend much time discussing it.

shaping Ella's experience, commenting that religion was 'not a thing, I think, that's the thing. It's not a big thing in my sphere, and consequently Ella's sphere of experience, except for what happens in school.' Reflecting on the religious diversity amongst pupils at St Peter's, he said Ella was 'obviously mixing with lots of kids, lots of different religious experiences at school, so she probably gets a lot more [input on religion in school]' than at home.

Kristen, another St Peter's parent, likewise drew attention to intergenerational shifts as she contrasted her own lack of interest in religion with her mother. She said her mother 'knows all about the Bible and the verses but I've never taken an interest in it'. Kristen commented that religion only came up in discussion at home in relation to the school:

> It's only through the school . . . For him [her son] if he said, 'Mum I believe in God', and he had his own beliefs then I wouldn't stop that. What he does is entirely up to him. I'll support him all the way through it, do you know what I mean? Apart from that, nothing's brought up. . . . Only in school it's a big subject, at Christmas time when they go to church. . . . All the Eid parties and stuff like that, he'll celebrate all that. Whatever he chooses to do that's entirely up to him. But I don't encourage it, you know?

Echoing this sense of generational shifts, Monica, a mother at St Peter's, spoke about how her parents used to send her to Sunday School as a child 'because that was what parents did', but said she had decided at a young age, 'sorry, it's not for me'. She commented that being interviewed for this study was the first time she'd ever had a conversation about religion or its place in her life with anyone, stating, 'no-one has ever asked me, "Do you have a religious . . . ?" It's never continued into a conversation. I always say things like, "Well, we're not churchy", or "Well, we're not really into that". It's never gone further.'

The children's comments were often revealing about how they picked up on religion's lack of salience for their parents. When asked how he thought his parents would identify in relation to religion, Callum from Sunnybank said,

> I think my mum will pick 'no religion' because she doesn't have a religion. She only thinks about washing-up. My dad might be a Christian, because he was christened, but he hasn't actually said it yet. My granddad might be 'none of the above', because he doesn't actually do anything. He just sits inside and watches the football and the cricket. My grandma might be 'not sure' because she might have been something. I don't know what it was. She hasn't actually talked about anything.

Even the small number of children who attended church regularly with their parents picked up on cues suggesting religion was less important to their parents than other things. Steve, who we met in the previous chapter, whose parents were liberal Anglicans, perceived his father as valuing snowboarding more than church, noting, 'the thing is, my dad loves nothing better than snowboarding, so he'll give up church for snowboarding'.

This sense of religion not mattering was not the case for all families: for some parents, aspects of religion were important in their lives, while a small number presented more overtly critical perspectives on religion to their children. For others, although discussions about religion did not *regularly* punctuate the weekly rhythms of family life, it was at times a matter for family discussion, as we will explore below. However, for the most part, everyday interactions between parents and children did not signal to the children that faith was something of personal significance to their parents. How then did the parents understand and experience their parenting practices in relation to religion? And when they did speak about religion with their children, what were they saying, and how?

'This Isn't What We Do': Normalizing Non-Religion and Non-Belief

Alice and Rich were the parents of Louise, who we met in the previous chapter, and were both middle-class professionals in their mid-forties. Explaining their non-religious identities, both used terms that also made clear their humanist stances. Alice identified as 'secular', 'atheist' and 'rationalist', and explained what these terms meant to her:

> Secular, I think, just because I'm a big believer in not having religion in state mechanisms of any kind. . . . Atheist: I take 'atheist' to mean 'without a god'. That's strictly, I think, what it means and that describes me because I don't have any belief in a god. Rationalist: I don't strictly know exactly what the definition of that is, but I like to think of myself as being a rational thinker. I like to think that I base my beliefs and thoughts on evidence.

Rich said that he would describe himself in the same way and added that he didn't like introducing the concept of belief in God, due to lack of evidence: 'one's base level should be to be sceptical, and you should only introduce belief when there is evidence of a thing. Since there is no evidence of a god, there is no reason to introduce the belief.'

During earlier adulthood, Alice had identified as Christian, but having children had sharpened her humanist sensibilities in terms of her awareness of shared human conditions of loving one's children, and she described how she had moved away from Christianity as she found it did not measure up to her humanist sensibilities. As she described it:

> Since having kids, I've come up against the reality of these entities that you love so, so much and you want to protect. You'd do anything to protect them. Yet, other people in the world have the experience of not being able to protect their children—with their children getting ill, being in war zones and not having enough to eat. What's the difference between them and me? It's not that I'm praying and they're not. It's just that I'm lucky that I've been born in a westernised, safe country and they're unlucky and they haven't. It's just luck. . . . I think those kinds of thoughts have really struck me since having kids . . .

Her critical move away from religion meant that she felt uneasy at her children being expected to participate in Christian practices from a young age. Alice commented that when Louise started nursery she had 'come home one day . . . saying that they'd prayed. I thought, "What? They're three. That's mad."'

Religion was something they discussed at home when Louise asked questions about things she'd learnt about religion at school. The way Alice described these conversations revealed how she and Rich were presenting scientific perspectives as an alternative to religious beliefs, and how their discussions about science were feeding into Louise's valorization of science. At the same time, Alice also articulated a desire for their children not to see religious beliefs as subordinate to science:

> ALICE: Because of the kind of people we are, we are very open to those kinds of conversations, so we talk about it [religion]. Because, also, we're both scientific people, we talk about scientific things quite a lot as well. Rich's background is physics, and Louise is interested in physics and stuff, so they've talked about the origins of the universe and all that kind of . . .
> LOUISE: I've decided I might want to be a physicist when I grow up.
> ALICE: Okay. Yes, so we do talk about that kind of thing quite a lot, but I am aware that I don't want us ever to become people who express any kind of negativity towards people who are religious or any kind of intellectual superiority because they might change their minds when they grow up. That's absolutely fine.

While Rich and Alice were conscious of their own atheism and discussed it with their children, they also reflected on how they wouldn't want to force their perspectives on their children, wanting their children to determine their own beliefs on the basis of evidence and reason:

ALICE: I agreed with Richard Dawkins when he said, 'There's no such thing as a religious child. There's just a child of religious parents', because children are so influenced, particularly if their parents hold very strong views. It's extremely difficult for a child to go against that before they become a teenager, I would say. I'm aware of the fact that you could have a similar argument for a non-religious child. You could say, 'Well they're not forming their own opinions. They're just parroting what their parents say.'

RICH: Well, yes, that's exactly what I was just going to say. It's completely pointless, because then it becomes the unbelief in God that's given to you by your parents rather than a rationalization based on evidence. The child needs to work that out for themselves.

Despite their desire for their children to work out their own beliefs, Alice and Rich also expressed a sense that atheism was the shared perspective in their home. Rich contrasted his own upbringing, in which his parents disagreed about whether God existed, and said, 'I grew up with that debate, whereas there is no debate here, is there?' Furthermore, as Alice and Rich articulated their own non-belief in the interview with Louise present, we glimpsed how these parent–child exchanges normalized non-belief, as in response to what they were saying, Louise was keen to burnish her atheist and non-religious credentials:

LOUISE: My religion is . . . I don't know whether there are such things, but what about Star Wars Mega Dragons . . .

RICH: I don't think that's an official religion yet.

ALICE: There should be. I'd sign up to that. [laughter] . . . I know what it's like to be a child because I have been one, and I know what it's like to have children. They are hugely influenced by their parents. Although, of course, I totally accept my children's current viewpoint about the world, I also realise that they're massively influenced by us and by what we say, because we talk about this sort of stuff quite a lot.

RACHAEL: You do? Does this come up in conversation?

LOUISE: There's no evidence for God . . .

ALICE: We have had discussions about God . . . especially because Louise
and Elena go to a church near their school, so they pray.

LOUISE: Well, I don't necessarily pray.

After Louise had gone upstairs to get ready for bed, Alice and Rich spoke
about how amongst their peers and colleagues, being non-religious was the
cultural default. Alice said:

I, personally, think that we mix with the kind of people where . . . I assume
everyone *isn't* religious, particularly at work. I'm always slightly taken about
when I realise that somebody— . . . There's a guy at work and he is very
religious. It was a while before I realised that he was very active in the
church. . . . When I found that out, I was like, 'Oh. Oh my God. That's
weird', but because I try very hard to be a tolerant person, I realise that
that's my problem. I made that assumption, and I shouldn't make that assumption about people.

Here we see a reversal of how in previous generations churchgoing and identifying as Christian were marks of 'respectability' (Day 2022). Rich's response
further indicates the cultural milieu they inhabit: despite their emphasis on
tolerance and desire not to see atheism as intellectually superior to religious
belief, this *is*, in fact, the way they see the world:

RICH: I don't know of any openly religious people. I'm sure I must work
with some. I don't know of any. Have we ever had any friends that were
religious? I can't think . . .

ALICE: Not properly churchgoing, regularly practising. I don't think so, no.

RICH: No. Yes, it tends to be more unusual.

ALICE: Despite what I said earlier when Louise was here about trying not
to be an intellectual snob, I think we are.

RICH: Oh yes, we definitely are. I mean, I am, but I try not to be, just in
the same way that I try to exercise and I try to be good. I try not to be
an intellectual snob, but sometimes, you fail.

Alice and Rich exemplified when and how many of the non-religious parents
were speaking about religion with their children: primarily prompted by the
children's asking questions about or mentioning their learning about religion
at school, parents were presenting religion as something *other* people do, while
at the same time seeing themselves as supporting their children's autonomy in
relation to religion and belief. We also see this dynamic in the comments of

Mary, the mother of Ada at St Peter's, who was raised in a mixed Protestant and Catholic household in Northern Ireland during the 1970s. Mary's experience growing up during the Troubles and her identity as a scientist not only informed her own non-religious identity but also how she discussed religion with her children. Mary said discussions about religion came up at home when Ada wanted to discuss what she'd learnt about in school, and said,

> MARY: . . . we'll discuss being Muslim in the same way we would discuss being a Christian, as in, this isn't what we do, despite the fact that both of her parents have been brought up in religious households.
> RACHAEL: So you kind of try and discuss them all objectively?
> MARY: Rationally . . . Sort of, 'This is what other people believe, and you can choose to believe it yourself, but this isn't something we do.' There's no, 'You're not allowed to' either. It's not, 'We don't do this as a family, we're not doing this together.' But if she wants to follow a religion, I hope she knows she could do, really. You have to be careful about that and how you say things really, as well. Religion's definitely discussed.

The parents who expressed the strongest anti-religious sentiments and consciousness of being atheist were usually those for whom religion had played a significant part in their own earlier life.[5] Of these, a handful said that they would not be comfortable with their children becoming religious. Erica, the mother of Jasmine from St Peter's, commented that her husband was 'very anti-organized religion' because of 'the corruption . . . and the hypocrisy that's gone behind it'. She said that if either of their daughters became religious, 'he would be really unhappy . . . I'm thinking more if it became slightly more evangelical, or even if they had children and wanted to get them christened . . . I think he would be really unhappy.' Alastair, the father of Ruby from St Peter's, commented that if Ruby were to come home and express 'really categorical religious positions, I'd be like, "where are you getting that from?" I'd want to know and I'd chase it down.'

However, most parents who expressed anti-religious views articulated a desire for their children to be free to choose their own path in relation to religion, even if that meant choosing to be religious. Danny, one of the few working-class parents at Waterside, was the father of Sophia, who we met in the previous chapter. Danny had attended a Roman Catholic school and

5. This resonates with previous studies demonstrating atheism has more salience for those for whom religion is more present in their culture or upbringing (e.g., Smith 2010; Zuckerman et al. 2016).

mentioned a friend who had been abused as an altar boy, and was highly critical of religion throughout the interview. He said that religion was 'the root of all war' and described the Catholic Church as 'probably the biggest criminal organization around' and as 'brainwashing, saying there isn't a Big Bang theory', before moving on to theodicy, commenting that God can't be 'all for peace and stuff' while 'killing thousands of people in the tsunami'. He then compared contemporary Islam with medieval Christian violence:

> As for what's going on now with the Jihad. People forget what we did, the English and the Crusades: we raped, pillaged and murdered nearly the whole world. We've moved on. I think they [Muslims] haven't moved on as a civilization. They're only doing what we did years ago.

Just as Sophia expressed a sense of religion as belonging in the past, Danny also said, 'it's more of an older generation who go to church, this, that and the other'. However, despite his own visceral distaste for religion, Danny wanted to enable Sophia's freedom in relation to religion, stating that if she 'wanted to do her first Holy Communion then I'd support that, she can do it. For me, I want Sophia to be independent.' In practice, both Danny and Sophia said that religion was not something they spoke much about. When asked whether it was discussed Danny said, 'not so much, but she does ask questions. I just give her my answer and say, "I don't believe in it".' This minimal presence of religion in Sophia's everyday home life thus contributed to her not seeing it as something important for her. Yet while, as we saw in the previous chapter, she expressed a sense of religion—especially non-Christian religions—as 'other', there was no evidence of her sharing Danny's moral critique. Indeed, she spoke about how she might herself be religious one day.

This dynamic of saying little about religion while at the same time privileging an ideal of children's freedom in relation to religion was present amongst many of the parents who expressed anti-religious sentiments. Harriet from Sunnybank spoke about living in the US 'Bible Belt' with her first husband, where they had regularly attended church and she had pretended she believed in God to fit in. Harriet said that in the UK, she had never felt being non-religious made her feel different to other parents, whereas in the US, she had felt judged by the Christian mums she encountered:

> People in the UK are a little bit more quiet about it. But in the US, because it was quite religious, and so you've got these stay-at-home mums who cook extravagantly salty and sweet meals, and just cook and clean all day. Then there's you, looking a mess, your house is a bit dirty, and you're just stressed

and stuff, and they . . . just used to make me feel like shit. . . . It [religion] was absolutely everywhere. So if you weren't religious, you were the social outcast.

She said that her ex-husband had

really strong religious beliefs that he wanted to be pushed down their [the children's] throats, and I didn't, because . . . they're really vulnerable. I don't want them having those kinds of anxieties, that if they do something wrong they're going to be punished or they're going to go to hell, or they're going to look at mum and dad and go, 'Wow, mum is having a glass of wine. She's going to burn in hell', you know? 'Aunty so and so, she's a lesbian.' . . . I just wanted them to not have all those worries and those concerns.

Because of Harriet's desire not to have these religious beliefs forced on her children, she said that since splitting up with her husband, 'I've never mentioned religion to them at all, but I never challenge religion either. So, it's just not a conversation we've ever had in this household, either anything against it or for it.' Thus with religion absent in discussion at home, the language her son used to articulate his non-belief in God (and his belief in science) was being resourced through school rather than home. Harriet described how a couple of years previously, her son 'came home and told me that he believed, well, he called it "revolution" but he meant "evolution". . . . He came home, he had this opinion, and I was just like, "Okay" . . . I didn't even necessarily encourage it. I just allowed him to have it.' She also took this accepting stance when her daughter described Christmas as 'Jesus's birthday' following a nursery nativity play.[6] She said, 'I don't shout that down. I just go, "Oh, that's nice. Is it? That's interesting." Like, I try and be neutral about it, because I don't want to force it, and I don't want to force them against it. I don't want to influence that.'

'Religious Residues': Where, When, and How Religion was Present

Everyday Conversations and Practices

While the majority of the parents identified as non-religious and did not believe in God, there were a number who belonged to a religion, and a number who believed in God. Reflecting the higher proportions of Christian identification

---

6. Though not uncontested, nativity plays are a common feature across UK primary schools.

in the broader north-west region where Sunnybank was located, it was not surprising that there were more Christian-identifying parents here than at Waterside or St Peter's. For most of these, their identification with Christianity expressed a 'nominal' belonging: they described themselves as 'non-practising', and did not, for instance, attend church other than for baptisms, weddings, and funerals. Just as some of the children identified as Christian—or were unsure about their religious identity—because of having been baptised, so for several parents, their Christian identity was 'natal' (Day 2011), conferred at birth through baptism, and not something they necessarily sought to pass this on to their children. However, due to the higher levels of Christian and Muslim identification within the area in which Sunnybank was located, religion was more of a live issue for parents in this fieldsite, both for those who belonged to Christianity and for those who had moved on. Being 'non-religious' was not perceived here by parents as the cultural default as it was by parents at St Peter's and Waterside. For example, Jake, Lea's father, described an instance where he had been completing a form at work, and a couple of his colleagues saw that he had written 'no religion', and commented 'they were really taking the mickey out of me, saying, "No? Are you just wandering about godless?"'

As well as the higher number of 'natal Christian' Sunnybank parents, the liveness of religion in the local area—which included both a significant Muslim population and relatively high levels of Christian identification—also led some parents here to share their critiques of religion with their children. We can see this dynamic with the parents of humanist-identifying Ryan. Ryan's mother, Jane, described herself as Christian 'since birth' and said she believed in a 'wider being out there . . . something looking down on you'. She described how as a child she had been 'forced to go to church every Sunday', and spoke about how the church school she had attended was 'proper Christian. Lord's Prayer every morning, Lord's Prayer every night . . . It was full on. That has pushed me out.' Jane said this experience had shaped her desire for Ryan to be free to choose his own path in relation to religion:

> I think it's because I hated it so much and I didn't want to get up every Sunday morning to go to church, and I didn't want to sit there, a full church school, and have that forced on him, you know what I mean? I believe it is important for him to choose his own path. . . . If he wants to believe, he can believe, and if he doesn't, then that is okay.

Yet while Jane and Ryan both indicated that they did not discuss religion with each other, Jane said that it was Ryan's father—whom she described as 'devout' in his atheism because of having been 'forced' to go to church as an altar boy—who was having conversations with Ryan about religion and belief. She said the two of them often had 'really intense' discussions about issues such as why God would allow children to die, and Ryan commented that he talked to his dad 'a lot about what I believe, and God, and all that stuff'. Ryan said he found it easier to talk to his dad about these kinds of things, and said that his dad would, like him, identify as humanist, but he wasn't sure whether his mum believed in God, noting that he didn't have these conversations with her. Thus, while Jane's Christianity was not being passed on, Ryan and his father were co-constructing their humanisms and atheisms together through their conversations.

Only a handful of the Christian-identifying parents attended church regularly with their children. Lisa, the mother of Steve, who we met in the previous chapter, started attending their local Anglican church in order to get their children into St Peter's Secondary School. In his interview with his friend Craig, Steve said that he and Lisa did speak about faith, while she also afforded him freedom of belief:

> STEVE: . . . my mum believes in Christianity, I believe in pretty much nothing. We just keep on chatting about it.
> CRAIG: Is your mum trying to get you to believe in Christianity?
> STEVE: Not really. She just lets me believe what I believe.
> RACHAEL: Is that important to you, that choice?
> CRAIG: Yes.
> STEVE: Yes, it is. Very.

Steve was present for the interview with Lisa, eating fish fingers as an after-school snack. Their interactions revealed something of the conversational dynamics through which Lisa accepted her son's non-belief, while at the same time articulating her own doubts, and also illuminating how Steve—like other children—felt confident in articulating his non-belief to his Christian parents. Rachael asked Lisa how she felt Steve would identify in relation to religion, and Lisa replied:

> LISA: I think Steve is a 'not sure', even though we do go to a Christian church, a Church of England church.
> STEVE: At school, what I said was 'no religion'.
> LISA: You say 'no religion'? Okay, then that's the one I would choose for Steve . . . Steve and Amanda [his sister] have a very scientific brain, so they find it very difficult to—you know, the stories in the Bible. He

finds it very difficult, and we've talked about this as well, you know, the parting of the sea. That's very difficult, as an adult, you know, as well as a child—

STEVE: It's quite hard to believe.

LISA: You know, gravity wouldn't allow that to happen, would it? Steve, when he was young, you know, he said things like, 'I don't believe in God.'

In contrast with Steve's perception that they spoke a lot about religion, Lisa said that religion was *not* something discussed much at home. She saw church rather than the home as where education about religion should take place:

Do we educate them [about religion]? I don't think specifically we do. We don't read the Bible, we don't pray. But I find it quite difficult to as well. Equally, I haven't actively thought about doing home study or anything specific. To be honest, I wouldn't know how to start doing something like that . . . I suppose, ultimately, I see going to church as being the place where that happens, for me, as well as for the children. Also, I probably don't think that I know enough specifically about the religion to teach it, as such.

The fact that religion was discussed relatively little at home—at least in Lisa's eyes—alongside the weekly ritual of church attendance contributed to the fact that Lisa and Steve had different perceptions of what it meant to be a Christian. Lisa saw her faith as interwoven with an ethics which informed her everyday practices in the wider community, for example, volunteering at a church-based food bank, and she described identifying as Christian in terms of 'being kind to your neighbours, your family, treating others as you would your own'. Steve however questioned her response, saying that he saw 'most of it [Christianity] is committing to go to church', something which he said he found 'quite boring'.

When asked whether they were intentionally seeking to incorporate a religious, secular, or spiritual worldview into how they were raising their children, Lisa spoke about how they regularly discussed science with their children, and compared this with her hesitancy in discussing faith:

When we're educating kids, we talk about a lot of things that you know the answer to. So, like, maths, we do a lot of maths at home. . . . We do a lot of science things, we've been watching *Blue Planet*, haven't we. . . . Religion is really difficult, because, you know, the idea of dying and going to heaven . . . that's quite difficult for me to—I think I do believe in it, because I believe that's where the soul goes, or the soul goes somewhere. Whether or not it's heaven or something called heaven, I find that quite hard. Equally, I do believe that all of us, the four of us, are very much science-y, maths. . . . [When] we were talking about some of the Bible stories, the parting of the sea, that's really hard, from my mind, to think that that's real, because of the things that we talk about, the maths, the science.

We see here that while Steve's parents were not actively enabling his articulacy in the language of faith, they were—like many other parents—enabling his fluency in empiricist and scientific grammars, and demonstrating through their everyday conversations that science and maths were things that mattered. This interweaving of science within his everyday home life, alongside his science education at school, were helping to shape Steve's intellectual affects in terms of his enjoyment of science. While Steve found religion boring, maths and science were important to him and—in his view—to the world more broadly, since 'almost everything involves maths', as he put it.

Lisa exemplified how autonomy was present in homes where parents identified with a religion as well as in non-religious homes. Furthermore, religiously identifying parents often portrayed their family's engagement with religion as enhancing their children's autonomy (Strhan et al. 2024). Nancy, Lewis's mother, identified as Church of England and said that she had always said to their children, 'we'll make it [religion] available to you. We're not going to say it's a load of mumbo jumbo, there's no point believing this, that and the other. I would never inflict my views on them. It's very much up to them what they want to do.' Nancy presented her decision to take her children to Sunday School when they were younger not, as we might perhaps expect from a theist worldview, with reference to religious beliefs or teachings but rather as amplifying her children's autonomy:

I think it was important for them to be introduced to that to allow them to make up their own minds. Not because I wanted them to follow a certain path or Nick [her husband] wanted them to follow a certain path, but just because I think unless you're exposed to something, you don't know whether you want it or not, do you? . . . How could they make their own mind up? And I'm kind of all about giving them their experiences to let them choose them. I would never say, 'This is your path because that's been my path.'

Just as religiously affiliated parents were accepting of their children's non-religious perspectives differing from their own, so too were the non-affiliated, other than the handful of more anti-religious parents who said they would be uncomfortable with their children becoming religious. Interactions between children and parents during the interviews were often revealing of how when parents discussed their own spiritual perspectives, the children did not necessarily share these, and their parents were accepting of their views. Delphine and Andrew, the parents of Rosie and Marisa, both identified as spiritual-but-not-religious. The ways they discussed their perspectives on life after death were suggestive both of how their understanding of 'spiritual-but-not-religious' were differently inflected for each of them, and also of how they validated their children's own differing perspectives. Delphine spoke first about how she had a 'pagan-y type' belief that 'when someone is born, it's time for [their] spirit to come into the world and work through stuff, and I think that everyone's life is a journey'. Marisa spoke about her beliefs being a bit like Hindu beliefs about karma. Rachael then asked Delphine what she thought would happen to the spirit after someone died, and she replied that it was like reincarnation:

> DELPHINE: . . . I guess a bit like past lives and things like that.
> ROSIE: I don't have a past life.
> DELPHINE: You don't think you do?
> ROSIE: No, because I'm a child.
> DELPHINE: Okay, I love your thoughts today.
> MARISA: No, but I think you wouldn't have a past life, you would have an opposite universe [laughter]. Sorry, I'm reading the *Northern Lights*—there's loads of different universes.
> RACHAEL: . . . And what about yourself in terms of do you have a belief in god or a higher power? And what do you think happens?
> ANDREW: I don't have a belief in a single higher power. And what do I think happens, I guess that's where I'm kind of comfortable with it being unknown, really. . . . So what I feel is known is that our bodies will decompose and either be burnt, you know, you would either become ashes or eaten by worms.

Revealing how his perspective offered its own form of wonder, Andrew said that this ontology

> opens up really lovely possibilities of what are all those other relationships going on between the worms and the earth and the plants and the minerals, you know. And how honourable it is to be able to become part of all these other worlds, these other things. . . . So within that apparently quite reductionist scenario, actually millions of other worlds open up.

Here we see how, with Delphine and Andrew's acceptance of their children's stances, all four members of Rosie's household were able to hold their own unique perspectives on matters of spirituality. This presence of differing views in the home, we would suggest, contributes to the children's reflexive processes of becoming, as they are encouraged to form their own stances through considering themselves in relation to others.

Several non-affiliated parents engaged in forms of spiritual practice with their children. Hattie, the mother of Lea from Sunnybank, said she was unsure whether she would identify as non-religious or Christian or somewhere between the two, commenting that she attended church as a child, 'but then I sort of went a bit anti-religion. I think, as I've got older, I've started understanding the benefits of religion and why people . . . have faith and belief.' Hattie said that as well as taking Lea to Messy Church[7] once a month, she regularly engaged in Buddhist practices, including meditating. The family regularly visited a Buddhist temple, and Hattie had recently bought Lea a 'Buddhism for Beginners' book. Hattie's husband Jake reflected on how, implicitly, the way they were raising their children was shaped by how aspects of religion were interwoven within the broader cultural landscape:

> I think we draw from different religions, but not in like a formal way. So, Lea goes to Brownies, so every now and again we'll go to church when they have something going on there, or we'll go to the Buddhist temple. . . . I suppose we draw from the surroundings and some of that is religious. But I don't think we'd put ourselves down as particularly attached to one religion, would we?

Jennifer, the mother of Zoe, who we met in the previous chapter, had moved away from the Catholic faith of her upbringing and now identified as spiritual-but-not-religious. Like Hattie and Jake, she expressed a sense that none of the usual survey options for religious identities captured her or her daughters' engagement with religion and spirituality, in which there were aspects of Christian practice at school, and yoga as a spiritual practice at home. Articulating why she felt 'no religion' was not the right term to describe her children, she said, 'they all do bits of yoga with me, you know, just the types of things that we talk about, really, about being kind to people, all that sort of stuff, you know, you feel like that's all part of something that's spiritual'. As well as yoga, Zoe revealed that she sometimes discussed Buddhist and Hindu

---

7. Messy Church is a global brand of informal activity and Christian-based worship sessions, aimed at children and young families (see Strhan 2019).

teachings with her dad, and commented that he had a shed with figures of the Buddha and Ganesha, as well as there being 'a big Buddha sitting by the television and then we've got another Buddha out in the garden'. These conversations and material culture in her home contributed to Zoe's positive appraisal of Buddhism, and she noted that if she had to choose a religion, 'I'd choose Buddhism, because I like Buddhas.'

These forms of spiritual practice were viewed significantly more positively by children than going to church. Louise, Zoe's friend, spoke about visiting a Buddhist Centre with her family and enjoying the meditation they practised there:

> We do this breathing exercise . . . it's just to calm us down. We close our eyes, and concentrate on our breathing, and imagine our worries floating away . . . I like it because they give you good advice on what to do if you have problems. It's not like church where you have to say prayers and stuff. It's not like that because they don't actually believe in a god, I don't think, so yes, I do like it.

While, as we saw in the previous chapter, Louise identified as 'no religion', she commented, like Zoe, that if she had to choose a religion, 'I'd choose Buddhism, because I don't think they actually believe in a god . . . Also, I think they're the only religion that hasn't had a religious war, and it's quite a peaceful thing, so I think that would probably be the religion I would choose.' The fact that Alice and Rich were normalizing atheism, while also encouraging Louise's engagement with Buddhist meditation, contributed to her seeing these practices as relevant to her and—in contrast with Christianity—cohering with her atheist cosmology.

Festivals and Rites of Passage

For many families, festivals and rites of passage were the main way in which religion was present in family life as a form of 'religious residue' (Beider 2022).[8] All the children and parents described how they celebrated Christmas and Easter. As well as the small number of families who were regular churchgoers, several non-affiliated families attended Christingle or nativity services at church and described these as meaningful to them. Kristen said she enjoyed attending the school nativity services held at the local church, stating, 'I do

---

8. Nadia Beider develops this idea of 'religious residues' (2022) through her quantitative analysis of the impact of childhood religious socialization on the religiosity of unaffiliated adults.

like it, going to church and all the little kids singing, I love all that. Beautiful.'
A small number of parents expressed a more ambivalent attitude towards
Christmas. Rich said that while they celebrated Christmas, he did not like the
fact it had, in his view, been appropriated by Christianity:

> RICH: . . . It just annoys me that they've glued this whole 'Birth of Jesus'
> thing onto it, because it is the Midwinter Festival for saying, 'We are
> surviving this winter. . . . This is our way of saying that we're strong
> enough to be happy for three days, give each other presents and do
> whatever is it that's a good thing.' I believe that's been going on for
> thousands of years, and then Christianity has been glued on top and
> becomes Christmas. I mean, we do celebrate Easter, but I don't
> particularly . . .
> ALICE: We do Easter eggs, but not massively.
> RICH: It's just because of your chocolate, really.
> ALICE: Yes, it's just because I'm a chocoholic. It's difficult because . . .
> everything is so commercialized and ramped up that it's impossible to
> escape. The kids know all about it. They do Easter things at school.
> We're not going to be the kind of parents that are going to say, 'No,
> we're not going to have any Easter eggs because we're not Christians.'

Rich commented that he hadn't shared this ambivalence about Christmas with
his children, stating 'I don't want my own hang-ups about it to go onto them.'
Most families expressed less consciousness of Christmas as distinctively
Christian: describing Christmas primarily in terms of spending time with the
family, giving gifts, and eating Christmas dinner. They often underscored that
there was 'nothing particularly Christian' about their celebrations, as Rosie's
father Andrew put it, or positioned their celebrations as 'very twenty-first
century secular', as Ella's father Miles described. The fact that most parents
located their celebrations of Christmas and Easter as 'not really religious' can
be seen as emerging from Protestant genealogies of religiosity framed primarily
in terms of religious belief decoupled from practice or community belonging
(Lauwers 2022: 6). This positioning of Christmas or Easter as 'secular' rather
than Christian thus expresses the ongoing cultural privilege afforded to Christianity through, for instance, the institutionalization of Christian holidays as
national holidays, and illuminates how this remains compatible with the rise
of non-religious identification and atheism, as Christian values inscribed
within Christmas become reframed as shared, universal values and opportunities for 'good fun' (Ferber 2012).

Religious residues were also present in the ongoing participation for many families in life-cycle rituals marking birth, marriage and death. While there has been a significant decline in baptisms in Britain since the post-war period,[9] several children in our study had been baptised. Their parents often situated this as having little to do with faith and much more about family belonging or an opportunity for a celebration. Reflecting on Sophia's christening, Danny said, 'everybody does it, don't they? Then you have a little get-together at your house or what have you.' For Kristen, having her children christened was also interlinked with ethnic identification (Day 2011):

> KRISTEN: They were both christened. It's passed down the generations. That isn't through my choice, that's a family thing.
> RACHAEL: I get that so that's more actually a family thing than it is . . . ?
> KRISTEN: It's tradition. It's an English tradition. You have a Sunday roast on a Sunday, it's tradition, you know? It's not the fact that I believe in it, because I don't.

A few families included parents from non-Christian religious heritages, all of which were mixed marriages or partnerships, with the other parent either of Christian or post-Christian heritage. These parents likewise situated their ongoing engagement with festivals or rituals as primarily linked to family belonging or cultural heritage. Despite no longer identifying as Muslim, Neera said they had an Islamic naming ceremony for their children because it was important to her mother. As well as celebrating Christmas, they also celebrated Eid, which Neera said was both 'an opportunity to . . . get the children to understand a bit about my cultural background, and things that I grew up with in that respect. It's important to my mum.' Siyuan also linked her family's participation in Qingming practices with family belonging and cultural heritage. Describing how since her father had died, they had visited China every April for the annual tomb-sweeping rituals, she described the practice as 'cultural more than religious', and valued their visits as an opportunity to spend time with her mother. Michael, who identified as Jewish, non-religious, and atheist, had grown up in an observant Jewish household, and said he was 'very fond' of his 'Jewish cultural heritage'. He mentioned that they had 'once or twice'

---

9. See, for example, statistics demonstrating the overall decline in baptisms and dramatic drop in confirmations in the post-war period: http://www.brin.ac.uk/figures/churches-and-churchgoers/church-of-england-baptisms-confirmation-sunday-school/ (accessed 30 April 2024).

been to London with his children to take part in a family Seder, but had 'literally never discussed it' with the children. While as a family they always celebrated Christmas, he commented that they only sometimes celebrated Jewish festivals:

> if I remember, I will light the candles [for Hanukkah] on one or two of those eight nights. Last December I completely forgot, and I don't care enough to make sure it happens. My wife was brought up in a non-believing C of E family. She'd never forget to do Christmas. I wouldn't have initiated Christmas myself when we got together. Had we never had children, it would have been each of us choosing whether or not to do these festivals or not. With the kids, it becomes more ingrained in the family anyway, so we do Christmas. We occasionally do one or more of the Jewish things, if I initiate it, but I often forget and I don't really care enough to make it happen. I like my Jewish cultural heritage, but I obviously don't care enough about it to make sure my kids get it as part of their [upbringing].

Sometimes non-affiliated parents improvised in fashioning their own rituals and markers of spiritual significance in their family lives, especially in relation to the children's births. Stephanie, the mother of Coco from St Peter's, said that they had not had their children christened but liked the Christian idea of godparents, and while her children did not have godparents, they instead had 'wise parents, wise women' who would take on the elder role that godparents had fulfilled in baptism rituals. Delphine and Andrew had created their own birth ritual though planting the placentas from Delphine's pregnancies in their allotment and garden. Delphine reflected on the meaning of this for her in terms of a sense of connection with the earth:

> I think just sort of giving it back to the earth, really. I mean Marisa's we planted a rose. . . . . And Rosie's we planted a plum tree. So yes, I guess that was a ceremony in itself, wasn't it? Definitely. . . . And the girls are aware of that, and Rosie particularly talks about, she says, 'It's my plum tree.' . . . Yes, so I guess that was almost a ritual in itself.

Where parents were improvising their own forms of spirituality through practices such as these, they were not created out of thin air, but rather suggest how religious repertoires continue for many parents to be stored as embodied dispositions which persist in shaping their desires, for example, to mark the birth of their children through particular ritual forms. These practices and the other religious residues present in how these parents were raising their children trouble binary understandings of religion and non-religion and reveal how individuals may connect with multiple religious beliefs, identities, and cultural traditions and also with their non-religious analogues (Manning 2015; Malone 2021; Blankholm 2022; Strhan et al. 2024).

Raising Humanists

We have seen, then, that parents' engagements with religion largely indicated to their children that it was not something that mattered much to them personally. And even if it did matter, they wanted their children to be free to determine their own identities and beliefs in matters of religion and spirituality. If they were not talking about religion, or at least, not talking about it much, what *were* they signalling to their children as matters of value and significance? The parents had a wide and diffuse range of interests and concerns in their lives, and did not draw on authoritative cultural scripts to narrate their hopes and desires in raising their children in the way that some religious traditions might refer to scripture or a particular set of teachings. Yet there were nevertheless a number of themes that resonated widely, which were resourcing the children's broadly humanist form of life.

Autonomy and 'the Reflexive Imperative'

We have noted above how parents accepted and saw themselves as supporting their children's autonomy in relation to religion and belief. Resonating with the imperative of personal worldview choice shared by the parents in Manning's study (2015), all our parents, without exception, underscored the significance to them of their children's freedom and self-determination, and wanted their children to be free to be explore, question, and determine for themselves their own beliefs and religious identity. Mason, who we met in the previous chapter, was one of the children who self-identified as humanist, and his mother Natalie likewise identified as humanist and was making Humanism consciously available to Mason. She noted that they had books about Humanism which Mason could engage with, and commented that she and her partner John spoke with Mason while watching the news about why a God would allow suffering. Yet at the same time, they also articulated a sense that they did not want Mason to just passively accept their Humanism, but to question and determine his own stance autonomously:

NATALIE: . . . I've shown him, I've got a few books on Humanism and it is one he can read if he wants to, but he doesn't have to. . . . No, we're not pushing him for or against, really, are we? We do encourage him to question things, because he's quite 'rules and regs' at school. He's very polite and he'll do what he's told and stuff, and sometimes I wish he'd just, 'Grr', rage against the machine a little bit, but he's polite, isn't he? I'd always encourage him to question, even if he questions us and he thinks we're wrong. . . . Yes, he needs to question, but he doesn't really question us much . . .

JOHN: . . . I want him to make up his mind about a lot of things because I hear him copying some things that I say, and I think I'm quite political. I'll suddenly start talking about things, and when he repeats it, I'll say, 'Well, why do *you* think that?' I want him to think, believe it himself, or not at all.

This emphasis on wanting their children to question in order to determine their own stances pervaded much more widely than just in relation to religion. Laura, Callum from Sunnybank's mother, said that this was an important part of their parenting:

One of the things . . . that both me and my husband believe quite strongly about is not just following what other people tell you do to, and to actually think for yourself about the world. . . . That idea of questioning and understanding why other people believe certain things but not being afraid to challenge them. . . . Not having to just follow people blindly without questioning *why* you do certain things. It is a conscious thing. . . . We've always made sure that we talk to our children in quite a grown-up way, suitable for their age, encouraging them to question the world, and to question authority.

Mary, Ada's mother, similarly underscored how her desire for her children to question what they were told was bound up with their becoming autonomous. She said she wanted her children to

Question everything. Don't accept what you're told. . . . Even thinking about behaviour, going back to your own moral compass, questioning what you're told, and doing things because you choose to not because someone else. Something we've always spoken about from a long time ago is who is the boss of her [Ada]. I've really tried to get her to realise that she's her own boss. . . . What I've tried to instil in her is, you're not showing this good behaviour because someone's told you do to it, you're showing this good behaviour because you believe . . . you've chosen that that is the right thing to do. . . . You are the person that makes the choice. That is always a choice, and a teacher or a parent can't make you choose one or the other—*you're* the person, at the end of the day, that makes the choice. That's going back to it being all about the self.

This strong desire to raise their children to question and form their own positions can be located within what Margaret Archer (2012) has termed 'the reflexive imperative' of late modernity. Reflexivity is defined here as 'the regular exercise of the mental ability . . . to consider themselves in relation to their (social) contexts and vice versa' (2012: 1). The imperative to be reflexive 'derives, quite simply, from the absence of social guidelines' (ibid.), as rapid social and cultural changes have brought into question traditional—including religious—norms and forms of authority received from older generations (Smith and Adamczyk 2021: 86–7). Archer argues that the perceived inadequacy of inherited traditions and guidelines 'intensifies throughout modernity, and especially during the transition to nascent globalisation, with the consequence that routine or habitual action becomes decreasingly appropriate for all' (2007: 61). As a result, 'personal reflexivity acquires an unprecedented importance in determining how we make our way through the world'. Socialization thus becomes, she argues, a process of 'relational reflexivity' as young people 'in the relative absence of authoritative sources of normativity . . . are increasingly thrown back upon reflexively assessing how to realize their personal concerns in order to make their own way through the world' (2012: 96–7). This entails learning to dovetail the personal concerns they encounter—at home, through schooling and through other social spaces they inhabit—into 'a sustainable *modus vivendi*'. Socialization is thus not done 'to' a child but is an active process of shaping a life, a weaving together of personal 'concerns' chosen reflexively from the natal, school and other environments into a form of life, prioritizing some things, subordinating and excluding others, with the child's relationships with others and the networks they are growing up within profoundly affecting what does and can satisfy and matter to them (2012: 97).

Analysing changes in American religious parenting, Christian Smith and Amy Adamczyk describe how this reflexive imperative should be seen in the context of the increased sense of autonomy that most individuals face compared with premodern human history (2021: 87). Most people, they argue, believe they 'can self-transform and in the process alter their station and experience in the world', and this reflexivity they argue, drawing on Archer, has become an imperative:

> People today essentially have *no choice* but to engage in its form of self-referential examination and appraisal. . . . To be a legitimate self in the contemporary social context *requires* self-reflexivity. Lacking self-reflexivity in today's culture means not only being clueless and shallow, but also in some sense being an inferior and incapable human being (Smith and Adamczyk 2021: 88).

We will explore in the following chapter how this reflexive ethic was encouraged at school, but it was also fostered by the parents through everyday interactions. Stephanie, Coco's mother, described how if their children

> come to us with concerns, we try and get them to provide the answers themselves, so look into themselves for the answer, which is quite hard to be able to have that sense of self-reflection and, obviously, it gets easier as you get older. They are both at an age now where we don't need to tell them everything, they can come up with a solution to something but we will help them through a situation if they can't come up with the answer themselves. We try and say, 'What do you think we need to do? There's a choice here, what do you think the choice should be? Which road do you think we should take?'

While individualist values of autonomy and reflexivity have, as sociologists have argued, permeated all spheres of social life and have shaped religious cultures, including approaches to parenting (Smith et al. 2020; Smith and Adamczyk 2021), humanism has a strong self-conscious association with ideas of individual autonomy and self-determination. This can be traced back to its Enlightenment lineage and understanding of humans as both rational and autonomous articulated by thinkers such as Kant and Locke (Taylor 1989; Fassin 2019). This humanist lineage emphasizes humans as 'autonomous agents' who should liberate themselves from arbitrary authorities—including religious authorities—and 'their aim should be self-realization' (Fassin 2019: 33). Alastair from St Peter's expressed this humanist unease with authority rooted in religious frameworks, stating that because religious leaders have 'power that can't be challenged . . . it's profoundly undemocratic', whereas 'at least you can question a scientific expert or an engineering expert'. Critics of humanism have noted that the moral universalism of these ideas has increasingly been seen as 'a Western form of symbolic domination' and that these ideas have often been used in the services of colonial oppression, including in the 'so-called exportation of democracy' (Fassin 2019: 33). Yet ideas of human autonomy, self-realization, and rational, reflexive deliberation remain, as we have seen, important values interwoven in how these parents—both religious and non-religious—were raising their children, shaping how the children thought of themselves as autonomous.

This emphasis on autonomy has important implications for why the children were growing up non-believing and (mostly) non-religious: while the parents were, for the most part, not indicating to their children that religion was a matter of significance, they were also affording the children's freedom to reject any form of religion that did not cohere with their personal 'journey' of self-realization. Thus, Buddhist meditation practices and celebrating Christmas—which parents were signalling as valuable—might fit with the atheist forms of life the children were inhabiting and shaping. However, other aspects of Christianity—such as church attendance—did not fit with what the children found desirable, enjoyable, or meaningful, and the parents, including those who were Christian, accepted their children's rejection of these aspects of religion as part of the children's right to self-determination (Stolz et al. 2016).

Humanist Epistemologies and Horizons

Historical accounts of humanism tend to foreground the Enlightenment emphasis on rationality, empiricism, and scientific method. Perhaps due to the public prominence of New Atheist figures such as Richard Dawkins who articulate a construction of rational, scientific, progressive atheism as opposed to irrational 'backwards' religion, this often feeds into perceptions of rational, scientific humanism as at odds with religious sensibilities—a stance that was expressed by some of the parents. However, if we follow the lineage of humanism back to the Renaissance humanist emphasis on *studia humanitatis*, we might see a humanist epistemology as not only about rationalism and empiricism, but also 'a celebration of the knowledge that humans have accumulated over time', including a distinctive appreciation for the humanities as part of the accumulated body of human knowledge of the world (Lee 2015: 162; Pinn 2015; Fassin 2019). In a sense, these contours of a humanist epistemology are slippery objects, both everywhere and, at the same time, hard to recognize as aspects of a distinctive way of encountering the world. However, many parents were clearly seeking to foster the children's empiricist and rationalist sensibilities as we have described above, while many were also encouraging an appreciation for wider forms of human knowledge.

When asked what worldview he was hoping to instil in his children, Greg, the father of Amy from St Peter's, said he hoped they would have a sense of 'the evolution of human history. There is a pile of books that I just give them to read which would give them a really fantastic overview.' He described how Amy's brother was developing this historical understanding through listening to podcasts about ancient mythologies, and mentioned that he was developing 'this idea . . . that humans believe in the concept of gods even though they're not real. . . . It's kind of like, for him, just part of the human narrative to believe in gods.' This valuing of human knowledge of the world was also infused with a humanist ethic of respect for individuals. Asked what would be the most important values when it comes to raising his children, Greg replied, 'One would be respect for each individual human. I think I'd also instil a value around knowledge. I think there is . . . a responsibility, given where we live in an extremely privileged upbringing . . . to make the most of the access to all that learning.'

This resourcing of humanist epistemologies meant that children were learning to interpret the world without any recourse to the supernatural, within a cosmology which centred the human. In the previous chapter, we suggested that this was part of the children coming to inhabit an 'immanent frame', anchored in this-worldly concerns and relationships, which we argued was not disenchanted but was rather a world of depth and fullness. Just as the children reflexively valued their relationships with their families and friends as sources of meaning, so too did the parents. As several children spoke about how they were already part of many groups and so had no need for religion, so the parents were enabling the children to take part in a wide range of activities in their everyday lives, and a sense of connection to these communities was also being fostered for the parents through these activities. Nancy, Lewis's mum said, 'we're a very sporty family. . . . We have the football family, we have the rugby family, Emma rides, so we have the stables', with the language of 'family' here indicating the closeness she felt to these community groups she was part of through her children's activities.

As well as these activities, the children's this-worldly orientation was also fostered by parents wanting to pass on to their children an appreciation for 'nature'.[10] Monica, a St Peter's parent, said:

10. In using the terms 'nature' and 'natural world' here and in subsequent chapters, we follow the children and their parents' vernacular usage of these terms. We note that analytically, a 'nature' / 'culture' separation is problematic (Latour 1993).

I think it's very, very important to appreciate what's around you, as in nature, fresh air, get away from the computers. . . . I'm always, always saying,
'We need to get out. We need to go and have a walk', just to appreciate that
it's not all in a box in front of you . . . I've got no problem with computers,
but also, there's a lot out there as well. Just get out. Go and see stuff, go to
the coast.

Nancy likewise said she and her family were drawn to the coast, commenting,
'We're very outdoorsy people. I think if we as a family are like, "Right, we want
to go out for the day, we all just need a nice day together", the first place we
would go to would be the beach. We like being out on the sea, out on the sea-
side', and she described being in these spaces as 'a calming feeling'. Gordon
spoke about his sense of awe and wonder at the beauty of 'the natural world',
and also mentioned that he had become involved in organizing a Woodcraft
Folk group, in which the group 'go out into nature and we do stuff like making
clay faces on trees and other stuff'. For Gordon, this group, however, was not
only about engaging with 'nature' but also about his desire, in response to the
growth of the far-right, 'to be a little part of the solution and the investment in
giving kids the opportunity of growing a different view'. Other parents, such as
Lisa and Jennifer, described watching nature programmes together with their
children as a way of seeking to foster an ethic of ecological responsibility.

   This valuing of nature and the more-than-human world was something that
was being taken up by the children, who often mentioned that they enjoyed
watching programmes about the environment or animals, reading books about
the planet, and several said they saw David Attenborough as an inspirational
figure, as we will explore in chapter 4. In their study of 'nature lovers' in Sweden, Denmark, and Estonia, David Thurfjell and his colleagues examine the
experiences of 'great transcendence' of otherwise secular people, defined in
terms of 'experiences of greater connection that are deemed to be out of the
ordinary' (2019: 207). They argue that transcendence is being relocated in
these societies 'outside of the church to, among other areas, nature' (2019:
209). While we did not probe deeply into how children or parents engaged
with 'nature', the ways they talked about their pleasure in 'nature' did not necessarily suggest these kinds of 'peak' experiences. Rather, 'nature' was for them
a more everyday site of connection, interrelatedness, and meaning, challenging older Humanist traditions which have emphasized human mastery over
nature. Resonating with these Scandinavian nature-lovers, the ways parents
were encouraging their children to value and enjoy 'nature', alongside and

interwoven with their humanist epistemologies, contributed to the children's this-worldly horizons not shrinking as religious meanings subside, but rather becoming expansive sites of depth and wonder.

These humanist ways of knowing and valorization of 'nature' which were threaded through both the parents and their children's lives overlap with some aspects of the two non-religious philosophical orientations which Taylor (2007) identifies as making up the 'secular age': 'exclusive humanism', associated with thought and rationality, and 'immanent counter-Enlightenment', associated with Romanticism and feeling.[11] Yet these two orientations were not separate for our children and parents. Many, like Gordon, articulated what we might see as the typical 'exclusive humanist' emphasis on empiricism and reason at the same time as living lives infused with feelings of awe and wonder at the beauty of nature, which we might associate more with Romantic sensibilities. There was no tension between these orientations in lived experience, underscoring how for the parents, like the children, non-religious worldviews were not mutually exclusive, and they combined aspects of different worldviews in creative ways.

Conclusion

Danièle Hervieu-Léger's (2000) influential theory of religion as 'a chain of memory' argues that in modernity this chain is being broken through a lack of religious transmission. It is certainly possible to interpret the picture we have presented above through this lens. However, rather than this image of a broken chain,[12] we would portray what is going on as the ongoing weaving of a braid of cultural memory by both the parents and the children. In this weaving, the colours of some threads—including many aspects of religion—are becoming fainter and fading as the process of braiding continues. At the same time, other colours and textures become brighter and more dominant, many of these associated with different humanist lineages—such as emphases on human autonomy, empiricism, and the valorization of science—which have been present in this interweaving over several generations now (Brown 2017; Day 2022). This process nevertheless still incorporates aspects of religion

11. See discussion in Lee (2015: 167).

12. See also Joanna Malone's (2021) study of non-believing older adults, which challenges Hervieu-Léger's image by highlighting forms of (non)religious change and continuity over generations.

alongside—and not necessarily in tension with—alternative non-religious practices, troubling binary understandings of religion/non-religion and religion/humanism which continue to circulate in debates about the place of religion and secularity in public life (Manning 2015; Lee 2015; Malone 2021; Blankholm 2022).

Previous theories about the rise of atheism and non-religion, often drawing from quantitative studies, have tended to distinguish between the role played by parental socialization and education. However, our parents' and children's narratives reveal that these may be easier to distinguish in theory than in practice, since what takes place in schools affects what takes place in homes. Children come home and discuss what they have been learning about at school with their parents, often prompting parents to reflect on these issues. Childhood studies scholars have drawn attention to how traditional socialization approaches have tended to present the child as the passive recipient of parental socialization and have contested the use of the term 'socialization', emphasizing the 'dynamic process of inter- and intra-generational negotiation of belief and morality' (Scourfield et al. 2013: 20). 'Transmission' should, they suggest, be seen as 'bi-directional or transactional rather than uni-directional' (Scourfield et al. 2012: 92), while other researchers have drawn attention to the importance of peers, media, culture, and other social networks in shaping young people's contemporary religiosities (Woodhead 2010; Singh 2012; Madge et al. 2014).

While we will explore further in the following chapters the roles played by schools, media, and culture, we agree that in the process of the children's becoming, the adults are also being changed.[13] Alice, Hattie, and Gordon, for instance, all indicated how being a parent had shifted in some sense who they were, drawing them away from some practices and beliefs and towards different ones. Anthropologist Tim Ingold notes how in traditional anthropological kinship charts, filiation might be marked 'as a line connecting two points, standing respectively for parent and child' (2018: 160). However, 'in real life'— and so, likewise, amongst our families,

> it is a process of becoming in the course of which, through 'growing older together' (Schutz 1962: 17), the child carries on the life of its parent, while progressively differentiating its own life from that which engendered it. Filiation is not the connection of parent *and* child, is it the life of parent *with*

13. This impact of having children in shaping the self-understandings of non-affiliated parents is also emphasized by Manning (2015).

child. Just as in musical counterpoint . . . so too, in the human family, lives lived in counterpoint are not 'and . . . and . . . and' but 'with . . . with . . . with'. And in answer—or responding—to one another, they co-respond. (2018: 160)

While our parents were providing cultural, moral, emotional, intellectual, and epistemological resources through which the children were co-creating their humanist forms of life, this process took place relationally: the parents were themselves in the process of becoming along with their children, as the children asked questions of them and vice versa, in an ongoing process of co-response.

3

Figuring out Humanism
and Non-Belief at School

IT WAS THE BEGINNING of a new school year and all the classes at St Peter's were lined up outside the main school hall one Friday afternoon in early September, ready to take their places for the school assembly. As the children walked in and sat down on the floor, Mr Forester, who was leading this assembly, stood up in front of them and said: 'Peace be with you' to which the children chorused in unison: 'and also with you'. Mr Forester then continued in Arabic, '*As-salam alaikum*', with the children responding '*Wa-alaikum-assalam*'. 'Well good morning, St Peter's! Hope we have all had a lovely week and got to do some nice things with your class. Today is our celebration assembly and we're going to be celebrating all the amazing things you lot have been up to this week!'

St Peter's had a list of core 'school values', with each value assigned to one of the three terms during the school year. During that term, one person in each class would be awarded each week with a 'values champion' certificate for demonstrating that particular value, with the class teachers announcing who was that week's values champion and explaining why that particular child had won the award, before inviting the child to the front of the hall to receive their certificate. That afternoon, Ridwan from Year 3 was awarded a certificate for his excellent work in class and demonstrating independent learning, while Gerry from Year 4 received his certificate for focusing in lessons and becoming a better learner. After all certificates had been handed out, there was a round of applause for all the week's values champions. Mr Forester then announced which class had won that week's 'attendance champion', with Year 3 announced as the winners. A child from the winning class, Lara, was chosen to pick one of three envelopes containing a mystery prize for the whole class. Lara selected an envelope and opened it, and with a cheeky grin said: 'twenty minutes extra playtime!' to which the rest of Year 3 exclaimed 'yessssss!'

Mr Forester congratulated the children and made some announcements about events happening in school over the following week. Beginning to draw the assembly to a close, he said, 'we are very proud of each and every one of you. You have learnt so much. Now we're going to take some time to think about our learning this week and if you want to say a prayer to God, *your* God, then you can. Or just sit and think about the words.' Some of the children then bowed their heads and placed their hands together in a posture of prayer, while others looked to the front of the hall or up at the ceiling, as Mr Forester read a prayer:

> Dear God, thank you so much for supporting our learning this week. We are thankful for our teachers and all the amazing lessons they produce and the fun we have in class. Please keep us safe this weekend while we get up to lots of fun things with our friends and family. Amen.

There was silence in the hall during the prayer, and a few children joined in with the 'amen'. 'Right then you lot', Mr Forester continued, 'have a great weekend. Stay safe and see you all on Monday.' Mr Forester then read out a closing saying, repeated at the end of every assembly: 'Our worship in this place has ended', to which all the children chorused in reply 'our service in the world has begun'. The children slowly left class by class, while a song about volcanos from a Pixar film played in the background.

To the reader unfamiliar with schooling in England, this assembly in a state-funded school might seem somewhat surprising, especially given widespread assumptions that Britain, like elsewhere in northern Europe, is largely secular. However, assemblies like these happened every day at St Peter's, while at Sunnybank assemblies took place most days and at Waterside at least weekly, as part of the legal requirement that all pupils in state-funded schools in England and Wales participate in 'acts of collective worship'[1] which, the law states, should be 'wholly or mainly of a broadly Christian character'.[2] This assembly was a fairly typical example at St Peter's, where assemblies always opened with the same Christian and Muslim greetings, followed by a talk on the theme for that day, then sometimes a song or hymn, with a prayer and moment of

---

1. The terms 'assembly' and 'collective worship' are often used interchangeably, with assembly the more popular term.

2. Education Reform Act 1988, Section 7.

reflection to conclude. The teachers were very aware of religious diversity at St Peter's—especially the significant proportion of Muslim pupils—and performed acts of collective worship which met the legal requirements while also attempting, in their view, to respect the pupils' religious diversity. However, there appeared little conscious awareness from teachers of *non*-religious diversity, inviting the question: how did non-religious children experience these acts of collective worship and the place of religion in everyday school life more broadly? And how did these different engagements with religion in school influence the forms of life they were growing up into and shaping?

Having shown in the previous chapter how the children's parents were resourcing a broadly humanist form of life, in this chapter, we turn to explore the significance of schools in shaping how the children were growing up non-religious and non-believing. While there is a growing literature exploring different ways in which religion is located in schooling,[3] there has been little research focused on non-religious children's experiences in schools or examining *how* schools may shape the distinctive textures of children's non-religiosity. Addressing this gap, this chapter demonstrates that schools play an important role in shaping how children in England come to think of themselves as non-religious and non-believing through the different ways they encounter religion at school. We begin by outlining the legal and policy contexts shaping how religion is located in English primary schools. We then explore how—despite the ongoing privileging of religion and Christianity in education frameworks— schools are making a humanist form of life available to children, which shapes what it means to children to be non-religious and non-believing. This form of life, as described in the previous chapters, centres principles of autonomy, individual rights and freedoms, and an epistemology that valorizes science, rationality, and empiricism as ways of knowing the world. The dominance of this worldview is, we suggest, not because of Humanist or Secularist groups' influence over education, but rather because these values cohere with wider educational policies and frameworks, especially dominant neoliberal education policies in the UK since the late 1980s onwards which have privileged ideas of reflexive individualism and choice. At the same time, these values cohere with how the parents were raising their children, so that the children

---

3. See, for instance, Madge et al. (2014); Hemming (2015); Strhan (2017, 2019); Kitching (2020); Guhin (2021); Benoit (2021); Singleton et al. (2021); Strhan et al. (2023); Shillitoe (2023).

are—across home and school—being provided with resources to figure out their own humanism and atheism, and to name these 'choices' as their own.

Religion, Education Law, and the 'Education Marketplace'

In contrast with countries such as France or the US where state-funded education is organized according to secularist principles of separation between Church and State, religion—and specifically Christianity—continues to occupy a prominent place in schooling in England. Churches here were historically the main providers of education before the nineteenth century and developed their own networks of schools. The idea of state-funded education was introduced in England and Wales with the Forster Education Act of 1870, which allowed public subsidies for Church of England schools, while the Education Acts of 1902 and 1906 established the 'dual system' of church and state schools in order to provide a national system of education (Hemming 2015: 4). The Education Act of 1944[4] then further developed this dual system, categorizing schools into 'County Schools' (entirely state-funded)—which since the School Standards and Framework Act 1998 have been termed 'Community Schools'—and 'Voluntary Schools', mostly designated 'voluntary-controlled' or 'voluntary-aided', which had formerly been church-funded but from that point onwards were funded in formal partnership with the state, while continuing to have some church governance.[5]

During the 1980s, neoliberal policies developed by the Conservative government under Margaret Thatcher significantly reshaped the educational landscape, with the 1988 Education Reform Act introducing the National Curriculum and a 'schools market' in which parents could choose schools, with the best schools expanding and the worst forced to improve or shut. Parents' ability to compare and choose schools was enabled through the introduction of standardized testing at the end of four 'key stages' of schooling and the publication of the test results and Ofsted inspection[6] results for each school.

---

4. The classification of schools in Wales is very similar to England, but different in Northern Ireland and Scotland. For further details, see Hemming (2015).

5. Voluntary-controlled schools were not funded by their religious body, though the church retained some governance, while voluntary-aided schools were partly funded by the state, with the faith body responsible for a percentage of capital works (Hemming 2015: 5).

6. The introduction of a national scheme of school inspections, with inspection reports to be published and available to parents, was established in the Education (Schools) Act 1992.

With the introduction of the National Curriculum, control of school curricula was centralized and shifted away from teachers. The new National Curriculum prioritized maths, science and English, which were established as compulsory 'core' subjects. The New Labour government subsequently expanded this neoliberal agenda of market reforms from the late 1990s onwards, further privileging ideas of parent 'choice' and reinforcing cultures of audit, testing, and governing by numbers and targets (Ball 2017). A side-effect of this agenda was that new opportunities opened up for faith groups as education providers in the schools market. In 2000, the Labour government announced plans to develop academies as part of a mixed economy of service providers which would enable greater parental 'choice', an initiative then expanded by the Conservative–Liberal Coalition in the Academies Act of 2010 and by the subsequent Conservative government (Dinham and Jackson 2012: 285).[7] Academies are state-funded independent schools operating free from local authority control, and are often run as part of academy trusts, including a significant proportion run by faith bodies, with the Church of England currently the largest provider of academies in England.[8]

Within this mixed economy of schooling, around a third of all state-funded schools in England are faith schools (Long and Danechi 2019). Of these the overwhelming majority are Christian, and most commonly Church of England. However, religion continues to play a role in all state-funded schools, reflecting how the historic settlement between churches and the state still shapes contemporary schooling (Hemming 2015). The 1944 Education Act made 'Religious Instruction' and 'Collective Worship' compulsory for all schools in England and Wales.[9] In the 1988 Education Reform Act, the term 'Religious Instruction' was replaced with 'Religious Education' (RE). This change signalled a shift away from exclusively Christian confessional education towards the introduction of teaching about a broader range of 'world religions', reflecting new forms of migration-driven religious diversity in Britain. Yet although the 1988 Education Reform Act retained the legal requirement

---

7. In 2015, the Conservative government announced plans for all existing schools judged to be requiring improvement by Ofsted to be converted into academies.

8. In addition to the types of school listed here, there are also grammar schools, private schools (including private faith schools), and special schools, but these are not the focus of this book.

9. The right of parents to withdraw their children from attendance at religious instruction and collective worship was also established in this law, Section 25(4).

for all schools to teach RE, it was not included in the National Curriculum, with local councils still currently responsible for deciding their own RE syllabus, while faith schools and academies can set their own. However, despite the move away from confessional religious instruction, Christianity remained privileged in law, with the 1988 act requiring that locally agreed RE syllabuses 'shall reflect the fact that religious traditions in Great Britain are in the main Christian, while taking account of the teaching and practices of the other principal religions represented in Great Britain' (Education Reform Act 1988, Section 8.3). Religious Education therefore today remains a compulsory part of the basic curriculum in England, with all children from ages 5 to 16 to be taught RE.[10] All schools in England and Wales are also still legally required to conduct daily acts of collective worship, which the 1988 act stipulated, as noted above, should be 'wholly or mainly of a broadly Christian character' in that they 'reflect the broad traditions of Christian belief' (Education Reform Act 1988, section 7; Shillitoe 2023).[11]

The schools we worked with reflected this legal framework. St Peter's was a faith school. Formerly a voluntary-controlled Church of England school, it had converted to academy status as part of a Church of England multi-academy trust. In practice, this meant little change in terms of the school's religious character, with the form and content of collective worship, the school values and ethos, and the RE curriculum unchanged. However, some parents expressed concern that becoming an academy might mean more prominence for Christianity. Justin, for instance, said:

At first, I was worried, especially when it was going through academization and [becoming] part of a diocese, kind of, academy I thought, 'Oh, my God. Right, here we go. They're going to be coming more hard line on the religious front.' I mean, that has not happened as yet, as far as I can see, but that would worry me a bit.

10. In local authority-maintained schools and in many academies in England, RE remains compulsory for all pupils aged 5–18. However, for those aged 16–18 in sixth-form colleges or other further education institutions, this provision does not apply. For further details, see Long et al. (2019: 5–7).

11. Hemming notes that while Ofsted and Standing Advisory Council on Religious Education (SACRE) reports indicate that the majority of primary schools in England comply with the daily collective worship requirement, many assemblies do not include much 'spiritual' focus, in contrast with secondary schools, 'the majority of which do not comply' with the requirement for daily collective worship (Hemming 2015: 12–13).

Waterside was not a faith school. It had, like St Peter's, converted to being an academy (from community school status), and was part of a multi-academy trust which included both faith and non-faith schools. No parents we spoke to raised concerns about the school becoming an academy. Sunnybank was a community school and therefore also not a faith school. At all three schools, RE and collective worship were part of regular school life, reflecting the legal requirements for schools in England.

In relation to the emphasis on parental choice underpinning the education framework described above, it is worth noting that the most common reason for parents' choice of school was location rather than the school's faith or non-faith status (Hemming and Hailwood 2018). No parent we spoke to from St Peter's said they chose the school *because* it was a church school. Neera was typical in explaining their decision: 'I think people should go to their local schools . . . I don't think it mattered that it was a C of E school.' She, like many other parents, was accepting of the fact that as a church school, religion was part and parcel of everyday school life:

> the fact that it is a C of E [school] doesn't bother us, or bother me at all. I accept that when you send your child to a C of E school, it's a Church of England school, and they will have religious practices. So, I'm completely okay with all of that. I'm quite happy for the children to go to the masses that they have, and for some of those religious values to be taught.

Neera added that the religious and ethnic diversity of the school also influenced their choice, commenting that the school has:

> so many people from different religions, different ethnic backgrounds, and different languages . . . which helps us all to get along. I think that's what makes it a good place to be. Ultimately, Benjamin and Soraya are not white children. They're kids who have got mixed heritage, and I think it's important for their psyches not to grow up thinking that they're white . . . they're mixed-race children, who have come from a Muslim/Catholic background. . . . All those things, I think, are really important.

This valuing of 'diversity'—seen as more important than St Peter's being a church school—was also emphasized by white parents. Miles, for instance, said,

> I think that the reason why I'm quite happy with her [Ella] in her school currently is not because it's a religious school . . . I think it has a fairly

inclusive and open-minded approach to religious education. . . . And the fact it is a diverse school with people of a variety of religious backgrounds and non-religious backgrounds, I think it's quite an exciting melting pot, a microcosm of society . . . I probably would prefer it if it had no allegiance to a [church].

Only Kristen saw the fact it was a church school as positive in itself. She said, 'this church thing . . . I think it's good. . . . If they want to learn all this, about God and stuff, then I think it's good for them because obviously they're learning. I haven't got a clue, you know? So when they bring me home things or tell me things, I'm like, "Bloody hell." I like all that.'

While St Peter's Primary School did not have faith-based admissions criteria, matters became more complicated for St Peter's parents when it came to choosing secondary schools (for children aged eleven to eighteen), since the nearby St Peter's Secondary School *did* have faith-based admissions criteria. Some parents—such as Erica and Lisa—began attending church with the explicit intention of getting their children into St Peter's Secondary when the time came. Other parents were very critical of the fact that their children could not attend St Peter's Secondary. Rich, who we met in the last chapter, said that this 'schools situation' had made him 'more secular. . . . They can't go to the local secondary school, and that's because I believe in rationality, so we're excluded.' He continued:

> RICH: We can't apply [to St Peter's Secondary] because . . . our
>   worldview is based on rationality. That has got to me.
> ALICE: It's got to me when Elena [Louise's older sister] has to get up so
>   early in the morning, she's tired, it's dark, and she's got an hour's walk
>   to school because she can't get into that school. It does make me
>   angry. . . . I, personally, think that schools should be entirely secular.
>   I'm not happy with St Peter's Primary being a Church of England
>   school . . . I just don't think that religion should be a part of education
>   because it means that religious groups are able to exert influence over
>   what's happening in the school . . . I think children should be free of all
>   that until they're old enough to make their own decisions.

The prominence of faith groups as providers in the education 'market' reflects the fact that the legal framework emerged in an era in which the churches were dominant players within education (Clarke and Woodhead 2015). In contrast with churches' historic power and influence, non-religious and secularist organizations have had less success in shaping education policies in England. Schools have been an ongoing focus of Humanist campaigns, and the Humanist movement (and before them, the Ethicists and Secularists) have been engaged in a century-long struggle in Britain against collective worship, the state-funding of faith schools, and about the content and form of Religious Education (Brown et al. 2023). The movement has made some headway, for example, in Wales, securing the inclusion of teaching about Humanism in the new Religion, Values, and Ethics education which has replaced Religious Education in Wales since 2022. However, with faith schools still making up a third of the total in England, and with the law on collective worship still unchanged, Humanist campaigns 'looks set fair for sustained activity' (Brown et al. 2023: 229). Yet despite Humanists having not achieved their overall aims to reduce the influence of faith groups in schooling, many children, as we saw in chapter 1, are growing up into a broadly humanist form of life. To what extent, then, and in what ways, was this being resourced through their experiences in school?

Developing Humanist Epistemologies at School

We saw in the previous chapter how many parents were discussing and valorizing science and maths in ways that enabled the children's fluency in—and attraction to—empiricist and rationalist ways of knowing. These epistemologies were being shaped in more pronounced ways at school than they were at home. Indeed, for children for whom there was little discussion of either religion or science at home, the language they used to articulate their belief in science (and non-belief in God) appeared to be almost exclusively resourced by school, exemplified in Harriet's comments, noted in the previous chapter, that her son had come home one day and announced that he believed in evolution. At all three schools, the children's empiricist epistemologies were being habituated through the timetable and rhythms of the school day, with morning lessons revolving around the three 'core' National Curriculum subjects— maths, science, and English—and if necessary, time taken from other curriculum subjects, such as RE, in the afternoon to further focus on these. The children's enjoyment of maths and science, exemplified by the comments of Lucas, Louise, and Steve in the previous chapters, were encouraged by activities such as 'Brain Gym', which was a morning activity at Sunnybank where children could be awarded up to ten minutes' extra playtime for successfully completing tasks, and 'Times Tables Rockstars' at Waterside, where children competed with each other on 'times tables challenges'.

With this central positioning of science and maths in the curriculum, it is unsurprising that the children were becoming empiricists and valuing science. However, it was from RE lessons that the children's articulation of their understanding of religion and science *as opposed* seemed to stem. The idea of a religion–science conflict tended to be introduced to the children in RE lessons focusing on theist—especially Christian—creation stories which were contrasted with scientific accounts, even if the teacher was keen to underscore that theists might believe in *both* science and religion. During fieldwork at St Peter's, Years 4 and 5 were learning about the Christian creation story in RE. In one Year 4 lesson, Charlotte, the class teacher, explained to the class, 'we are going to think about the creation story and what Christians believe, as that's what we're doing this term'. She began by asking the children if they could describe the creation story and what happened on each day, and went on to explain that 'some Christians believe it took seven days, and some people believe in the Big Bang and this is what scientists believe'. A number of children raised their hands at this point. Jake put his hand up and said that he believed in both the Big Bang and God and that we developed from monkeys into humans, but that God could have started it all off. Another child raised her hand and said she was unsure. Charlotte nodded and said, 'Yes, some people think only the Big Bang happened and some people believe only the creation story. Some people believe the Big Bang and that the creation story is just a story but God is behind the creation and the Big Bang. You can believe in something and have faith in something but you'll always have lots of questions.' She went on, 'some people don't believe and that's okay. You might change your opinion throughout your life. And remember we're learning that's what Christians believe.'

Charlotte then introduced the activity for the lesson. In three different areas of the classroom were signs: 'agree', 'sometimes agree' and 'never agree'. Charlotte explained she would read a number of statements about the story and the children would have to stand near one of the statements depending on the extent to which they agreed or disagreed. She emphasized that we all have different beliefs and opinions 'because we're all different and that's okay and it makes the world a more interesting place', and reminded the children not to simply follow their friends when deciding if they agreed or not. The children walked eagerly around the room for each statement, deciding whether they agreed and discussing the statements with each other. Although the children were not asked to state their religious identity in this exercise, it nevertheless provoked discussion about who was and who was not religious, as well as also introducing children to the idea that Christian creation stories might conflict with scientific accounts. The following week, the children were given an activity following on from this, in which Charlotte asked them to cut up different statements—such as 'science has all the answers' and 'God is the Creator of the universe'—and to decide where to glue each under two separate columns in their exercise books, headed 'All Christians believe' and 'No Christians believe'. Although, as in the previous week's lesson, the aim of the lesson seemed to be to encourage the children to understand that many Christians believe in *both* science and creation, the way that this was being set up through initially presenting a binary conception of theism and science as opposed appeared to lead the pupils to take away from these lessons the idea that belief in God and science were in conflict.

This idea of religion as at odds with science was also implicit in the fact that the teachers sometimes equated non-religion with science when we asked whether non-religious worldviews were taught in RE. Mrs Aspin from St Peter's said, 'the further up the school we go . . . we've been looking at the science view as well, I mean, you know, that can be opposing the religious view'. Children's accounts were consistent with this. For instance, Louise showed how she was developing an idea of scientific approaches as intrinsically non-religious through the way the curriculum was presented:

> In the last few years, I haven't been liking RE because they're constantly talking about religious stuff. I know it's called Religious Education, but there are other beliefs, like the Big Bang theory and stuff. But this year, I was kind of a bit more glad because in the creation story, they also did it about the Big Bang. They didn't just do creation story and, like Jesus and God and stuff, because that's what they always do. They never seem to do stuff that other people believe in. I know that I'm not the only person who doesn't believe in God. Loads and loads of people in my class don't, but they never seem to talk about that; they just talk about the religion.

As well as this subtle equation of science and non-believing perspectives, there were also lessons encouraging the children to understand belief in God as a phenomenon that was either supported by evidence or—as most of the children we spoke to came to conclude—not. At each school, the children had lessons in which they debated the reasons why people believe or don't believe in God. Describing these lessons at Sunnybank, Mrs Fordham said, 'They're forming their own views and opinions and . . . basing it on science. . . . When we do, "Is God Real?" [in RE], it's from a scientific point of view: where's the evidence?' And even when this was not the focus of the lesson, children saw these lessons as providing opportunities to discuss whether there was evidence to support belief in God. Delilah described an RE lesson at Sunnybank in which she had raised these questions, stating, 'we were learning about [the] Christianity God. I said, "Excuse me, how do you know that he's real?" "It said in the Bible." "Yes, but the Bible doesn't have any proof though, does it? . . . It doesn't show you that it's real though."'

Although the children encountered the term 'agnostic' as well as 'atheist' and 'theist' during these lessons, there was little emphasis on agnostic ideas about the limits of knowledge or 'unknowability' as desirable in how these lessons were taught, and no discussion of a subjectivist non-religious worldview which values individual experience as a way of validating knowledge (Lee 2015). Rather, the content and pedagogical techniques used in these lessons—with pupils evaluating statements on the basis of evidence—expressed a humanist emphasis on the knowability of the world, which then manifested in the children's perception of religious beliefs as lacking evidence or as illogical, as we saw in chapter 1. The children's comments sometimes revealed a lack of understanding of what theists would understand as 'evidence' in support of their belief, while also highlighting the significance of RE in potentially leading children to evaluate and reject belief in God. Minnie from Sunnybank commented, 'when I was younger, my mum said God was real, so I believed in God then, but then when I started coming to school and learning about RE, I just thought maybe he isn't real, because there isn't a photograph of him'. Her friend Amber responded, 'there isn't proper proof of God yet', to which Minnie replied that if proof was found, 'obviously I'll believe in God then'. Thus, we see how the idea that the children were encountering in RE—that what is real is what can be evidenced—could feed into how the children articulated their atheism as related to empiricist ideas.

Becoming (Self-Conscious) Non-Believers

As well as contributing to the children's narratives of their non-belief in God being due to their empiricism and belief in science, RE was also significant for many children in crystallizing their awareness of their non-belief and non-religious identities. In other words, while many children were non-religious and did not believe in God *prior* to RE lessons, with religion relatively absent in their everyday lives outside of school, RE lessons were one of the main ways in which they encountered religion, which in turn, contributed to their awareness of their own *non*-religiosity and *non*-belief. This dynamic means that RE plays an important role in shaping how these children come to understand what 'religion' is and how and why it matters to (other) people. Annie and Sophia from Waterside, who we met in chapter 1, discussed how religion might be 'special' to some people, and when asked how they knew this, replied that they knew this because of a video they'd seen in RE:

> ANNIE: . . . religion might be really special to them because some people do pray like every night about anything they've had today and every night to every day. I'm not really sure, but I have watched a video.
> SOPHIA: Yes, in school.

Thus, while many of the children were not discussing religion very regularly at home, religion was much more present in their schools, with curriculum materials and RE lessons shaping how they came to think about what religion was, while also prompting their reflection on their own identities and beliefs in relation to religion. Ryan from Sunnybank described how he had come to identify as a humanist after learning about Humanism in RE:

> RACHAEL: So you were saying before you learnt about Humanism, you didn't know it was there?
> RYAN: I didn't think there was such things as like humanists, when you didn't believe in God or anything, you just had no religion whatsoever. So until we actually did learn about humanists, I didn't know. . . .
> I am happy about being a humanist but I didn't really know about Humanism until we learnt about it. I was a bit, you know, wobbly before we thought about humanists because, like, I didn't really believe in God in the first place but I just . . . it's a bit hard to say and stuff.

While we saw in the previous chapter how Ryan's humanism and atheism were being co-constructed through conversations with his father, we see here how school also shaped Ryan's articulation of his humanist identity. It is worth noting that the only children who *consciously* identified as humanist were at Sunnybank, where the children had learnt about Humanism in RE, in contrast with St Peter's and Waterside, where there was no explicit mention of Humanism by pupils or teachers during our fieldwork.

Although children such as Ryan found that learning about Humanism of-fered a grammar to reflect on and articulate their own worldview, most children commented that they received little substantive teaching on non-religious worldviews in comparison with the dominance of teaching about

Christianity and 'world religions'.[12] Mason from Sunnybank said, 'the thing I don't really like about RE is that I think . . . there was only one lesson I can recall out of the whole of the school that was about, like, humanists and non-religious people'. Isabella and Emma, also from Sunnybank, said that they would like non-religious viewpoints to be included in RE:

ISABELLA: I don't like RE at all. We just learn about Muslims and Jewish.
EMMA: And Hindus.
ISABELLA: And Hindus. Other religions. And people really don't have religions, they don't speak about them. It's like, you're leaving them out. I just don't like it. . . . It upset me because it makes other people upset when you leave those people who don't have a religion out. . . . Some people might want to know about people who don't have religions, what they do, or something.
EMMA: That would be very interesting. . . . Or it could be very interesting. That should be something that we do in RE.
ISABELLA: I know.

However, while non-religious worldviews were not being covered in depth in RE in the way that Christianity and 'world religions' were, more abstract ideas about non-belief in God—and reasons for belief and non-belief in God—were discussed. When asked whether non-belief in God was discussed in RE, Lewis and Dan from Waterside replied:

DAN: Yes, it is quite a lot, actually.
LEWIS: Well, sometimes it is. Sometimes there are big discussions about if you believe or if you don't believe.
DAN: And there's usually quite a lot of arguments after.
LEWIS: Yes.
RACHAEL: So, what have you discussed and what would you talk about?
DAN: Well, I wouldn't go into the arguments. I don't really want to argue about stuff like that. So I just stay away.
LEWIS: I don't know really. We, probably, have like a discussion about, like, have agreements and disagreements. So, someone would probably give their opinion and then someone who didn't believe will probably give their opinion.

12. Amongst RE practitioners and policy-makers in England, there is growing recognition of the importance of RE including teaching about non-religious worldviews, and proposals for RE to be replaced by 'Religion and Worldviews' (CoRE 2018; Hutchings, Benoit and Shillitoe 2022).

The boys mentioned a lesson in which they had learnt the terms 'theist', 'atheist' and 'agnostic', and said their teacher had read out some statements and they had to identify which stance the statement aligned with and stand by the sign with the correct term on it. Dan described the lesson as 'pretty good' and Lewis concurred. These boys' comments are revealing of how RE lessons addressed children in ways that asked them to perform recognizable religious/non-religious or believing/non-believing subject positions (Kitching 2020), while also normalizing a broadly Protestant construction of 'religion' focused on individual, propositional beliefs. At the same time, their non-participation in these 'big discussions' suggests that the framing of these subject positions in RE in terms of arguments about belief/non-belief in God did not necessarily resonate with or interest them.

As well as encouraging the children to take a stand in relation to belief/non-belief in God, RE lessons also often encouraged the children to position themselves in relation to a binary understanding of religion and non-religion. During a Year 3 RE lesson at Waterside, the children were asked to think of as many festivals and ceremonies as they could and write them on sticky notes. The class teacher asked them to stick these on a large piece of paper, which she had divided with the headings 'religious' and 'non-religious'. She then led the class in a discussion about how the children had categorized particular holidays, ceremonies, and festivals as religious or non-religious. Birthdays, Mother's Day, and Flower Day were unanimously placed by the children in the 'non-religious' column, but there was animated debate about Christmas, with many children commenting that they were not religious but still celebrated Christmas.

Although not aimed at encouraging the children to take a position as religious or non-religious, this activity nevertheless reproduced a binary relationship between religion and non-religion, and prompted the children to reflect on where they stood in relation to these categories. This mode of address, asking the children to reflect on, name, and articulate their beliefs in relation to recognizable subject positions, permeated different pedagogical activities. Henry, from Waterside, described an RE lesson in which they were asked to position themselves in relation to religion and belief when completing a worksheet which asked them, as he put it, '"Who do you believe?" and "Why do you believe that?" and stuff . . . and then, "What religion do you believe in?"' He commented that he had put 'no religion'.

RE lessons were therefore encouraging the children to reflect on where they stood in relation to religion and belief in God, crystallizing their awareness of their non-religion and non-belief. The fact that the children—as they

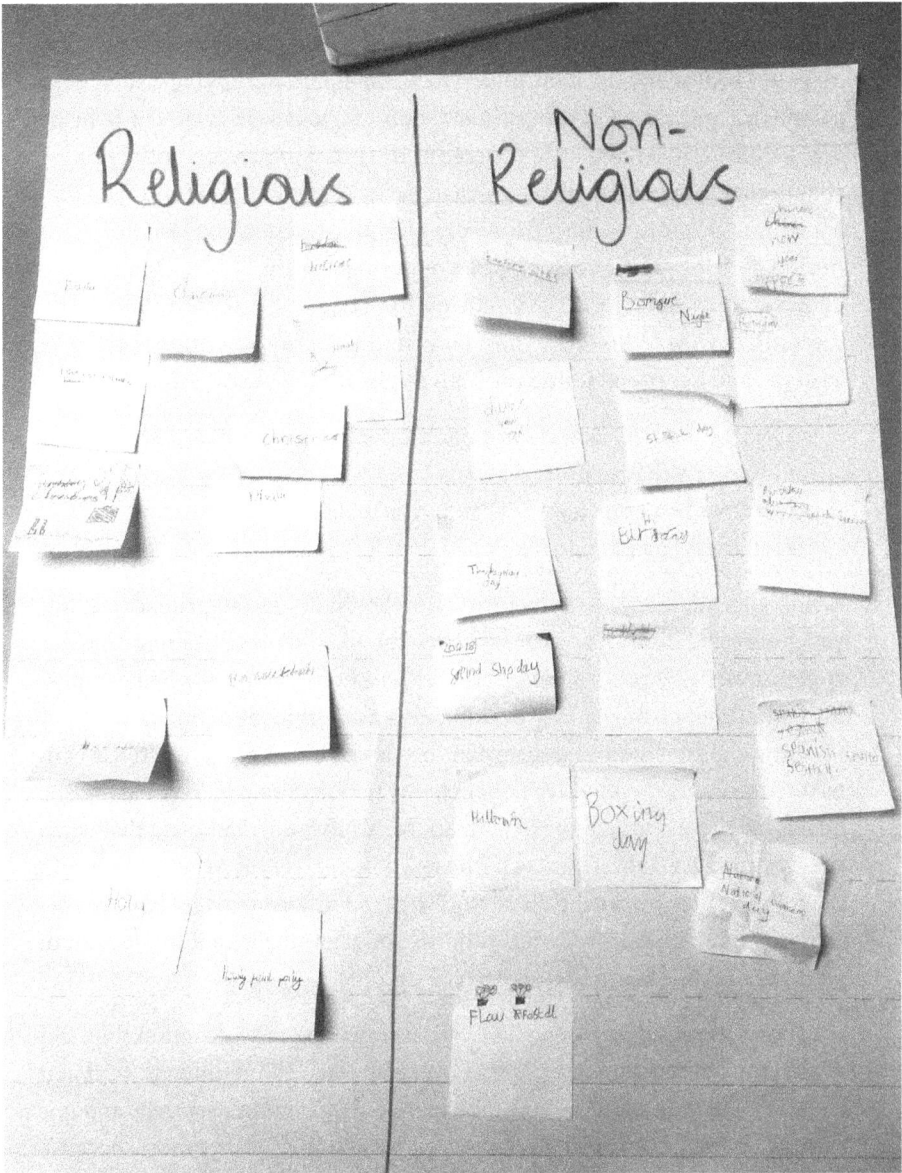

FIGURE 3.1. Photo taken during a Religious Education lesson at Waterside, in which the children were asked to write names of festivals on sticky notes and then place them under 'religious' or 'non-religious' headings

themselves noted—received relatively little teaching about non-religious worldviews, in contrast with the dominant focus on teaching about Christianity and 'world religions', contributed to non-religion occupying a somewhat paradoxical position. On the one hand, non-religious worldviews were being marginalized, receiving little classroom time in comparison with learning about religious practices, beliefs, rituals, festivals, and texts. Yet on the other hand, non-religious perspectives were also privileged in the sense of being treated as self-evident outlooks, not requiring the kind of explanation and understanding through RE that religions do (Lee 2015). Several children expressed this view. When asked how they would identify in relation to religion, Yasmine and her friend Cameron, both pupils at Sunnybank, said:

> YASMINE: I don't know if I'm a normal person, a Christian, a Muslim . . .
> RACHAEL: What's a normal person?
> YASMINE: You don't have a religion, you're just a normal person.
> CAMERON: You have no religion.

Echoing Céline Benoit's study (2021) of religion in English primary schools which revealed how many primary school pupils were constructing religious communities as 'other',[13] here we also see how non-religion was being implicitly naturalized through being positioned as a self-evident outlook.

Some children indicated that what they learnt about religion actively contributed to their atheism, as the opportunity to reflect on religious and theistic beliefs led these children to reject them. Isla from Sunnybank said that when she was younger 'I didn't know if I believed in him [God] or not, so I was in the middle. But now that I do a lot of work on it, I don't really believe anymore . . . I don't have a religion.' When asked what she meant by 'do a lot of work', Isla replied that in RE lessons,

> talking about religious people . . . it's just making me uncomfortable, so I don't believe in God any more. . . . We also learn about different stuff in it [RE], like in India there are some people that are on the streets, and it is making me uncomfortable, so I don't believe in God any more, because there are lots of people in India that live on the streets. . . . Some of them have been dying.

While Isla's answer is open to different interpretations, we take it to imply that her atheism is linked to RE lessons prompting her to reflect on global

13. This also resonates with Strhan et al. (2023).

inequalities, which thereby raised questions of theodicy for her. Other children commented on how the presentation of theistic perspectives in collective worship also led them to question and reject these. Molly and Rosie from St Peter's spoke about a school assembly led by the local vicar, Revd Sally, in which they said that they had been told, as Rosie put it, 'God controls you to do all the good stuff, and then you do every single bad thing.' Rosie elaborated further:

ROSIE: . . . [Revd. Sally] said, 'Have you ever made something that you really hated? That wasn't God, that was you.'

MOLLY: I don't really get how if God is so perfect, why do we make mistakes and why do we have to be the bad of everything?

While concerns are often expressed that RE or collective worship are a subtle form of religious indoctrination, our children's comments imply—perhaps paradoxically—that the asymmetrical ways in which religion and non-religion were being presented in RE were encouraging the children to reflect on and become more aware of their *non*-religious beliefs and identities, as they were being shaped as subjects who were continually asked to take a reflexive stance in relation to their beliefs and identity, interwoven, as we will suggest below, with a broader cultural imperative of autonomy. At the same time, we would also suggest that the relative lack of teaching the children received about other-than-religious worldviews can be seen as a 'hermeneutical injustice' (Fricker 2007) in the sense that non-religious children were not being provided with interpretive resources to make sense of their worldviews in the way that members of some religious communities are within schools.[14]

'Giving Them the Tools to Question for Themselves': Reflexive Individualism and Autonomy at School

Previous studies have suggested that the shift towards ideas of children's autonomy which have become dominant in many educational settings have fed into declining religiosity through giving children freedom to resist efforts by their parents to raise them as religious (Stolz et al. 2016; Klingenberg and Sjö 2019). Yet we know little about how ideas of 'autonomy' become entwined with particular aspects of religion and belief in everyday school life, or the role this

---

14. See further discussion about the importance of including non-religious perspectives in RE in *Religion and Worldviews: The Way Forward* (CoRE 2018) and Strhan and Shillitoe (2022).

plays in shaping children's non-religious worldviews. In the previous chapter, we saw how parents—both religious and non-religious—were encouraging their children to question and form their own positions as reflexive, autonomous subjects, as part of the 'reflexive imperative' of late modernity (Archer 2012). These same ideas were also pervasive at each school. Indeed, the children being asked to reflect on their own beliefs, the reasons for their beliefs, and to articulate their religious or non-religious identities, as Henry described above, epitomize how a norm of personal reflexivity is inscribed in everyday educational practices.

As the children were encountering at both home and school an imperative of personal worldview choice and autonomy, they were also encountering a variety of differing stances in relation to religion. Through learning to reflect on themselves in relation to these encounters, the children came to see themselves as actively choosing and determining their own (non)religious identities. Molly and Rosie illustrated how they were conscious of this sense of their own autonomy in relation to religion as increasing as they grew older:

MOLLY: If I was in Reception and you were talking about this I would have definitely said 'I'm Muslim because my dad is'.

RACHAEL: Sure, but as you got older—

MOLLY: I've realized that religion is something that you choose to be, you don't inherit it. I mean you could inherit it but you choose to inherit it. You choose to be what you are.

ROSIE: When I was younger I thought I had to be a Christian, because I went to a Christian school, but now I know I don't really have to be anything. I can just believe what I like and I can choose. I don't have to follow what school I go to, what people believe in. I don't have to do that just to fit in. I can choose whatever I like. I used to think that I had to be Christian to fit in as well, otherwise everyone would not like me, but then I realized Molly likes me and she knows I'm not a religion.

MOLLY: I thought the same thing too.

ROSIE: I have a lot of friends even though I'm not a religion and then I realized I could just believe whatever I liked.

Here we see how school presented Molly with the idea that there were wider (non)religious possibilities opening up to her that she could choose besides her father's Muslim faith. We also see how both girls were reflexively discerning the significance of their friendships and belonging—which they recognize as important goods in their lives—in influencing the potential desirability of (non)religious identities.

The teachers we spoke to at all three schools described developing reflexive autonomy as a fundamental aim of RE, resonating with how the children and their parents emphasized 'choice' and self-determination in relation to religion. Waterside's headteacher, Ms Buck, said that educating children about different religions enabled choice: 'how do you have choice if you're not sharing the different beliefs?' Miss Logan, a Sunnybank teacher who identified as Christian, also articulated this, as well as emphasizing tolerance and autonomy:

I think one of the main aims, I see, in primary school, now, is tolerance. Teaching tolerance for other religions, I would hope that that's something that we're teaching children. Educating children to live in a multicultural society. Helping them to question themselves, as well, and what their thoughts on religion are. Like I said, I was never pushed into going to church or having those [Christian] beliefs. I think children have to make up their own minds about what it is that's out there. . . . Hopefully, we are giving them the tools to question for themselves and make their own minds up.

While the children did not necessarily always like RE, they shared this idea of the subject as enabling respect for different religions and some children articulated this idea of RE as enabling their 'choice'. Lea from Sunnybank said she thought the aim of RE was 'to learn about different religions. . . . Because you might not be a religion and you might want to change to be a religion. It's not just about when you're little. . . . You can believe when you're older.' Similarly, comments from Sam at Sunnybank about how he *could* believe in a range of religions or scientific theories expressed his self-understanding as a subject who has agency to determine his own stance from a range of religious 'choices' he had learnt about in RE:

I could believe in Hinduism, or God, or evolution. Mostly, every religion that is out there, I could believe in one of those, but I don't know which one to choose to believe in. I've thought about Hinduism, because if I go to Hindu temple, magic happens. If you were Hindu you go to the Monkey God and pray to him, you get strength. . . . If I believe in God, I'd go to church every Sunday, and I don't know anything else about being a Christian. All you do every Sunday is you just sit down in a church. They do have festivals and celebrations though, so that might be fun. Then, if I don't believe in any religion and I just believe in the Big Bang or something like that, I don't know what's going to happen.

This ethic of choice in relation to religion was not just about freedom for the self to choose, but also about freedom for others. When Izzy, a pupil at

Waterside, was asked what they learnt about in RE, she replied, '[that] people can believe in anything they want', and her friend Teddy added that their RE teacher 'always says, "not everyone is the same. People are different religions."'

As well as permeating RE, the reflexive imperative to consider oneself as an individual in relation to one's social contexts and to identify one's own personal concerns was interwoven throughout broader school life. As we saw at the start of the chapter, children were rewarded for being 'independent learners'. This reflects what education theorist Gert Biesta describes as the 'learnification' of education in which the fundamental issue of education becomes 'entirely redefined as a question of individual *adaptation and adjustment*' rather than a matter of political and structural issues and collective responsibilities (2016: 67). Understandings of education as concerned with the progressive development of autonomy stretch back to the Enlightenment and a secular–liberal vision of an ideal society of rational, autonomous actors (Seligman 2014; Strhan 2019). However contemporary schooling—in England and elsewhere—intensifies this individualistic ethos through its entwinement with neoliberal education policies which shift attention away from the importance of relationships and wider social contexts in educational processes towards instead a narrow emphasis on the individual reflecting on and taking responsibility for their own 'learning' (Biesta 2016: 15). Under neoliberal governance, the role of the education system is to equip children 'for their future role as productive, self-reliant citizens through the knowledge, skills and values conferred' through schooling (Pimlott-Wilson and Coates 2019: 269). These principles—interrelated with the privileging of the market as regulator of all forms of activity—shape how we understand the world, 'our relations with others and ourselves—our mentality of government and self-government', producing an imperative to optimize the self (Ball 2017: 218). In neoliberal times, the ideal individual is thus one 'for whom life is a conscious, reflexive project of the self and to whom it may seem plausible that, barring accidents, the individual is primarily the author of what befalls them' (James et al. 2010: 631).

This interweaving of reflexivity, autonomy, and the language of learning and individual 'choice' and self-determination shaped how children were being addressed as subjects at each school. In an incident at St Peter's for example, a group of Year 4 boys had been playing their own version of the video game Fortnite in the playground, which had led to an argument as the boys filed in for their afternoon lessons. Miss Kitson noticed their arguing, asked the boys for more details, and expressed her disappointment at the boys in terms that required the boys to reflect on their 'choices' and to take responsibility in dealing with the situation: 'This is not how we treat each other, is it? Do we think we are making the right choices? We need to get ready for our afternoon learning, but I am not happy. You boys go to the Independent Learning room and talk this through yourselves. You're in the juniors now, and we expect better from you.' This phrase 'are we making the right choices?' reverberated throughout teachers' engagements with pupils, for instance when Year 5 were not following instructions during a history lesson, and Ms Aspin asked whether they were 'making the right choices', then asked them to sit and 'reflect for five minutes' on their actions and to 'take responsibility' for them.

Ideas of individual responsibility and self-determination were also interwoven in the emphasis at each school on 'resilience', reflecting the wider rise of 'resilience training' in schools and non-formal education programmes in Britain and elsewhere utilizing concepts such as resilience, grit, and determination (Mills 2021). This growing emphasis on resourcing children's 'resilience' has its roots in neoliberal grammars of individual responsibility and self-reliance, which shift attention away from wider structural inequalities that shape the conditions of students' educational and emotional worlds (ibid.). We can see this emphasis at Waterside, when Ms Buck spoke about how the school's 'core value' of 'courage' was about encouraging the children's resilience, which she described as part of a 'growth mindset'. She said, 'We've got the most lovely children—so polite, well-mannered, respectful—but if something isn't correct or something doesn't go quite how they would expect it to, they really struggle with that. They've not got that bounce-back ability', which was why they had situated it as a 'core value' in the school. Children were encouraged to reflect on this value—and develop it within themselves—through lessons such as Personal, Social and Health Education. A Year 3 lesson exemplified this, when the children were asked to think of examples of people or traits which made people 'resilient' and to design their own resilience 'superheroes', with the aim of encouraging the children to recognize the importance of individual 'resilience' and taking responsibility for their own emotions and self-development. These 'resilience superheroes' were arranged to form a wall display in the classroom. Parents sometimes said that they liked this ethos of the children being encouraged to develop a sense of their individual responsibility for their learning. Cassandra and Liam from Sunnybank, for instance, commented that their son's '[school]work at the minute is really poor, and it's going to impact on his SATs',[15] and valued the fact that the teachers had 'tried to say, "The choices

15. SATs are Standard Assessment Tests taken at the end of Key Stages 1 and 2 in primary schools.

that you're making, they are going to impact on your SATs and your test results for later on in life. The decisions you make, you have to stick by them."'

Collective worship and assemblies were also occasions through which ideas of individual choice, reflection, and self-determination were made explicit to the children. In the example discussed at the opening of the chapter, Mr Forester made clear to the children that whether they engaged in prayer was a personal choice. Mr Horton from St Peter's also articulated his understanding of school prayers as offering the children space for 'reflection', describing the purpose of the prayers as 'just to give the children that moment of reflection, that moment of calm. Again, it's not a forceful "you have to say *Amen* at the end", it's just that quiet moment of reflection.' Several children seemed to have taken up this idea of prayer as an opportunity for individual reflection and self-development. Coco from St Peter's said, 'I do listen to the prayer that the person who's doing the assembly is saying. I'm not necessarily saying it to God, because I don't really believe in him that much. So I'm . . . just saying it to, you know, myself, to help me and everyone else become a better person in any way.' Her mention of 'and everyone else' suggests that while Coco is herself developing an ethic of individual reflexivity, she also situates her hopes for herself relationally alongside hopes for 'everyone else' in ways that interrupt the narrow neoliberal focus on the individual at the expense of the relational.

It is perhaps not surprising to find this emphasis on becoming a reflexive, autonomous self so pervasive in primary schools, since these are values that are largely taken for granted within and beyond contemporary liberal democracies (Archer 2012; Watts 2022). While ideas or autonomy and self-determination are by no means unique to non-religious forms of life, they are nevertheless, as noted in the previous chapter, strongly associated with Humanist histories, especially the Enlightenment lineage of Humanism associated with thinkers such as Locke, Hume, Rousseau and Kant, who emphasized humans as rational, autonomous actors who should strive to 'free themselves from religious authority and arbitrary power' in the pursuit of self-realization (Fassin 2019: 33). These ideas were occasionally positioned as Humanist by the children. Discussing ideas of moral decision-making, Amber from Sunnybank said that Humanists 'just think to themselves if it is right or wrong' to do something. Her friend Minnie then asked Amber if she was a Humanist, since she didn't believe in God, and Amber replied, 'I don't even know. I might be. I do think to myself . . . might as well just be a Humanist.' Yet these values have extended far beyond self-conscious Humanism. In their history of the Humanist movement in Britain, Brown, Nash and Lynch note that what they term humanist values—including the valuing of individual autonomy and individuals' rights to self-determination—have *become official* in legislations, international treaties, and other forms of 'official' policy (2023: 249). This becoming 'official' includes conventions and policies shaping children's lives, from the United Nations Convention on the Rights of the Child to schools' 'values statements' and professional ethics codes for teachers, as well as within higher education, underpinning our ways of thinking about the world.

When thinking about how these children are growing up into a broadly humanist form of life, more significant than whether or not these values of individual autonomy and self-determination are named as Humanist is the fact that these values—which pervade within and beyond schools—contribute to the children coming to understand religion and belief as matters of individual, personal choice. While these values certainly can cohere with religion, at a fundamental level, they can nevertheless be seen as ultimately secularizing in the sense that they locate authority and decision-making in the 'secular', this-worldly realm of human life and affairs, rather than subordinated to religious interpretations, authorities, or theologies rooted in the Beyond.

This secularizing logic applies to schools as institutions as much as to children inhabiting these school worlds. While, as noted above, some parents and organizations such as Humanists UK express concerns about the role of faith groups in education, the three schools we worked with were all shaped by a broadly secularist consensus that the primary role of schools is to 'produce modern child (and/or colonial) subjects, and neutrally facilitate the refining of their capabilities for rational, authentic selfhood and cultural and economic exchange' (Kitching 2020: 134). Indeed, several teachers spoke about how they sought to embody and exemplify this idea of 'neutrality' when facilitating discussions about religion. Mrs Fordham from Sunnybank spoke about how during RE lessons, she was 'very careful' to ensure that she does not say 'we believe' rather, that 'Christians believe' or 'Muslims believe' and said that in terms of how she positioned herself when facilitating discussions with children, 'it's very much a neutral, "I don't have any belief".'

'This School is Aimed Towards Christianity'

This logic of secular 'neutrality' was not, however, the whole story. Alongside this idea of schools as refining the children's reflexive, autonomous selfhood, particular aspects of religion—and specifically Christianity—were being positioned in the schools in ways that sat in tension with this dominant ethos, with the children often expected to participate—or look as if they were participating—in Christian practices.[16] This was especially pronounced at Sunnybank, despite it not being a faith school. One of the teachers, Mrs Macfarlane, spoke about how children were expected to engage with prayers during assembly:

> RACHAEL: So, when they have the moments of prayer, is that seen as a choice . . . ?
>
> MRS MACFARLANE: No, we would expect everyone to respect that it's prayer, so they should bow their head, they should be silent. In the juniors, I would say they're told to put their hands together, but if someone didn't put their hands together, as long as they were still, it wouldn't be an issue. They don't have to do anything other than show respect to people that are wanting the minute's quiet. It's a bit like a minute's silence, isn't it? You expect everyone to be silent, you don't have to agree with it, but it's about respect, if that's what everybody is doing.

Teachers often corrected children's behaviour during prayers if they deemed it unacceptable. During the prayers in one assembly, two boys were turning around making subtle faces and gestures to each other. Picking up on what was going on, their teacher waved at them to get their attention, then mimed the posture expected of them: heads down, eyes closed and hands together. As soon as the teacher did this, the boys followed suit and closed their eyes, bowed their heads, and clasped their hands together in a posture of prayer.

Several children criticized these expectations.[17] Vic commented that he disliked school prayers, and especially the enforced expectations of how they should sit with heads bowed, and noted that his mother had shared his sense that this enforced participation was not right. He said, 'If you sit up they [the teachers] tell you off, but then my mum said, "You should let people not pray and sit up if they want to." So yes, that's what I don't like about assemblies.' Vic

---

16. See also Hemming (2015); Strhan et al. (2023).

17. This strongly resonates with findings from the 'Becoming Citizens of Postsecular Britain' research project, which examines the relations between religion and citizenship in primary schools in England, Scotland and Wales, and has found that *both* non-religious children *and* children from non-Christian faith communities are often critical of the dominance of Christianity in different aspects of school life, especially prayers, hymns, and RE lessons (see Strhan et al. 2023).

said that to conform to the school norms, he did bow his head, and his friend Harry added that he did not like the singing in assemblies, and commented that 'when someone's not Christian', the prayers 'would be a bit offensive to them'. Jake and Lucas also described what was expected of them during prayers, with Jake describing what prayers were like as follows:

JAKE: 'Hands together, eyes closed. Dear God, let us be pleased for the safe drinking water we have in this country, Amen.' That might be a prayer. That's actually one of the prayers she said.

RACHAEL: And do you both take part in the prayers?

JAKE: Yes, everybody does. She says, 'Hands together, eyes closed' and you do that. No, you don't say anything; the headteacher always says something.

RACHAEL: But do you have to take part in them?

JAKE: Yes, we all have to put our hands together, I suppose.

LUCAS: Even though I can sense a very strange vibe at some point, when people are like, 'Do we have to do a prayer?'

Here we see how although the teachers were articulating an ideal that freedom of religious choice was being developed through RE, in practice, Christianity was still afforded prominence over other religious and non-religious worldviews in both collective worship and RE, reflecting the national legal framework for these aspects of school life.[18] Children were aware of Christianity's privileged status. Jake and Lucas commented on how Sunnybank—despite not being a faith school—projected an assumed Christian collective identity:

RACHAEL: So even if you don't believe in God, then, do you still take part in the prayer?

LUCAS: Yes.

JAKE: Yes.

LUCAS: Which I find a little bit annoying.

JAKE: Most schools do that, or most primary schools, anyway . . .

RACHAEL: So why do you think primary schools do them?

JAKE: Because they want you to get into the life of Christianity.
    This school is aimed towards Christianity. You can tell, can't you?

---

18. This echoes other studies examining aspects of religion in primary schools in England, especially Hemming (2015); Bénoit (2021); Strhan et al. (2023); and Shillitoe (2023).

LUCAS: Yes, it's very subtly told. Like when we did about places of
worship [in RE], what was the very first thing they showed us? Church.

JAKE: Yes, and when we learn about religion, first religion we learn
about?

LUCAS: Christianity.

JAKE: We learn about Christianity for like seven lessons, and then we
learn about Sikhs for two lessons.

LUCAS: I know.

JAKE: And then we learn about Muslims for one and a half lessons. And
then we go on a different subject and we learn about Christians first
for a long period of time, and then other religions for a short period
of time. But you can tell—

LUCAS: And also they go, 'Dear God, Amen.'

JAKE: Yes, we do proper prayers.

LUCAS: So very powerfully, it's basically, 'We are Christians. We always
believe in the Christian faith.'

Christianity was also afforded prominence at both Waterside—although
RE took place with less frequency here than at Sunnybank—and at St Peter's,
which is unsurprising given the latter's Anglican affiliation. Laura Aspin, the
deputy headteacher at St Peter's, spoke about how, through using terms that
they felt would be appropriate for Muslim pupils in the school, they sought to
make the Christian values and ethos of the school 'universal':

Because we're a Christian school and an Anglican school . . . our assemblies
do have to have a Christian element. But what we try and do is marry it up,
so we don't do things like, like when we pray, we always pray to God, rather
than Lord, because Lord isn't kind of something that they say in Islam, but
they use God, or Allah, so . . . try and make it a bit more universal.

Mr Horton stated that while the school ethos at St Peter's was centred on
Christian values, he saw these as 'underpinning every faith, every religion'.
While teachers were aiming to ensure the inclusion of Muslim pupils through
incorporating Arabic blessings alongside Anglican prayers, they also expressed
a wider tendency in contexts where it is the majoritarian religion to perceive
Christianity in terms of a universal that transcends its own boundaries and, as
Lori Beaman puts it, 'imagine[s] itself as representative of everyone, even
when they themselves do not find themselves adequately or at all represented'
(2017: 64). Christianity was also present in the schools in other ways, including

the celebration of Christian festivals, and visits by Christian clergy and speakers to give assemblies. St Peter's organized regular school visits to the local church for services and had 'reflection' spaces in every classroom, usually including a Bible, a cross, some pebbles or flowers, and a 'worry box' where children could write down any worries. In practice, while such spaces were rarely used for reflection and more frequently co-opted as additional marking space, they nevertheless reveal the materiality of how Christianity was present, if often unremarked upon, in everyday school life.

Just as we saw in the previous chapter that some parents positioned Christian festivals as 'secular' rather than 'religious', so also teachers sometimes presented traditionally Christian practices, such as prayers during Christmas services, as having 'no religious connotations' to them, as Mrs Hampson from Waterside put it.[19] She described how the headteacher would light four candles during assemblies in Advent, and positioned this as 'used more in a countdown to Christmas, rather than in a religious way'. These ritual repertoires associated with Anglican liturgies which the teachers could situate as 'not really religious' express the 'privilege of banality'—a phrase coined by anthropologist Elayne Oliphant to conceptualize the 'inequalities that allow certain religious symbols to achieve the status of the ambient, while others are marked as religious and refused access to the background' (2021: 18).

It is notable that it was more liturgical traditions of liberal Anglicanism that could achieve this ambient status. Evangelical Christianity, however, could not. At Waterside, some parents contacted the headteacher to complain about an evangelical youth group, Bright Lights, visiting the school to lead assemblies. While it is relatively common for external speakers to be invited to speak at assemblies in English schools, there have been national media reports about parental concerns at evangelical groups visiting schools (Strhan 2019: 134–5). Yet it was not only parents who were unhappy. As a teacher, Ms Anderson was also critical, describing the assemblies as 'frighteningly indoctrinating-y'. She said that at the end of these assemblies, the Bright Lights visitors would 'always say, "Oh, we're going to say a prayer. If you agree with what we say or if you believe in what we say, then say Amen at the end."' She saw this as 'tricking' the children, as she put it, as they felt 'peer pressure' to say 'Amen'. Furthermore, some Waterside parents did not view liberal Anglican clergy speaking in assemblies as merely ambient: Ms Buck and Mrs Hampson both noted that some parents had complained about the local vicar leading assemblies because, Mrs Hampson

19. See also Malone et al. (2024).

explained, his use of 'us' and we' to describe Christian beliefs 'presumed that everybody believed. Some of the teachers did agree it was quite heavy-going.'

Alongside this presence of Christianity at all three schools, most teachers described their schools as making a reasonable attempt of accommodating children's non-religious forms of life, describing the Christian values as 'shared' or 'universal' and thereby accommodating the non-religious or else emphasizing that they were taking a 'neutral' stance in relation to religion. Miss Kitson, from St Peter's exemplified these ideas of the 'inclusion' of the non-religious, stating that the school values:

> are Christian values, but they're actually values that you would hope every-body would want. We cater for everybody. Not every assembly . . . is reli-gious. It's more about we're taking that religious value and we're exploring it. I think the way we word things as well. We quite often say, 'Christians believe', or, 'Muslims believe', instead of saying, 'We believe'. My friend works in a Catholic school, and they would say, 'We believe this', and, 'We believe that'. We don't do that here. It's more like, 'Christians believe this'.

This perception of a stance of secular neutrality as a way of 'including' the non-religious was also expressed by Mrs Hampson at Waterside, who said:

> I think we cater extremely well for non-religious children because I don't think there's anything that is pushed. I don't think there's one religion that's taught more than any other. In some ways, I think we teach Hinduism or Islam more than we do Christianity sometimes in our RE lessons.

The idea that teachers expressed that they were catering well for non-religious children through their performance of 'neutrality'—while at the same time not engaging with the form and variety of non-religious worldviews—reflects the still dominant public perception of 'non-religion' or 'atheism' as the absence of religion rather than as 'substantive' forms of life (Lee 2015). This 'subtractive' grammar—in which 'non-religion' is presented as 'insubstantial' compared with religion—was evident in a lesson at St Pe-ter's in which the Year 5 class were completing a task about themselves enti-tled 'Where are we from?' and had been asked to write down on sheets of A5 paper the name of the country they'd been born in, the languages they spoke, and the religion they belonged to.[20] While the teacher, Jane, was introducing

20. This example is discussed in Shillitoe and Strhan (2020) and Shillitoe (2023), and took place during Shillitoe's doctoral fieldwork at St Peter's in 2015.

the activity, one pupil raised his hand and asked, 'what do you do if you don't have a religion?' Jane replied, 'For those who don't have a religion, don't put anything. Just leave it blank.' As Rachael chatted with the children about what they had written and put their pictures on the classroom noticeboard, one girl, Maisie, aged nine, handed her picture over. It read: 'My name is Masie, I come from England and we speak eglish But my granddad is from Irland so I am a quarter Irish. I don't realy have a religion but I join in with the prays at school most of the time.' Maisie explained to Rachael that she 'wasn't sure' if she was religious and did not think her parents were religious and she did not go to church, but said she liked to join in with school prayers, and so felt it was important to write that down when reflecting on her belonging. Shrugging her shoulders and smiling, she said, 'I don't know. I don't think I do have a religion.'

However, while the teachers did not appear conscious of this asymmetry of how religion and non-religion were woven within the fabric of school life, the children *were* conscious and critical of the ongoing privileging of both Christianity and theism in school life. Owen and Nicole from Sunnybank criticized RE as not relevant to them as atheists:

OWEN: I don't get why, in RE, we have to learn about God and we don't even believe in him. What's the point?

NICOLE: Exactly. You have to learn about it because it is a subject at school and you have to learn about things that you don't like doing.

OWEN: Yes, but if you don't think it's real, what's the point about learning about it? We don't have any interest in it, we don't care about God. We don't think it's real.

Will from Waterside also articulated his view that the subject was often irrelevant to him, stating, 'I don't believe in anything that any religions really believe in. . . . Because I'm not Christian and I'm not like any religion, and I find it a bit annoying that I have to do something that's not really that important to me.' He then expanded on his critique of RE as it was currently taught:

Because all you need to do is like, you know what they do, and just respect them, and not like make fun of them. That's all you really need to do. And like, really, it's kind of being nosey about what their gods are called and stuff, doing RE. So, technically, I really don't like it.

Tim, his friend, commented that he had enjoyed learning about Roman gods, and Will concurred, 'if it's history, really, I'm fine with it'. When asked what they meant by RE being 'nosey', Will said, 'why do we need to know what they do at their weddings? It's like *their* wedding'. Tim agreed, commenting 'why would you want someone else to know about your religion?' They added that in learning about religion, children might end up laughing at it, noting that one classmate 'does a bit of laughing at things, like at different religions'. It is possible to interpret these boys' critique of RE as 'nosey' as showing how they have developed a liberal, secularist understanding of religion—based on a Protestant conceptualization—as an individual, private, and personal matter, which they feel RE transgresses.[21] A further possible interpretation is that they disagree with the fact that RE constructs religion as something that *requires* understanding and explanation. In their view, the most important thing is to respect others, and acquiring this respect for others does not, as they see it, require extensive detail about others' religiosity. Indeed, their comments about their classmate suggest that they see learning about others' beliefs as potentially leading to *dis*respectful engagements with religion. Thus, their dislike of RE stems not only from the fact that it is dominated by teaching about religion but also from how the curriculum's presentation of religion can—in their eyes—implicitly undermine respectful engagements.

Other children's critique of collective worship gestured towards the tension they felt between being required to participate in hymns and prayers and the pervasive ethic of freedom in relation to religion they had internalized. Mason from Sunnybank commented that the Christian hymns they had to sing in hymn practice were 'a bit unfair on people like me and Kevin, but also on Muslims . . . I think that . . . Muslims and non-religious people [should] have a bit of a choice, that we didn't have to do hymns.' Chris and Sam from St Peter's also expressed their sense that their freedom was undermined by school prayers:

> CHRIS: I absolutely hate prayers. We have to do it every day in assembly, every time. They don't give us a choice whatsoever . . .
>
> SAM: Yes, sometimes we really have to.

---

21. The analysis in Strhan et al. (2023) of religion and citizenship in two contrasting primary schools in England notes that this construction of 'religion' as private and personal was present in a school with low levels of ethnic and religious diversity—a characteristic shared with Waterside—but not at a 'superdiverse' primary school with high levels of religious diversity, where pupils were happy to talk about religious belief and practice.

Yet Chris and Sam did not passively accept being told to write prayers, and revealed how the children could demonstrate their refusal of the Christianity they were being asked to accept:[22]

> RACHAEL: You have to write prayers for assembly?
> CHRIS: Once, I wrote 'Dear Bob'.
> RACHAEL: Dear Bob?
> SAM: I spelt 'God' wrong on purpose once in one of my prayers.
> RACHAEL: You spelt God—on purpose?
> SAM: Yes. I made my G look like a J.
> RACHAEL: So, Jod?
> SAM: Yes. [Laughter] Then I think the teacher thought it was just a spelling mistake. . . .
> CHRIS: I wrote 'Dear Bob' on purpose.
> RACHAEL: Dear Bob? . . .
> SAM: And then you just write 'Goodbye' at the end, not 'Amen'.

Some children refused the teachers' expectations that they bow their heads for prayers. Claudia from Waterside commented that when she was younger, she used to bow her head and put her hands together, but now 'I just listen and I don't really do anything'. She commented on how her Muslim friend Meera also did not bow her head, and she expressed a quiet solidarity in their subtle refusal of school prayers: '[Meera] doesn't do them either, and we kind of just look at each other and just smile at each other. Because usually everyone's heads are down, so we can just see each other.' In contrast, other children, such as Rhiannon and Pearl, indicated that they perceived bowing their heads as a choice they were making to show others respect:

> RHIANNON: I just think it's polite, yes, that's what I do.
> PEARL: Polite and respectful.
> RACHAEL: So you do it because it's polite.
> RHIANNON: Yes, and respect, you respect other people's religions as well.

Mason indicated how he saw bowing his head as a mark of respect, while also acknowledging the force of teachers' behavioural expectations, and how at the same time, he passed this time for prayer in individual reflection. He stated, 'I don't put my hands together, but I just bow my head so it's, sort of, in respect.

---

22. See also Shillitoe (2023) and Strhan et al. (2023) on children's agency in relation to collective worship.

Plus, I might get into trouble. So, I just bow my head down and I just think about what the day is about, and any troubles I have, which is very rare.'

Through these instances we see how the children were articulating their own critiques of aspects of religion in school that did not align with their own values and beliefs.[23] We would suggest that the children's consciousness that these aspects of religion are those they do not share helps crystallize their non-religious identification and non-belief. At the same time, their ability to critique and subtly refuse forms of religion with which they do not agree, or in other cases to explain how their participation in prayers aligns with their own value of respecting others, demonstrates their being shaped as reflexive subjects with a strong sense of their own—and others'—autonomy.

Conclusion

While previous studies have emphasized the role of changing parental social-ization in patterns of religious decline, this chapter has revealed how schools can play a significant part in shaping children's perception of themselves as non-religious and non-believing. We argue that *both* parents and schools are resourcing the children to figure out their own broadly humanist form of life. In schools, the children's humanist epistemologies are being shaped through the prioritization of maths and science in the curriculum. This feeds into these children becoming atheist through creating a sense of humanist epistemology and knowledge gained through science and logic as having priority over theist ways of knowing and believing—with religion and science being constructed as in tension through the RE curriculum. While the children were being en-couraged to see religious beliefs as something you might determine yourself, they saw knowledge gained through science and maths as non-negotiable. As Molly and Rosie expressed this:

> ROSIE: With maths, there's like the right answer or adding numbers, but there are rules to follow.
> MOLLY: In RE there isn't really a right or wrong . . .

At the same time, the subtle equation of 'science' and 'non-religion' that was happening in RE, and the positioning of non-religious viewpoints as requiring no understanding or critique, fed into the children coming to perceive

---

23. See also Strhan et al. (2023) for further discussion of how both religious and non-religious children articulate critiques of the place of religion in schools.

non-religious worldviews as self-evident and 'normal'. While they were en-couraged to see religion as something to be questioned, explored, and exam-ined, the children were not being encouraged to think about their humanist and other non-religious worldviews as their own form of 'existential faith' which might sit alongside religious faiths (Connolly 2005). At the same time, the emphasis on individual autonomy in relation to religious identity and belief reinforced amongst the children the dominant 'secular' framing of reli-gion in liberal democracies as one option amongst others (Taylor 2007). More-over, religion was often perceived as a matter of private, personal choice—and one which the children deemed important to respect, even if they themselves concluded that such an option was illogical or unsupported by evidence.

As discussed in the previous chapter, Margaret Archer's conceptualization of socialization as 'relational reflexivity' (2012) helpfully captures how these children were becoming non-religious subjects through their multiple engage-ments with religion as they make their way through formal education. Schools here, alongside families and other communities that children belong to, are 'sources of mixed messages and sometimes messages that do not mix' (2012: 106) from which children and young people learn to discern reflexively which ideas, beliefs, values, and concerns they are taking on as their own. In this chapter, we have seen how the children are receiving a range of messages about religion which often did not mix, especially the messages of individual au-tonomy and religious freedom and an assumed Christian identity interwoven in practices such as prayers and hymns. Developing as reflexive subjects with a clear sense of their own autonomy, many children came to reflect that they did not like the imposition of forms of religion that sat in tension with this ethic of freedom, and this, we would suggest, further fed into the development of their self-conscious non-religiosity.

Mrs Reid from Sunnybank commented that this ongoing dominance of Christianity did seem anachronistic, stating, 'I suppose it's just the history of the school. I mean, I really don't know. It [Christian prayer] happens in every school, doesn't it? Even though we are teaching all religions, it does seem a little bit ironic, doesn't it? That we still focus on Christian prayers.' It is worth noting that the majority of teachers we spoke to identified as non-religious, including some who were highly critical of what they described as the 'hypocrisy' and intolerance of organized religion. While they did not share these views with the children, largely seeking to model secular 'neutrality' in how they spoke about religion, some teachers commented that they did mention their own non-religion or non-belief to the children. Mr Wilson, from Waterside, said:

I'd say that in a lesson to kids, I'll say, 'Look, I'm not religious. I'm just telling you . . . what some people believe. This is what Christians believe, or
some Christians believe', say, 'I'm not telling you that you should think that
or not . . .' It depends on the lesson really, I guess, and the content. I say,
'Well, I'm not a believer', so I will do that in lessons.

Other teachers identified as Christian. Although they did not necessarily share
their beliefs with the children, this was something that the children often
picked up on, for instance, Mason commenting that one of his teachers was
Christian because she wore a necklace with a cross. Thus, from leading Christian
prayers and hymns in collective worship to sharing their own non-belief in RE
lessons, the teachers were themselves in their interactions with the children
embodying a range of possible stances in relation to religion and a/theism,
despite the legal and institutional privileging of Christianity.

Although Humanist organizations have largely not achieved their aims to
reduce the influence of faith groups in education (Brown et al. 2023), the experiences of children in our research suggest that despite the continued place
of religion in school curricula in England, schools are nevertheless making a
humanist worldview available to children, which intertwines with the humanist epistemologies and values that their parents also share. This worldview is
not, as we have noted, being expressed in terms of discrete creeds, texts, rituals
or practices in the way in which children are being taught about religion.
Rather it is seen in how the teachers, parents, and children express an
epistemology that valorizes rationality and science as ways of knowing the
world, and principles of reflexive autonomy, individual rights and freedoms.

While Archer locates this pervasive cultural emphasis on reflexive autonomy as characteristic of late modernity, we have situated this dominant ethos
also in relation to neoliberal emphasis on the self as a reflexive project. It is
worth highlighting again that an ethic of autonomy can be consistent with
religious as well as non-religious lifeworlds, and that this ethic has been shaped
by religious histories. Anthropologist Webb Keane (2007) has explored how
the emergence of secular 'modern' autonomous subjectivities was associated
with particular historical Protestant practices, which emerged through religious conflicts and colonial encounters, which objectified 'belief' as an internal state. Keane discusses, for example, how Christian creeds such as the
Apostles Creed begin with the first-person assertion 'I believe', and in repeat-
ing the creed, Protestants report their alignment with this belief publicly, and
thus the practice of saying creeds 'entails a normative tilt towards taking

responsibility for those words, making them one's own' (2007: 71). In this sense, Keane shows how Protestant language practices had a 'centripetal' force in the kinds of subjectivity they created, which helped shape the emergence of the secular, individualized, autonomous subject of 'modernity' (Bialecki 2011: 682). Thus, while the ideal of the autonomous reflexive self has often been associated with a particular narrative of secular modernity, there were also sticky Protestant residues in how children were being encouraged to identify, articulate and express their own beliefs and in how the children came to emphasize themselves as the ultimate arbiters of their belief.

While our study did not focus on them, there were, of course, theist children attending the schools we studied, who were experiencing the same school curriculum as our non-believing children. While we cannot claim this with certainty, we would speculate that they likely shared many of the same epistemological stances and values as their atheist classmates, and that their religious faith was sustained through religious engagements at home. Mrs Fordham, for instance, commented that the faith of Muslim children at Sunnybank was supported by active religious socialization they were receiving outside of school. She said that the Muslim children were 'very very strong [in their faith]. They will also practise it as well. They go to mosque. . . . They know things. They've got a much deeper knowledge of the world . . . And it's few and far between that you'll get a Christian child who has the same conviction with their faith by the time they leave primary school.' Given that we currently know relatively little about religious—as well as non-religious—children's experiences in relation to their faith in primary schools, her comments point to the importance of further research examining differences and similarities in how children of 'all faiths and none' respond to and locate the significance of the dominant worldviews they encounter in school. Yet while many aspects of the humanist values and ways of knowing are likely to have been shared by religious and theist children, we would suggest that these ideas were especially significant for understanding non-religious childhoods because they were the ideas and values through which the children in our study themselves made sense of, articulated and gave an account of what it means to them to be non-religious and non-believing.

4

The Aesthetics of Godlessness

CHARLOTTE AND LILY were eight-year-old girls from Sunnybank. As they drew pictures of the things that they saw as important to them, including unicorns, their houses and pets, Charlotte spoke about how she 'believe[d] in fantasy, like unicorns and stuff like that'. She went on, 'I love unicorns because they're bright and they're colourful and they're magic', and she suggested to Rachael, 'maybe . . . can we have a research [project] on unicorns a little bit?' Lily commented that she didn't believe in God, whom she described as 'just an invisible God who lives in the sky', and commented that she used to believe in God, 'but now I don't, because I'm eight.' She added, 'But I still believe in unicorns. Big fluffy unicorns dancing on rainbows.'

As they spoke about RE lessons and their own non-religious identities, Charlotte commented, 'I like Hindu images, because the images are . . . really decadent.' She said that she thought that her parents, like her, would identify as 'no religion', but that her nan was Christian, and that she sometimes spoke about God and Jesus with her. She added that she wouldn't tell her nan that she didn't believe in God, because 'I don't want to upset her', so instead she would tell her she was uncertain about her beliefs. When talking about RE, the girls commented that they had enjoyed making a Christingle out of oranges and sweets when learning about Christmas; 'we got to eat sweets', as Charlotte noted. Both commented that their own non-religious perspectives were not discussed in RE, and Lily said she found the subject 'super boring and when Ms Fordham talks about God, I don't believe in it'. She added, 'but I do believe in two things . . . unicorns and fairies'. When asked how they thought their closest friends would identify in relation to religion, Charlotte said that like her, they would be 'no religion', and Lily added, 'they are kind and they love unicorns'.

Rachael asked the girls whether they'd ever been to a church or place of worship, and Charlotte replied that she'd been to a wedding and Lily said that 'everyone at school has been to the church down the road'. Rachael asked them how they found these experiences. Lily replied:

LILY: Boring.
RACHAEL: . . . What made it boring?
LILY: Because all we had to do—
CHARLOTTE: Sit on hard seats really. That's just it.
RACHAEL: Sit on hard seats.
LILY: Sit on a seat, look at the front and just be like this.
CHARLOTTE: Yes, but when some people want to rest their feet, other people get to, but when you're sat there along with a teacher, they tell you not to. You know those like little fluffy cushions which you pray on? When you're sat on a row with your teacher, you don't get to sit on one.
LILY: It's just like: sit up, sit down, bye-bye.

Atheism and humanism have often been stereotyped as matters of the mind and intellect rather than of bodies, feeling, and things. However, Lily and Charlotte's comments indicate that the textures of their non-religiosity are embodied, material and felt. For them, the experience of going to church in its materiality and physicality—sitting on hard, uncomfortable seats, looking up at the front—is something they *feel* as boring, while they like the tactile Christingle oranges and sweets. This non-religiosity is also interwoven with visuality: they are not drawn towards the image of an invisible God in the sky, but like the 'decadence' of Hindu deities. At the same time, the enthusiasm they express when talking about unicorns and fairies—unlike religion and God—evokes their feelings of enjoyment and interest in these subjunctive modes of belief, which they share with their friends. Perhaps, as Charlotte suggests, a research project on unicorns would be fun.

Dominant ideas of non-religion and non-belief as immaterial emerge in part from how these phenomena have, as discussed in previous chapters, historically often been grasped primarily in relation to the absence of religion, rather than having their own substantial cultural—including material—formations (Lee 2015). As anthropologists Jacob Copeman and Mascha Schulz note, conventional portraits paint secular humanism as a disembodied, dispassionate, 'hyper-intellectual exercise that is antithetical to aesthetics' and therefore 'unconcerned with, indeed divorced from, matter, affect and the senses'—a portrayal which is somewhat 'ironic given the normative commitment of secular humanists to materialism' (2022: 23). Some scholars have linked these portraits of non-belief, non-religion and secularity to a particular Enlightenment narrative. In this story, the development of the autonomous self of Enlighten-ment modernity meant a focus on 'individuality, interiority and inwardness'—putting 'mind over matter' and 'thoughts and ideas over things' (Engelke 2019: 200). This is also interwoven with ideas of disenchantment and its depiction as an 'iron cage' of emotional emptiness—a story of 'sober philosophers and scientists grinding down religious superstition and revealing humanity's emo-tionless, rational core' (Schaefer 2022: 22). Charles Taylor's account of disen-chantment, for instance, situates the disciplined, buffered individual self as inhabiting a secular age in which calculative, instrumental rationality domi-nates (2007: 542). Within anthropology, there has been recognition of this story's bias in terms of European intellectual history (e.g., Copeman and Schulz 2022: 20), and thus of the importance of acknowledging how particular ideas of the self as an autonomous, rational, self-contained individual emerge through contingent material practices, shaped in particular times and places, including through colonial encounters. Webb Keane, for instance, urges ex-amination of how the 'thoughts, beliefs, and values' associated with 'secular modern' selves are always supported and instigated through 'bodily habits, clothing, kinds of media and the visual imagery they support, the layout of buildings and cities, ways of talking, all that makes them plausible and habit-able' (2013: 164–5).

Pushing back against stereotypes of non-religion and atheism as primarily intellectual, immaterial phenomena, a growing number of qualitative studies[1] have drawn attention to their affective, embodied, emotional, and material qualities.[2] Much of this work has however been framed in terms of the nega-tive aspect of the *not*-religious qualities of these phenomena—for instance, how critiques of, or indifference towards, religion are expressed through media, objects, or practices (Lee 2019a). However, as Engelke notes, this 'nega-tive aspect of secularity's not-religious or other-than-religious character is partial . . . because we do see secular ontologies and epistemologies emerging on their own terms, putting forward specific combinations of values, emo-tional sensibilities and affective registers' (2019: 205). Thus, rather than ap-proaching non-religion as the 'negation or absence of religion or as a neutral

1. Within history, Alec Ryrie's *Unbelievers* (2019) also examines emotional histories of doubt and non-belief.

2. See, for instance, the recent edited collections by Scheer et al. (2019); Beaman and Stacey (2021), and Copeman and Schulz (2022), building on earlier work by Lee (2015); Engelke (2015b); Binder (2016); Copeman and Quack (2017); and Eccles and Catto (2017).

ground', we might instead shift our focus to how 'non-religiosity is produced and made tangible and socially significant in different contexts' (Copeman and Schulz 2022: 6).

Exemplifying what it would look like to get hold of non-religion as something affective, embodied, and tangible, Donovan Schaefer's *Wild Experiment* is underpinned by the question: how does secularism *feel*? (2022: 22) Analysing historical case studies—including the writings of David Hume, Friedrich Nietzsche, William James, Charles Darwin, and Max Weber, alongside the Scopes Trial and the New Atheist movement—Schaefer challenges ideas that rationality and feeling are separate, and reconceptualizes rationality as defined by affective processes. As Schaefer expresses this:

> In all its forms, secularism[3] washes over us, rewriting the parameters of how our bodies feel their way through the world. Thought—the play of ideas, concepts, reasons, and evidence—is emotionally alive, neither immune to the public domain nor detached from it. If formations of the secular have something to do with the reconfiguration of frames of knowledge, they have everything to do with changing how the world feels.... Certain affective forms are nourished, cultivated, detailed, disciplined, refined to a level of sculptural precision. Others are left to wither and fall. (2022: 105–6).

Schaefer's focus on historical cases invites the question: how are particular *felt* ways of navigating the world produced within atheism and humanism in the contemporary moment? Children's experiences are a particularly important site for addressing this, since they make these processes of formation explicit, opening up how frames of knowledge and the feelings associated with them come to arrive through particular routes and be configured in particular ways. Although Schaefer does not focus on children, his work makes clear the significance of childhood in the formation of non-religiosity. He draws on the insights of Silvan Tomkins in articulating how 'raising children means shaping what they find interesting in the world. This can mean admonishing them to keep away from the bank of a river or pointing out an exciting plant or animal' (Schaefer 2022: 68). In this process, particular 'interests are rewarded and nourished, others are obstructed and shamed ... by imposing "barriers to interest or enjoyment"' (2022: 68–9). And this, we suggest, raises important *empirical* questions about how affective, embodied, and material registers are

---

3. Schaefer follows the common North American use of 'secularism' which largely overlaps with much of what we have been referring to as non-religiosity.

implicated in nourishing particular interests, patterns of belief, and ways of knowing in children's lives, and how other paths are being closed off.

This chapter therefore addresses these questions, focusing on the interrelated formation of atheism, non-religiosity, and humanism. In doing so, we draw on anthropologist Birgit Meyer's approach to religious 'aesthetics'. Aesthetics here is used not in the narrow sense of referring to the beautiful in relation to the arts, but emerges from the Aristotelian notion of *aesthesis*, as a means of organizing our 'sensory experience of the world and our sensitive knowledge of it' (Meyer 2012: 165). Meyer's aesthetic approach emphasizes how religious subjects are shaped through a structured process in which the senses are tuned in particular ways to form a habitus, entailing not only 'a strong emphasis on specific, privileged, sensory and extra-sensory perceptions but also the tuning down or anaesthetization of other senses or sensory perceptions' (2012: 167). Meyer's interest here is in how a religious sense of the transcendent—and the tuning down of other senses—is 'fabricated' through particular practices, materials and forms (Copeman and Schulz 2022: 21). Shifting our attention instead to *non*-religious senses and sensations, this approach invites attention to how the children's immanent, this-worldly senses of faith are fabricated (2022: 22).

In a sense, we have already begun to answer this question over the previous chapters. The ways in which the children spoke—or didn't speak—with their parents about religion, together with the ways in which both parents and schools were encouraging the children to think of and experience themselves as autonomous individuals, always took place through *embodied* acts of conversation and pedagogical practices, interwoven with particular emotional registers. The absence in most of the children's lives of practices such as regular churchgoing which were more common amongst their parents' generation meant that their senses were in many ways being 'anaesthetized' as Meyer expresses this—that is, *not* being tuned in ways that would lead them, for instance, to experience the sacred in sacraments such as Mass or practices such as prayer. This meant, as we saw in the previous chapter, that their affective sensations during prayer were those of boredom, with some children feeling that prayers were imposed on them in ways that jarred with their sense of autonomy. Moreover, the pervasive privileging of ideas of autonomy we saw in the previous chapters also emerges through being enmeshed in particular spaces, places, and practices, in which religion and theism are at the same time also being socially constructed with particular textures which click—or don't click—with how the world feels for the children.

This chapter explores the aesthetics of the children's non-religiosity, atheism and humanism—and how these were interwoven—through focusing on the feelings, sensations, embodied practices, affective registers, and forms of media and materiality implicated in its fabrication. We begin by exploring the feelings and practices through which the children and some of their parents come to situate themselves as other-than-religious, for instance, senses of indifference to religion, but also sometimes stronger sensations such as disturbance or disgust at traditional Christian iconography and ritual. We then turn to move beyond these 'negative' modes of non-religiosity to explore the 'substantive' aesthetic formation of central aspects of their humanist form of life, including their subjunctive modes of belief and enjoyment of nature and science, and underscore the importance to the children of these immanent connections, attachments, and shared affective registers of pleasure and enjoyment.

Feeling Other-Than-Religious

How, then, were the textures of the children's non-religiosity and non-belief in God produced, embodied, and made tangible? Despite the emphasis on 'neutrality' towards religion that many teachers expressed, the idea that there is a 'neutral' ground in which expressions of religion or non-religion appear is a fiction (Chalfant 2022). The forms of religion which were present in the children's lives were situated in relation to the much more pervasive material expressions of humanism they were encountering, which shaped how they came to engage with the religion they encountered. This humanism was ubiquitous and 'banal' in the sense that Michael Billig uses the term to express the power of given, unremarkable material forms, such as the 'unwaved flag' (Billig 1995; Lee 2015). In each of the schools, for instance, human achievements were made visually and imaginatively available to the children throughout the everyday spaces and rhythms of the school day. This included school noticeboard displays celebrating individual and team sporting achievements and musicians, and assemblies in which the children were invited to sit and listen to narratives celebrating the achievements of historical or contemporary figures, accompanied by PowerPoint images of these exemplary humans. For instance, during Black History Month at St Peter's, the teachers decided to make all the assemblies during the month focus on the achievements of particular individuals, accompanied by music from artists involved in anti-racist activism, such as Aretha Franklin or Nina Simone.[4]

---

4. This focus on exemplary individuals is not unique to contemporary educational landscapes. School history textbooks, for instance, have followed the 'great man' path for many years.

This focus on exemplary individuals was also materially and visually present in the books the children read, both at school and at home. The popular *Goodnight Stories for Rebel Girls*, for instance, which many of the children told us they enjoyed reading, tells the stories of 'one hundred remarkable women'. Teddy from Waterside said that of all his many books, his favourite was *Rebel Girls*. When asked what was good about it, he replied, 'it's just got lots of different girls, and they all do really good stuff, like helping each other'. His friend Izzy commented that she also had a book she enjoyed called *Girls who Rock the World*, featuring Florence Nightingale, Harriet Tubman, Frida Kahlo and others. These women were united, she suggested, through their being 'brave'—suggesting how reading the book was encouraging her to reflect on the moral quality of courage exemplified in the narratives of these women's achievements.

As well as this celebration of 'remarkable' humans, each school held weekly assemblies celebrating the children's achievements, which might be linked to their behaviour, the school values, academic success, or something they had tried hard to accomplish. Thus, throughout the children's everyday school life, it was people and their achievements and struggles to overcome adversity which were celebrated and which the children were being encouraged to perceive as matters of importance and interest. Although Humanist discourses and histories were not made explicit in the framing of these stories, posters, books, or music, they were nevertheless fabricating a humanist form of life, centring what matters in the this-worldly realm of human history and affairs, and resourcing the children's moral imaginations with ideas of human achievement and progress in different spheres of life, from struggles against racism to science, art, music, and sport.[5]

Alongside this pervasive humanism, religion—and specifically Christianity—was also present in material, tangible forms, both implicit and explicit, through which the children were learning to understand what 'religion' and 'belief in God' were and to feel that they did *not* themselves necessarily share these. While as we saw in chapter 1, the children tended to articulate their atheism using Christian propositional grammars of (non) belief, the forms of Christianity—and other aspects of religion—which they experienced in schools were not just abstract doctrines. In his study of children's schooling in Ireland, Karl Kitching describes how a non-religious

5. This echoes Hemming's study of religion in primary schools, which noted a pervasive 'generic humanist position' (2015: 116) shaping the ethos of the community school he studied in northern England.

child, Cormac, was 'experientially enmeshed in Catholicism through repeated encounters with a variety of objects and spaces, despite his nonbelief'
(2020: 117). It was therefore 'through these objects and spaces that Cormac
apprehended and swerved from religiosity and local church rituals' (2020:
117–18). Compared with the normative Catholicism in the Irish schools
Kitching studied, religion was somewhat differently emplaced in the schools
we worked with. But it was nevertheless still present through material, spatial,
visual, and embodied forms which shaped how the children were swerving
away from it. Yet the threads of their entanglements with religion were looser
than Cormac's enmeshment in Catholicism, and were in places coming apart
altogether, especially where humanist and Christian threads were felt as pulling against each other.

We saw in the previous chapter how particular forms of Christianity perco-
lated in the schools through prayers, collective worship, Christian festivals,
and the RE curriculum. Alongside these, the children also visited churches for
school church services, as well as occasional RE trips to other places of worship, such as gurdwaras or mosques. As well as these entanglements via school,
there were also a minority of children, such as Steve, who attended church
regularly with their families, and a larger number who attended churches occasionally, for weddings or christenings. At the same time, church halls served
a local community function as venues for hire for activities such as arts or
dance clubs, children's birthday parties, Cubs and Brownies—with several
children commenting that they had been in a church when attending Brownies, Beavers, or Cubs. How, then, were the children responding to the visual
and material forms of religion they encountered in these spaces?

For some children, aspects of Christianity were somewhat 'banal' in the
sense that Elayne Oliphant (2021) situates Catholicism in France as 'banal'—
occupying, in contrast with Islam, an unmarked background space, achieving
'the status of the ambient' (2021: 18). We noted in the previous chapter that
some forms of Christian practice and materiality in the children's schools
were able to achieve this ambient status, such as the Advent candles at Waterside, or the classroom prayer spaces at St Peter's. This was also the case for *some*
children's engagements with Christian materiality outside school. For instance, several children regularly participated in Messy Church, which is an
organization that facilitates informal crafts-based activities for children and
families, oriented around Christian teachings. Several children spoke about
how they liked these activities, with their enjoyment more focused on the
materiality of the craft than the specific Christian teaching they were learning

about. Izzy from Waterside described an activity in which she had designed and made her own cross:

RACHAEL: So, with Messy Church, was it to do with religion then or . . . ?
IZZY: No, not really.
RACHAEL: No? So, you don't have to be religious to go Messy Church?
IZZY: No.
RACHAEL: What kind of stuff do you make in Messy Church?
IZZY: We make anything, really. There are different activities, so last time
    we went, it was an Easter-y one and so we made an Easter wreath with
    the story in a circle, and then we also made a cross with glitter. So, it
    had a cross made out of masking tape and then we had to cover the
    other bits with glue, and then sprinkle glitter all over the gluey bits and
    then we took off the masking tape.

Izzy's description of Messy Church can be seen as an instance of how Christianity is made 'banal' in the sense that Izzy sees it as 'not really' to do with religion. The Christian meaning was not lost on Izzy, but was a 'background' element to the practice. More foregrounded for her were the glitter and glue. When Rachael specifically asked her why she was making a cross, Izzy's reply demonstrated she was aware of the underpinning Christian narrative here:

RACHAEL: Why were you making a cross?
IZZY: Because Jesus, he died on a cross.
TEDDY: That's not nice.

This contrast between Izzy's reply and her friend Teddy's comment indicates that this Christian practice was *not* 'banal' for children like him who didn't participate in these kinds of activities, but rather jarred with his moral sensibilities.

Teddy's response is revealing of how particular aspects of Christian visual and material culture did not achieve an ambient status for many children and parents. Nancy, a Waterside parent who identified as Anglican, commented that when her daughter had learnt about Easter at school, she 'really didn't like the lesson at all when they talked about him being nailed to the cross, because she just didn't like that idea. Not because of its religious context, just because why would you do that to somebody?' Laura, a Sunnybank parent, also reflected on how her daughter found the image of Jesus being crucified in relation to Easter upsetting, and said she had 'a very difficult conversation with my daughter about Easter. Soon after Christmas, somebody bought her an

Easter book, and that was pretty horrific.' Laura commented on the fact that her generation had been brought up immersed in these Christian imaginaries in a way that was different from her daughter's imaginative repertoire:

> Well, you go from baby Jesus to Christ being crucified on the cross. It's quite dramatic, isn't it? I remember talking to some of my friends and my dad, with his faith, and they said, 'Yes, well, we were brought up with that, so that was no shock to us.' But obviously to my children that was quite a shock.

Laura commented that she was proud of her children's emotional response to the violence of this Christian imagery:

> that really emotional reaction to what happened to another person, rather than the fact that this is Jesus. Just that emotional human response. I was very proud of them to respond like that, because if something so horrific happens to a human, whether you believe they are the Son of God or not—

Here we see Laura's humanist pride in, as she puts it, her children's 'emotional human response' to what she sees as the dehumanization of another. Parents too expressed visceral responses to Christian iconography portraying human suffering. Natalie, the mother of Mason at Sunnybank, who identified as humanist, commented that when visiting a potential Catholic secondary school for him,

> there were crucifixes in every room that we went in.... For me, as a non-religious person, it's not a nice image, because it's a man who has died on a cross.... [They were] at the head of the classroom, and every classroom we went into, that's what was there. It freaked me out, I just wanted to get out of the classroom ... because there wasn't a lot else on the walls, but that was there. It wasn't big, but it's a man on a cross who has died and looks like he's in pain.

Like Laura, Natalie also expressed her consciousness of generational differences shaping the felt textures of these encounters with Christian imagery. She commented that non-religious children of Mason's generation would not perceive a crucifix in the same way as older generations, noting that 'for a child who isn't religious', they would see an image of a man in pain, rather than an object evoking transcendent meaning: 'They won't see, "he died for us, and it's sacred". That isn't the eyes he'll be looking at it through, is it really?'

Alongside unease in response to Christian visual repertoires portraying human suffering, parents sometimes expressed their felt dislike of Christian institutional spaces in terms that gestured towards their sense of a tension between an ethos of formality they saw embodied in churches and their own humanist ethic of freedom and authenticity—an ethic we will explore further in the following chapter. Faye, a Waterside parent reflected on her feelings of unease while visiting a church school as a potential secondary school for her children:

> So, they've got a chapel there that they [the children] actually go into for sessions. I wasn't keen on that really. It freaked me out a little bit. That makes me sound really weird, but I think I have a bit of a thing about the whole church environment. Whether it's the formality of it or whatever, often church settings I find a bit cold and bit creepy. It just turns me off really in that sense.

Faye—unsurprisingly—did not send her children to this school, but instead chose a community school, illustrating how parents' affective responses to material forms of religion meant they did not want their children exposed to these forms.

As well as parents' comments about their own and their children's felt responses, several children also expressed feelings of disturbance, disgust, or dislike at aspects of Christian visual imagery, spaces, and practices. Daisy and Gia from Sunnybank spoke about visiting a church for a christening. When asked how she had found this experience, Daisy replied 'disturbing'. Rachael asked her to elaborate, and Daisy replied:

> DAISY: . . . the guy who christened the twins . . . he had no experience. It was his first time. He was filling in for somebody. He didn't really know how to do it. He put the water over her head but it got in her eyes and her mouth. He'd moved it back and it poured quite fast and got it on us. What I found disturbing was you could see some body parts in the church that you weren't really supposed to see.
> GIA: Yes, like you see bits because they've only got something covering their bits. You can see their belly buttons and other stuff.

Rachael, somewhat concerned, asked the girls to explain what they had seen and who they were referring to:

> RACHAEL: Whose body parts can you see?
> DAISY: There were people on the wall. I'm not sure who.
> RACHAEL: Not real people?
> GIA: No, not real people.

DAISY: They were statues.
RACHAEL: Oh, right.
GIA: There are things on the windows.
RACHAEL: So, images—?
GIA: Of God.

The girls were referring to crucifixes—or 'little statues of God on the cross', as Daisy described them—and the stained-glass windows in the church. And it was clear that they did not experience these visual representations of Jesus's exposed body as 'banal', but rather as something outside their usual visual repertoires which they found disturbing.

Pearl from Waterside expressed a sense of disgust as she spoke about taking part in First Communion:

> I did eat the bread once, but I don't want it anymore because that's his body. That's what I thought before, because I thought it was his actual body and his blood . . . I thought it was a bit disgusting that we would drink that, drink it and eat it. I was only quite young then, so I did think it was disgusting.

As well as these aspects of materiality, some children also expressed their felt dislike of the idea of God, conceptualized in particular ways. Amy from St Peter's said that she felt the idea of 'someone just looking down on you all the time' was 'a bit creepy . . . like when you want privacy, why would you want someone just looking down on you?' She went on, 'I wouldn't want someone looking down on me all the time', and her friend Edith concurred, commenting she didn't need God because 'you've got your parents and stuff to look after you'. These different affective responses demonstrate how in contrast with the 'banality' of Catholicism that Oliphant observes in France, Christianity does not fully occupy this unmarked 'ambient' status in the lives of these children. Their comments reveal how as the colours of Christianity grow fainter in the ongoing weaving of cultural memory, so too does the ability to situate particular images, objects or forms of material culture within wider Christian histories and frameworks of interpretation (Hervieu-Léger 2000). As Natalie commented about Mason, 'that isn't the eyes he'll be looking at it through'.

There were also other material and embodied aspects of the pervasive Christianity that the children encountered in schools which did not necessarily generate *strong* negative affects of disturbance or disgust, but through which the children nevertheless perceived Christianity as a form of life they did not share. At Sunnybank, for instance, a number of the children commented that they thought their headteacher was Christian due to the way she spoke and acted. Bethany commented:

> BETHANY: I think the headteacher is religious, and they like having the prayers.
> RACHAEL: What makes you think the headteacher's religious?
> BETHANY: She sounds and looks like she's religious. I'm not saying you have to look like something's religion. But she just does.
> RACHAEL: Go on, tell me a little bit more. . . . What do you mean she sounds and looks like she's religious?
> BETHANY: She wears stuff that you would expect people—like nice clothes. Saying, like, 'Thank you, God, for all the clothes that we have.'
> RACHAEL: What religion do you think she is?
> BETHANY: Christian, Church of England.
> RACHAEL: What makes you think she's Christian, Church of England, as opposed to any of the other religions?
> BETHANY: Because I just think she is, and she likes doing Christian prayers.

Bethany's comments are suggestive of how children were perceiving the Christianity they did not share not only through the kinds of propositional theistic beliefs we explored in chapter 1 but also through particular affective registers, such as the way the headteacher spoke and how this manner of speaking conveyed a *liking* of prayers.

The presence of Christianity in the schools also had auditory dimensions, and it was sometimes through these that the children were swerving away from belief. Like Charlotte and Lily, Louis from Waterside enjoyed aspects of the school Christingle service but did not enjoy the songs:

> I quite like it [Christingle], except the singing. Because I don't really like singing. It's just because they're kind of like slow songs and more about religious. Sometimes when I'm singing them, I'm thinking that I don't think it's true—what it says in the songs and what God's doing.

These feelings of disliking Christian songs were also expressed by children in relation to attending churches for baptisms or weddings. Hayden from Sunnybank said that he had been to a church for a baptism, and when asked how he had found the experience, he replied: 'I didn't like it because people were singing, but because I'm not really Christian, I had no idea what was going on. My mum was like, "Ssh, be quiet." Then, I was like, "Can I play on DS?"'

Moreover, it was not only children who expressed feelings of unease or dislike in response to religious soundscapes. Michael, the father of Henry from Waterside, who identified as Jewish, non-religious, and atheist, commented:

> I could never sit in a religious place and sing religious words because I would feel like I can't even utter those words unless I believe them. No one else in my family gives a toss. They enjoy singing and they sing four-part harmonies all the time anyway. They'll sing anything. They don't care. They'll enjoy it for the music, whereas for me there's a moral thing in there.

Michael's comment, like Louis's, suggests how singing religious songs you don't believe in might violate a humanist ethic of authenticity, a value we will explore further in the following chapter, and perhaps also underpinning the fact many children did not like having to sit quietly with heads bowed while school prayers were said. These auditory dimensions thus fed into the children's grasping and swerving from Christianity.

While some parents expressed their own discomfort with particular religious aesthetic forms, there were also instances when parents expressed unease about their children engaging with particular material forms of religion. Anthony, a Waterside parent, initially positioned himself during his interview as open to talking to his children about religion, and said, 'I don't mind talking to them about religion.' He then commented on how a 'very religious' evangelical friend had given his children a book about Christianity. He said:

> the first time I read it I was just kind of, 'I can't read this it's so . . .' you know, it's a religious book, a religious children's book. I struggled and really didn't fancy reading it ever again, and then Emily picked it up the other day and she was like, 'I want to read this.' I kind of said, 'No'.

Through these comments, we see how although Anthony initially positions himself as open to talking about religion, his response to the book reveals his embodied, emotional reaction of dislike towards particular forms of Christianity, meaning he does not want to read the book to his daughter. This reaction then, we suggest, was subtly conveying to his daughter that the subject matter of this book—Christianity—was not a matter of interest, enjoyment, or importance. Here we see how despite parents' strong emphasis on the idea of their children having choice and autonomy in relation to religion, in practice, particular ways of knowing and feeling associated with religion were being closed off.

Other instances also demonstrated how despite parents' articulated desire to embody a 'neutral' stance when speaking about religion with their children, religion was sometimes materially situated in the home in ways that were not neutral. Harriet, a Sunnybank parent, emphasized during her interview how despite the fact that she was critical of religion, she did not seek to pass on this critique but rather to embody a stance of 'neutrality' with her children in relation to religion. At the end of the interview, as Rachael was about to leave, she spotted a hologram of the Last Supper wedged behind Harriet's toaster. Seeing Rachael's interest, Harriet asked if she would like to see her toilet, and said this might also be of interest. The walls of her downstairs toilet were covered in framed pictures and paintings of religious imagery and figures within Roman Catholicism and Mormonism. On the windowsill above the toilet were numerous pieces of religious iconography, including small statues of the Virgin Mary, crucifixes, and rosary beads. When asked why she had decorated her toilet like this, Harriet laughed and said she wasn't really sure why, and added 'well, I like to make my boyfriend uncomfortable when he goes to the toilet'.

This kitsch, irreverent staging of religion in Harriet's toilet indicates how religion might be materially present in the home as something to be made fun of even while at the same time parents saw themselves as embodying a stance of neutrality in how they were speaking about religion with their children. However, while aspects of Christian iconography might be present as something to be made fun of, aspects of Buddhist and Hindu material culture were sometimes present in a slightly more reverent sense, such as the statues of Buddha and Ganesha which Zoe said that her father had in his garden shed. As we noted in chapter 2, the material presence of these statues in her home, normalizing Buddhism as something her father valued and was interested in, appeared to contribute to Zoe's draw towards Buddhism, and she commented that if she had to choose a religion, 'I'd choose Buddhism, because I like Buddhas.'

When thinking about these sometimes unremarked upon visual and mediated aspects of how children came to feel themselves as other-than-religious, it is worth noting that a few parents commented that they discussed religion with their children in relation to particular news events. They did not specify what these events were, and we did not ask them at the time. However, the ways in which Joe, a pupil at Waterside, equated Islam and terrorism suggests that at least some of these news stories discussed with parents may have concerned terrorist incidents, in which links were being made between Islam and terrorism:

JOE: I can't be friends with terrorists though. I don't get why terrorists are only Muslims.
RACHAEL: Do you think they are?

JOE: Yes, they are. I know they are. It was on the news. Terrorists are only Muslims because, like let's say a Muslim who was wearing all black, if he was just robbing houses and didn't kill anyone or scare anybody, he would be a robber. But if he went out causing crimes and fighting people, then he would be a terrorist.

Whilst Joe's was not a viewpoint that other children explicitly articulated, his comments reflect how the children's—and adults'—imaginaries of religion are 'shadowed by discussions of terrorism because of the popular media links that are being made consistently between them' (Hickey-Moody 2023: 151). Although this was not how religion or Islam were represented in the school curriculum, the presence of popular media in the children's homes—whether news programmes or the radio on in the background—articulates and feeds these kinds of linkages between religion and terrorism, rather than, for instance, making links between particular cultures of 'protest masculinity' and terrorism (ibid.). At the same time, comments from other children suggested that some parents were perhaps trying to challenge these linkages and ways of perceiving religion. Mason from Sunnybank commented that he had discussed the Manchester Arena bombing with his parents, and said, 'people started calling Muslims names, and they were being a bit racist, and my mum and dad were talking with me [then] about, well, religion, sort of'. These then were some of the material, affective registers through which children—and their parents—were grasping religion and 'swerving away' from it, situated within a wider pervasive humanist culture.

Feelings for Maths, Science, and Nature

Alongside these ways of relating to aspects of religion, the children's faith in science and appreciation of the natural world were being nourished through other affective registers. In chapter 1, we described how the enjoyment that many children felt in maths and science challenged stereotypical ideas of science, rationality and empiricism as primarily pursuits of sober, detached rationality. We described in chapter 2 how through everyday conversations, their parents were nurturing the children's interest in science and 'nature' as matters of interest and importance. At the same time, as we explored in chapter 3, the schools were also seeking to encourage their enjoyment of maths and science through playful, fun activities, while these subjects were also positioned as areas of non-negotiable importance through the priority they were given in the school curriculum.

This sense of science and maths as matters of importance was interwoven in how Craig and Steve from St Peter's spoke about them. Craig commented that 'maths is my favourite [subject] because it's to do with science', and noted that when he was older, he wanted 'to be a professor of science or something which involves a lot of science and maths'. At the start of the interview, when they were talking about things that were important to them, they identified 'family' and 'school' as important to them and Craig explained:

> CRAIG: School is just so important, because think about it, if you hadn't gone to school . . . if someone else had, they would be like, 'what's two add two?' and then you'd be like—
> STEVE: Seventeen [laughter]
> CRAIG: No, but then you wouldn't even know what numbers were. So you'd be like, 'what are you even saying?'

The boys' interaction here reveals how they situate mathematical ways of thinking as fundamental to what it means to be educated. But maths and science were not just of intellectual importance to Craig and Steve: they were also defined by affective registers of enjoyment and interest, and interwoven in their friendships and in material culture beyond the school curriculum:

> CRAIG: . . . me and Steve really *get* maths, like a lot. I think that's the reason why we're always best mates as well.
> STEVE: Yes, so that's how we're friends.
> CRAIG: Guess what he got me for my birthday? He got me a whiteboard with a pen, a maths set and stuff. . . .
> RACHAEL: Did you like that?
> CRAIG: Yes.
> RACHAEL: Was it special?
> CRAIG: Yes, because it's from him.

The children's narratives also sometimes revealed how their faith in science was associated with particular modes of visuality which shaped the children's sense of science as more persuasive than the visual imaginaries they associated with theism. Zoe from St Peter's mentioned how her father's magazines had shaped her belief in evolution rather than God:

> I always thought it [belief in God] didn't really make much sense because I always thought that people were evolved from things like monkeys because my dad used to get these . . . *National Geographic* magazines. There were

things about evolution in there, which sounded more true or more realistic than God and the creation story.

Zoe's friend Louise concurred, and commented on how the visual representation of evolution in these magazines played a role in the formation of her faith in science:

> LOUISE: I was going to say about evolution—it just makes more sense to me that the monkeys that look like humans—because you know in the magazines, they always put, like—so there's the monkey or gorilla thing, then it's kind of slowly evolves to be more intelligent and stuff and stand upright. That kind of makes more sense to me.
> RACHAEL: Seeing it like that?
> LOUISE: Yes.

The phrase 'made sense to me' here evokes how these scientific visual cultures 'click' (Schaefer 2022) with how the world feels for Louise and Zoe, in a way that 'God and the creation story', as Zoe puts it, 'didn't really make much sense'. Moreover, several of the children, when asked to draw pictures of things they believed in, drew images, such as those shown in Figures 4.1 and 4.2, of how they imagined the Big Bang, underscoring how these scientific accounts were for them interwoven with particular visual repertoires.

As well as their attraction towards scientific theories and the enjoyment many experienced in science and maths, several children also spoke about the pleasure they got from engaging with and learning about nature, animals, and non-human life forms. Lucas from Sunnybank expressed his atheism as related to his enjoyment of learning about nature, as well as his sense of affinity with Charles Darwin, stating:

> I don't believe in God. I believe in evolution. . . . Well, I've always been sort of a nature guy, haven't I? I've always been a bit like Charles Darwin—attracted to nature, wanting to learn more about it. And I'm with Charles Darwin: I don't think that God created everything.

When asked about whether they had ever found anyone particularly inspiring, several other children also mentioned scientists who embodied this sense of science and nature as matters of interest and importance, such as Einstein and—more commonly—the biologist and broadcaster David Attenborough. The BBC television series *The Blue Planet*, which was being broadcast on BBC1 when we were conducting our fieldwork, was also a popular response when

FIGURE 4.1. Child's drawing representing the Big Bang

FIGURE 4.2. Child's drawing representing the Big Bang

we asked the children whether they liked to watch any particular TV programmes. Bob, a pupil at St Peter's, expressed his enjoyment of nature programmes and their importance to him:

> BOB: I love David Attenborough. Do you know who Steve Irwin is?
> There's a TV show called *Bindi's Bootcamp*; I love watching that. I just
> love Steve Irwin—all I watch on YouTube is just all the zoo tours by
> Steve Irwin, all of that stuff.
>
> RACHAEL: So why do those particular things inspire—why are they
> important to you?
>
> BOB: There's a movie called *Crocodile Hunter*, that's a movie with Steve
> Irwin in it. I have that movie at home. . . . Loads of wildlife is so
> important to me, and so is all of the Irwin family and all that stuff.

Several parents noted that they watched *Blue Planet* with their children, and
said that they saw watching and discussing it together as helping to cultivate
a sense of care for the planet. When asked whether she intentionally drew on
any particular spiritual, religious, or secular worldview when raising her
children, Jennifer, Zoe's mother, said she watched programmes like *Blue Planet*
with them:

> we're watching *Blue Planet*. . . . So, things like that which are about looking
> after the environment. Obviously, they've got their bit at the end where
> they tell you what's going on. I was telling them last week . . . 'Really, this is
> you guys now.' You know, they're the ones to be looking after our planet.
> So, we've talked a bit about plastic this week. Oh, it terrifies me. Did you
> see last week's *Blue Planet*? . . . They did about plastic at the end. It was just
> horrendous. . . . So, we do *Blue Planet*, we talk a lot about the environment,
> mainly . . . being kind to each other. That's a big thing, isn't it?

These comments about watching *Blue Planet* gesture towards how the
children's humanist form of life—centring meaning and significance in this-
worldly experience—may be cultivated by sensations of awe and wonder (Lee
2019a). Media historian Alexander Hall (2019) describes the high-budget BBC
nature programmes of the twentieth and twenty-first centuries—with their
rich visual splendour—as inviting feelings akin to a 'religious' awe in response
to the beauty of nature and humanist narratives of existence (Hall 2019: 158;
Lee 2019a). Indeed, we might see the act of watching these nature programmes
together as a family at home on a Sunday—when they tend to be scheduled
in a prime-time slot—as for many families replacing churchgoing as an act of

FIGURE 4.3. Child's photo of Forest School

worship, cultivating a sensation of the sacred in relation to a *humanist* reverence for nature and science.

More mundane affective registers of enjoying nature also emerged through the children's narratives. For example, when asked what was important to her at the start of the interview, Gabby from Waterside mentioned Forest School—a space at the back of the school grounds—and explained:

> It's like a forest at the end. Sometimes in the summer we get to go down there and play in the forest. . . . Sometimes I see children having lessons in there and I think that's quite good, because then you can get out to do lessons and get some fresh air whilst you're in it.

This enjoyment was something the children also expressed during the photography activity, when we asked them to photograph spaces, places or objects that were important to them, and several photographed this wooded area in school as a space they enjoyed and spoke about their memories of playing with friends and the games they had created together in these spaces.

Materializing the Subjunctive

Affective registers of enjoyment and pleasure also defined the children's subjunctive modes of belief. Jasmine from St Peter's had been really excited for Rachael to interview her mum, Erica, so she could show her the vast collection of unicorns and unicorn teddies she had told her about. When Rachael arrived at their Victorian terraced house a short walk from the school for the interview, Jasmine was excitedly standing at the bottom of the stairs, beckoning Rachael upstairs. Erica was midway through inviting Rachael towards the kitchen, when Jasmine interjected and asked if Rachael could come upstairs quickly first so she could show her all her unicorns. Rachael and Erica laughed, with Erica nodding and asking if Rachael would like a cup of tea. Running upstairs with Rachael following behind, Jasmine mentioned she had some new 'really cool' unicorn pyjamas. And indeed, as promised, Jasmine's room was awash with unicorns. As Jasmine gave Rachael a whistlestop tour of her collection, she documented each object and where it came from: 'and this pencil case is from Smiggle, and this is my favourite teddy, which Father Christmas got me . . .' As well as unicorns, there were fairies, wands, and all sorts of magical and mythical creatures and objects.

As described in chapter 1, subjunctive *as-if* modes of belief in supernatural, magical, or fantasy figures were important for many children. During nearly all the interviews, the children would at some point discuss fairies, ghosts, unicorns, mermaids, or dragons, and at the start of the interview, when asked to draw things that were important to them, many drew pictures of these, alongside other things, such as their pets. These magical and supernatural figures were interwoven throughout the visual background of the fieldwork, featuring on everyday objects such as the children's pencil cases, backpacks, lunch boxes, water bottles, watches, books, hats, and coats. While this may seem unremarkable, in understanding the aesthetic formation of the children's subjunctive beliefs, the pervasiveness of these figures in media and consumer culture is significant. Ella articulated how her belief in

FIGURE 4.4. Child's drawing of a dragon, cat, dog, and sunshine

unicorns was resourced by this ubiquity of unicorns in the media and culture they encountered:

ELLA: I started to believe in unicorns because I just saw loads of stuff with unicorns on.
RACHAEL: Yes, there's a lot of stuff about now with unicorns, isn't there?
ELLA: One time I was in a shop and there were unicorn pyjamas for adults.
RACHAEL: Oh wow, maybe I should've got them.
ELLA: I got a unicorn adult dressing gown, because it nearly fitted me.

These subjunctive beliefs and their aesthetic formation were gendered. For instance, Alex and Gabby from Waterside compared the feminized aesthetics they associated with fairies with the patriarchal figurations they associated with Christianity. Alex commented that she thought of fairies as 'girly . . . stars, hearts, that kind of thing' compared with how 'when you think "God", you think power up in the sky, and lightning, that's what I imagine'. She went on, 'I think people should also believe that there should be another God that's a woman . . . instead of just being the man God.' Gabby commented:

FIGURE 4.5. Child's drawing of a fairy and a unicorn cake,
with rainbow, hearts, and sunshine

when you think of Christianity you never hear any mention of other gods. It's just the one main God. It's a man, and it's the same with Jesus, it's a man. It's kind of going back again. Women weren't allowed to vote. We don't think that's fair, especially as girls, we don't think that's fair, well I don't, anyway.

These comments exemplify how the aesthetics associated with these subjunctive beliefs 'clicked' with how the world feels for many of the children in ways in which traditional Christian visual imaginaries—and the gendered figurations within these—did not.

On an affective level, these subjunctive beliefs were important sources of pleasure and happiness in the children's lives. This pleasure infused the animated ways children spoke about fairies, ghosts, and unicorns, often smiling as they spoke. Annie and Sophie from Waterside discussed their beliefs in ways that convey both Annie's attachment to fairies and how this was resourced through popular culture:

> ANNIE: I'm into fairies. . . . I believe they're real. Even though part of me thinks they're not real, part of me thinks I really want to tell this other side they're real. I don't know why that does that.
>
> RACHAEL: So, like part of you thinks fairies are real, and part of you kind of gets frustrated with the other part?
>
> ANNIE: Yes. So right now, I'm just getting a mix of feelings, like, 'They're real. No, they're not. They're real. No, they're not. They're real. No, they're not. They don't exist.' I think they're real though, sometimes.
>
> RACHAEL: So, tell me about fairies then.
>
> ANNIE: Well, . . . I started liking them because of this programme I have called *Tinkerbell*. There are lots of different series. . . . I really love those films. Well, they're really special because I've had them for a long time, and . . . I've loved them for ages and ages and ages. And also, the films like—I believe what they say . . . even though I've never seen a fairy before—
>
> SOPHIA: You can still believe.
>
> ANNIE: It doesn't mean that they're not alive. It doesn't mean they're not real, because you could see them like now. Like one could pop into the room.

Annie's *wanting* to believe in fairies—and this desire being resourced through films—resonates with how novelist Zadie Smith describes children's media as encouraging a belief-in-belief which 'has no denomination . . . it belongs to a generalized American faith that long ago detached itself from any particular monotheism, achieving autonomy in and of itself' (Smith 2018: 119). Describing a trip to the cinema with her children, Smith notes, 'Believing in belief is what makes Luke a Jedi and Cinderella a princess and Pinocchio a real boy, and my children have been believers of this kind from the earliest age—ever since they could say "Netflix". This is the lesson: If you believe—it will be real!' Our children's comments suggest that this is not a uniquely American faith. Parents also commented on their children's believing-in-belief. For instance, Paula, a Waterside parent, said that her daughter Eliza 'believes in . . .

the gods of YouTube . . . And she has always made it clear that she wants to believe in things and we aren't to disabuse her of that notion.'

These subjunctive modes of belief were encouraged through friendships as well as popular media. Annie spoke about how her belief in ghosts was shaped through her friendship with her classmate Minnie and, indirectly, the television programme *Creeped Out*:

> I believe in ghosts, now that Minnie has made me believe in ghosts. Well, she hasn't made me—I believe in ghosts . . . I'm not scared at school, but that's because I'm with Minnie and she's an expert on this stuff. But my mum said nothing is true—[that] she [Minnie] just makes this all up. But I don't believe that because I believe that she's . . . not making it up, but she's watched this programme called *Creeped Out* which she hears it all from.

Although Annie's mother was trying to dissuade her belief in ghosts, Annie's comments reveal how children are active in sustaining each others' subjunctive beliefs. This belief in ghosts—which was common amongst the children—can be located as part of what Christopher Partridge has described as an 'occultural turn' in western culture. This idea evokes how secularization in western societies is accompanied by a shift towards an 'occultural' cultural milieu that is essentially other-than-Christian, and includes a spectrum of beliefs and practices, including beliefs in the paranormal and spiritual practices, such as yoga and meditation (Partridge 2005: 2). This milieu 'both resources and is resourced by popular culture' and is seen in the popularity since the 1990s of television shows such as *Buffy the Vampire Slayer* and the Harry Potter series, as Lynn Schofield Clark (2003) explored in her study of US teenagers' fascination with the supernatural and paranormal.

In reflecting on these subjunctive—including occultural—beliefs which were resourced through a range of cultural forms, we would underscore that their significance for the children was bound up in their relationships with each other. They can therefore be situated, as noted in chapter 1, as part of a magical humanism, in which the meaning and significance of these beliefs is rooted in the this-worldly realm of human relationships, and these beliefs are not necessarily felt as in tension with faith in empiricism and science. These subjunctive beliefs often functioned as badges of social belonging. For instance, as noted at the start of this chapter, when Lily from Sunnybank was asked how she would describe her friends, she replied: 'they are kind and they love unicorns'. Moreover, the children's interactions in the interviews often gestured towards how these beliefs were—in contrast with belief in God—experienced as socially desirable, as we see with Izzy and Teddy:

IZZY: Pretty much everyone believes in mermaids.
RACHAEL: Pretty much everyone believes in mermaids?
IZZY: Yes.
TEDDY: Including me.

Although parents mostly did not explicitly comment on these kinds of beliefs in the interviews, they were also helping to sustain them through enabling the children's access to media and culture which resourced them. In relation to her belief in unicorns, for instance, Ella commented:

ELLA: On Facebook my dad showed me a picture of when it was a girl's birthday. She went horse-riding and they made the pony blue, and made it look like a unicorn.
JASMINE: Oh awesome.

These magical creatures also formed the toys, clothes, and games which parents, grandparents, aunts, and uncles bought the children as gifts, expressing their love, belonging and connection. Thus, while parents were in many ways contributing to the anaesthetizing of structures of feeling associated with religion in their children, they were enabling the aesthetic formation of these subjunctive beliefs, even if it was the children themselves who were active in creating and sustaining these with each other. Although we did not focus on their experiences, we think it likely that most of these forms of attachments were shared by their religious classmates.

The children's engagements with these magical and supernatural figures via media and consumer culture might be dismissed by some as part of the commodification of childhood. However, we would interpret their attachments to these figures as part of their social citizenship with each other (Pugh 2009). The children were intensely concerned with and focused on their everyday social worlds, and this was expressed in the importance to them of their friendships and peer relations. Thus, talking about unicorn dressing gowns and cuddly toys, ghosts, *Tinkerbell,* and *Creeped Out* are means of fostering their social relations and place within these. These figures and objects are entangled in the children's conversations as they tuck into their sandwiches or school dinner, and shared knowledge about unicorns, fairies or ghosts is important for how they play together at breaktime. Through these engagements, friendships are made, sustained, and sometimes challenged, and the children practise cooperation, collaboration and conviviality as part of the ongoing process of becoming.

Conclusion

Reflecting on what secularism feels like, Schaefer notes, 'The secular isn't the extraction of emotion and the injection of feelingless science. . . . It is, instead, no more and no less than an effort to build new formations of feeling—in part, by fashioning new modes of knowing' (2022: 22). In this chapter, we have described some of the 'formations of feeling' through which the children become other-than-religious, and how their humanist ways of knowing and believing are imbued with felt textures of enjoyment, pleasure, and interest, and are resourced through particular media, visual and material cultures. We have demonstrated how, in contrast with stereotypes of atheism, non-religion and Humanism as primarily intellectual pursuits, the children's non-religion and non-belief have particular felt, affective dimensions. In this sense, non-religion and atheism are 'not so much about the eradication of feeling as the replacement of one template of feeling by others' (Schaefer 2022: 84). These shifting 'templates of feeling' are expressed in the fact that for many of the children, the religion that they encounter does not *feel* right, or does not 'click' with how the world feels for them, and this is expressed in emotions such as boredom, disgust, disturbance, or lack of interest. These changing templates are bound up with the fact that religious ways of feeling and 'chains of memory' are not being nurtured in the way that they were in the childhoods of many of their parents' or grandparents' generations (Hervieu-Léger 2000), while at the same time, their humanist formations of feeling *are* being nourished, through their families, schools, everyday interactions, and wider media and culture.

Within religious cultures, aesthetic forms are often centred around particular repertoires of embodied practices and pedagogical forms, such as bible-reading, singing hymns, and listening to sermons within conservative evangelical culture, or Muslim practices of prayers, fasting, pilgrimage, and alms-giving. Moreover, socialization within these religious cultures often involves the intentional habituation of these practices amongst children (Scourfield et al. 2013; Strhan 2019). However, while there were shared patterns and textures of feeling amongst the non-religious children, their experiences and practices in relation to these were not uniform, because they were not organized around a particular religious institution or discrete body of texts or practices. Thus, while science did appear important in some sense to most children and many expressed the pleasure they felt in science, not *all* the children necessarily enjoyed it. Similarly, while many believed in ghosts and fairies, not *all* did. These differences in experience arise from the fact that the cultural forms and practices resourcing their other-than-religious form of life were diffuse, decentralized, and pervasive—from pedagogical practices emphasizing their autonomy explored in the previous chapter, to the books they read, the television they watched, and the posters on the school walls celebrating human achievements. In this sense, their humanism—like Schaefer's description of the secular—'isn't just one thing. It's profoundly multiple, arriving from many directions and leading down many roads' (2022: 106).

In their study of how children come to articulate environmental knowledge, Richard Irvine and colleagues draw on the work of Christina Toren (1993) to describe how children are both 'products and producers of history, and their engagement with the world is a process of continual meaning making as knowledge is constituted afresh in the course of their own lives' (Irvine et al. 2019: 724). Drawing on their experiences at home, with friends, from media and consumer culture, and from school, as children 'explore their environments, they make observations and connections. It is a process of figuring out.' In this chapter, we have seen how in these connections that children are making, as they draw together seemingly disconnected aspects of their experience— arriving from many directions—this 'figuring out' is always imbued with particular affective sensations and textures. Thus, when Gabby and Alex compare— and in doing so, connect—the aesthetics of fairies and Christian monotheism, they express a sensation of dislike, as they swerve away from Christianity.

This process of making connections and drawing seemingly disparate elements together to fashion a form of life has been conceptualized by numerous scholars as a process of 'bricolage'. Drawing on Lévi-Strauss's (1966) conception of bricolage in relation to myth-making, Véronique Altglas describes bricolage as a process of fabricating and 'tinkering' with materials that are at hand, with 'unpredictable and contingent results' (2014: 476). In his study of the religion, beliefs, and spirituality of young adults in the US, Robert Wuthnow describes them as a 'generation of tinkerers' or bricoleurs, who put 'together a life from whatever skills, ideas, and resources that are readily at hand' (2007: 13). And the possibilities for tinkering are growing with the proliferation of cultural forms, information, and 'exposure to diverse cultures and networks' (2007: 15). Unlike 'religious professionals' who might 'approach spirituality the way an engineer might construct a building' (2007: 14), the children in our study are also—like Wuthnow's young adults—bricoleurs who improvise as they make do with what they can, which depends on the aesthetic forms that are made available to them by their parents, schools, friends, media, and popular culture.

Altglas notes that studies within the sociology of religion have often used the concept of bricolage to highlight individuals' religious creativity in crafting eclectic religious and spiritual styles and identities. She argues that they have thereby missed how processes of bricolage are 'driven by a consistent quest of self-realisation which, as such, reflects wider norms and incentives of Euro-American societies' (2014: 475). This ethic of authenticity and self-realization, which we explore in the following chapter, also underpinned the children's forms of bricolage. Interwoven here was a reflexive habitus, which as noted in the previous two chapters can be located as part of the 'reflexive imperative of late modernity' (Archer 2012) and which was being formed in the children's schools and homes. Through this reflexivity, the children were able to recognize and evaluate particular aspects of material and visual culture as important to them, and other aspects—such as the forms of religion they encountered—as mostly not part of who they were.

Despite the seemingly disparate components through which the children were fashioning their form of life, the *importance* to them of their attachments stood out as something shared by all the children. Whether it was nature documentaries, unicorn pyjamas, celebrities ranging from David Attenborough to Ariana Grande, the maths set a friend had given, or a photograph from a family holiday, their attachments to these things *mattered* to the children (Hickey-Moody 2023). They expressed this mattering through their emotional registers of excitement and enthusiasm as they spoke, laughed, and drew pictures of these things, and the phrases 'I love' and 'I just love' resonated throughout the interviews as the children described these attachments.

These affective registers of enjoyment and pleasure were central to the form of life that the children were fashioning. In his study of organized British Humanism, Matthew Engelke notes the importance of happiness and pleasure for Humanists, arguing that 'Humanism in contemporary Britain is driven by a passion for the pursuit of happiness' (2015: 70). Engelke's organized Humanists understood happiness as part of the struggle for Enlightenment values, and positioned this happiness in contrast with religious values. Thus, rather than a religious promise of future happiness in a transcendent hereafter, 'the time to be happy is now', as Stephen Fry says in a Humanist video, 'and the way to find meaning in life is to get on and live it, as fully, and as well, as we can' (cited in Engelke 2015: 74). The pleasure, enjoyment, and happiness the children expressed in relation to their attachments to science, nature, or unicorns were not self-consciously positioned by the children as at odds with religion. Indeed, these forms of feeling may be important to *all* children, whether religious or not; as Anna Hickey-Moody notes, pleasure 'is a key means through which children become who they are' (2023: 130). And yet through these pleasures of connection and attachment, they were in a sense expressing this humanist ethic of finding meaning and happiness in life as they got on and lived it, as fully as they could, with the resources they found at hand.

5

The Shifting Ethics
of Non-Religion

AFTER PLAYTIME one afternoon at St Peter's, the Year 4 class lined up outside their classroom ready for afternoon lessons. Miss Morris, the class teacher, asked the children to hang their coats up, grab their water bottles, and sit down at their desks for the PSHE[1] lesson. The children were divided into groups of eight. As they were settling down, Miss Morris explained to Rachael that the school had invested in a resource called Jigsaw, which provided lesson plans and resources for PSHE. That afternoon's lesson focused on 'stereotypes and identities'. Every table was given six laminated sheets of A4 paper, each with a picture of a person. Under each picture were half-completed statements for the children to discuss in their groups, such as, 'Girls are . . .', 'Boys are . . .', 'Sporty People are . . .' As they began their discussions, Miss Morris stressed to the children that there were no right or wrong answers.

Rachael sat with the green table as they discussed the 'Boys are . . .' statement. The children shouted suggestions, including 'human', 'have the same rights', 'different to girls but have the same rights', and 'different to girls but the same importance'. They then discussed the 'Girls are . . .' statement, offering similar suggestions, all indexing ideas of gender equality. After ten minutes, Miss Morris asked the class to gather on the carpet to share their suggestions together. After a couple of groups had fed back their ideas, Miss Morris commented that their responses demonstrated that 'no matter what you look like, you're all important'. However, the cordial atmosphere was somewhat interrupted when Miss Morris invited responses to the 'Girls are . . .' statement, and one child responded '. . . stupid'. The other children responded with

1. Personal, Social, Health and Economic Education.

audible gasps and open-mouthed expressions of shock. Defusing the situation, Miss Morris commented, 'okay, well that's his opinion and not everyone agrees with that, judging by the gasps. And just because you think something doesn't mean it's true.' She went on, 'It's important to respect other people's opinions. They are entitled to think what they want.'

This lesson exemplifies both how the school was actively seeking to habituate an ethic of equality and how this ethic was already seen by most children as a given, and they experienced any transgression of this ethic as outrageous. At the same time, we see how, in attempting to manage the tension created by this transgression, the teacher referenced a liberal ideal of individual freedom of belief and opinion. The differing moral threads interwoven in this interaction—emphasizing ideals of human equality and individual freedom of belief—have a strong association with both liberal humanism and with narratives of religious decline. In his study of how individuals living through the 1960s in Europe and North America became atheist, Callum Brown (2017) argues that a humanist moral culture—which centres ideas of human equality, individual rights and freedoms, bodily and sexual autonomy and an ethic of care—is displacing western Christianity. Positioning the human as the source of moral knowledge, this humanist moral culture is secularizing in the sense that it decouples morality from religious teachings about rewards in an afterlife, and separates ethics from religious authorities and institutions, 'with a basic tolerance towards belief and unbelief, and a receptivity to materialist understandings of the world and the human condition' (Brown 2017: 169). Sociologists and historians have situated tensions between Christianity and an increasingly dominant humanist morality as a driver for secularization in western societies from the 1960s onwards, as individuals increasingly come to experience churches' teachings and institutional stances as morally unacceptable, especially in terms of conflicts with a humanist valorization of individual freedoms and equality, and an ethics of care and compassion (Woodhead 2016, 2017; Brown 2017; Day 2022).

While numerous scholars have traced the roots of these 'secular' humanist ethics within Christianity,[2] humanist moral sensibilities feeding into nonbelief do not emerge uniquely from Christian genealogies of the secular. Studying non-believers of Muslim origin in Egypt, Samuli Schielke (2012) demonstrates that his participants' non-belief was also based on moral discontent with religion—in their case, unease with a revivalist religion which

2. See, for instance, Taylor (2007); Keane (2007); Erdozain (2016); Ryrie (2019).

promised happiness and justice, but delivered 'oppression and suffering' (2012: 312). Underlying his participants' critique of religion, was their 'trust in the capacity of human moral judgement' (2012: 311), and Schielke highlights the similarity between the *moral* roots of contemporary Egyptian non-belief and how English freethinkers in the late nineteenth and early twentieth centuries turned away from faith on moral grounds.[3] Schielke argues that these similarities should not, however, lead us to locate the origins of Egyptian non-belief in European moralities: he notes that Islamic genealogies of atheism also reveal the development of humanist ethical sensibilities based on a similar 'conviction that human reason is sufficiently capable to differentiate between right and wrong and that there is no need for prophets and religions, which in the end cause only confusion and war' (2012: 311). Overall, Schielke positions contemporary Egyptian non-belief as 'about developing a lifeworldly certainty that turns the loss of divine presence into an accomplishment with the help of a trust in human agency and judgment' (2012: 317), resonating with how our children also spoke about their belief in their own and others' agency.

Schielke's work draws attention to the contingent formations of humanist moral orientations in particular times and places, and challenges dominant genealogies of humanism and secularity as intrinsically rooted in Christianity. It also opens up possibilities for attending to how the formation of non-belief through different historical lineages—such as those emerging in England and Egypt—may lead to unexpected resonances. While there has been a growing body of quantitative literature documenting the values associated with non-religion,[4] Schielke's research demonstrates the value of fine-grained qualitative attention to the moral narratives that people draw on when articulating their non-belief and paths away from religion. The majority of qualitative studies exploring how humanist values rub up against—and spur dissociation from—religious cultures have focused on the experiences of adults who were growing up in European or North American contexts at a time when Christianity was the cultural default.[5] We know relatively little about the ethics interwoven in the non-religious worldviews of the younger generations of second- and third- generation atheists in countries such as England where being non-religious and atheist are now 'the new normal' (Woodhead 2017). How, for instance, do these 'cradle nones' (Bullivant 2022) conceptualize,

3. See, for instance, Budd (1977); Brown et al. (2023).
4. Zuckerman et al. (2016) and Kasselstrand et al. (2023) both offer useful overviews.
5. See, for instance, Zuckerman (2011); Brown (2017); Day (2022); Turpin (2022).

respond to, and live with religious and other kinds of difference? What are the values that are interwoven in their everyday actions and interactions, and how do these compare with their parents?

In attending to these questions, this chapter is in conversation with literature in the sociology and anthropology of ethics, morality, and values. Morality,[6] as Marcel Mauss describes, is fundamentally about 'the art of living together, and . . . recognised by the presence of the notion of the good', while values express what is considered desirable, good, or proper in human life (Mauss 2007: 156; Henig and Strhan 2022). The sociological study of values, ethics and morality deepens understanding of this art of living together and of what comes to matter to people as good or desirable, and how and why. It also entails, as Michael Lambek suggests, attending to how people 'do in fact live and acknowledge that living, and how the living of discrete lives resonate with one another and with the ideas, words, and practices available for living them (at certain times, places, and class positions), as well as the particular challenges, constraints and hindrances to them' (2015a: 9). As Schielke notes, this means attending also to 'the complex, inconsequent and often highly contradictory way ethical practice works in everyday life' (2009: 164). These issues also inevitably bring us into the realm of the political. As human existence is always plural and the realm of ethics is 'inextricably interpersonal (both other and self directed)', concerned with how our lives are lived and organized with others, so the ethical is always interwoven with the political (Schielke 2009: 10; Strhan 2012; Fassin 2015).

In reflecting on ethics and morality in relation to non-religious children, it is worth noting that non-religious and non-believing identities have historically often been stigmatized as immoral (Lamont 1992; Ryrie 2019). Ryrie notes that the ancient Greek word *atheos* (without God) was 'a term of abuse, applied in ancient times to people like Socrates, condemned for his supposed rejection or neglect of established religious norms' (2019: 7) and over subsequent centuries in Europe 'atheist' became 'a usefully elastic term of abuse' (2019: 9). While not necessarily used with quite the same pejorative force, this stigmatization of atheism nevertheless still persists in many contemporary cultural contexts, for instance, in anti-atheist sentiments in the United States and elsewhere (Gervais 2014; Edgell et al. 2016; Thiessen and Wilkins-Laflamme 2020).

6. We use the terms 'morality' and 'ethics' largely interchangeably in what follows, following Webb Keane's observation that a strict separation of these terms is difficult to maintain, reflecting 'the dialectical relations between [these] modalities' (2010: 65).

A growing number of studies have sought to challenge these portrayals through documenting the ethical principles associated with the non-religious or non-believing.[7] At the same time, younger generations are often stereotyped as a 'selfish, individualised "Generation Me"' or a 'snowflake generation' (Catto 2014; Katz et al. 2021), while younger children are often perceived as ethically immature, for example, positioning them as recipients rather than givers of care. Because of these figurations of childhood and youth—alongside anxieties about the cultural decline of traditional values associated with religion—childrearing and education are often sites of intensified focus in politicized public debates about moral values, with parents' protectiveness of their children becoming easily entangled with anxieties about lost innocence, the future, and a changing culture. This process is exemplified in right-wing culture warriors' obsessive focus on schools and the idea that schools and children are being 'infected' and 'indoctrinated' by 'woke values and culture'. In these debates, the moralized, sentimentalized construction of children as embodiments of the future, and of innocence and purity, effaces the lived experiences of actual children, who aren't blank slates but individuals, each with their own history, which they themselves are in the process of shaping (Malkki 2015: 96; Toren 1993; Strhan 2019).

In conversation with the growing number of studies challenging negative stereotypes of the non-religious as selfish and self-absorbed, this chapter examines how non-religious children are themselves active in articulating, reflecting on, and enacting particular values in their lives, and how their ethical sensibilities towards religion and belief relate to their parents' stances. What ethical stances do non-religious children—who have received less religious socialization than their parents' generation—express as they make their way in societies that are marked by growing religious diversification? What does it mean to them—and to their parents—to live *well* together in relation to religious and other forms of difference (Derrida 2012; Beaman 2017a)? In answering these questions, we draw together how ideas of authenticity, autonomy, choice, and respect in relation to religion were privileged by the children, parents, and school staff, with 'choice' and 'respect' emerging as the two most prominent ideals participants spoke about in relation to religion and belief. While ideas of 'choice' in relation to religion are often portrayed as narrowly

---

7. See, for instance, Schielke (2012); Bengtson et al. (2013); Zuckerman (2014); Zuckerman et al. (2016); Copeman and Quack (2017); Ryrie (2019); Zuckerman (2019); Brown (2017); Day (2022).

individualistic, we argue that the ways children talk about 'choice' reveals how for them 'choice' is interwoven with an ethic of respect for the other.

We begin by situating the narratives of 'choice' articulated by the children and their parents in relation to expressive individualist cultures, in which autonomy and authenticity are central values. We then turn to explore how many of the parents expressed a moral critique of religion as anti-autonomy and anti-authenticity, and how for some parents, this experience of religion as constraining freedom had sharpened their desire to enable their children to become autonomous, authentic selves. We argue that this strong valorization of autonomy is infused with a moral concern for equality, and explore how many parents also described their move away from religion as related to their moral critique of religion as anti-equality, especially in relation to gender and sexual orientation. We note that the children did not, however, criticize religion in these terms, and consider how they articulated an ethic of equality in relation to different kinds of difference. We situate their ways of thinking about equality in relation to long-term shifts towards child-centred approaches to parenting and education, which implicitly shape how the children are growing up with a strong egalitarian ethic and sense of their own and others' rights and freedoms.

Through comparing how the children and their parents talk about 'respect', we argue that ethical sensibilities in relation to religion are shifting somewhat amongst the non-religious in England, as moral critiques of religion and the language of 'tolerance' expressed by parents are giving way amongst their children to an ethic that is primarily articulated in terms of respect for religious difference, within a wider social context of growing religious and ethnic diversity. Considering how these ethical orientations are expressed in everyday life, we describe how the children's interactions within school settings are a form of conviviality across categories of social difference, and also note the ambivalences and avoidances present within this conviviality. Overall, we argue that interwoven in the children's lived humanism was what we term an ethic of 'ordinary' equality.

Narratives of Choice and Authenticity

As we explored in chapter 1, the children took it as given that religion and belief were—or, at least, should be—matters of individual choice. Occasionally, children's comments revealed how this view of belief was slightly different from their parents, who could be conscious of a more normative force of Christianity. Sam from Sunnybank, for instance, noted that his mother had told him not to tell any Christians that he didn't believe in God or that he believed in evolution, as that would make them 'scared'. Sam, however, thought that his mum's instruction to keep quiet about his non-religion was 'crazy' as he put it, and he commented that Christians would not get scared, but would 'just think, "okay, you believe what you want to believe, and we believe in this religion", or whatever religion they believe'.

Sam's comments are indicative of the dominant cultural positioning of religion as a matter of personal choice which we have explored across previous chapters. This idea of religion becoming a matter of choice rather than duty is a well-worn theme in narratives of an epochal shift from former ages of faith towards our contemporary 'secular age'. As Charles Taylor expresses it, 'The shift to secularity . . . consists, among other things, of a move from a society where belief in God is unchallenged and indeed, unproblematic, to one in which it is understood to be one option among others, and frequently not the easiest to embrace' (2007: 3). While the ideal of individual choice runs deep in imaginings of a 'progressive' secular modernity, pitted as the 'autonomous adversary of "revealed religion"' (Rose 1997: 127), many sociologists agree that it was following the Second World War that 'choice' became a central value within North America and western Europe. Alan Ehrenhalt's study of 1950s Chicago expresses this sentiment:

> Most of us in America believe a few simple propositions that seem so clear and self-evident they scarcely need to be said. Choice is a good thing in life, and the more of it we have, the happier we are. Authority is inherently suspect; nobody should have the right to tell others what to think or how to behave (Ehrenhalt, cited in Taylor 2007: 479).

The rise of 'choice' to become a sacred article of faith is part of the long-term shift towards individualism providing the 'common moral vocabulary' of America and other liberal democracies, expressing how we conceive of ideas of freedom or justice in terms of individual freedoms or rights (Bellah et al. 1985: 22–6; Manning 2015: 144). Intertwined with the commodification of more and more areas of social life and with the growth of identity rights movements, the distinctive form of individualism that arose in the postwar mid-twentieth century and remains pervasive today is an *expressive* individualism (Bellah et al. 1985; Manning 2015; Watts 2022). As Manning describes it, this ethos saw 'the ultimate purpose of American independence as exploring and expressing one's true inner self. The good society is one that facilitates this freedom for every individual' (2015: 145). Taylor described the moral sensibility of expressive individualism as an 'ethic of authenticity', an expressivism which 'infiltrates everywhere', from beer commercials in the early 1970s instructing us to 'be yourselves in the world of today' (2007: 475) to contemporary children's T-shirts printed with the Disney Princess Elsa enjoining us to 'Be True to Yourself'. Within this moral framework, 'each one of us has his/her own way of realizing our humanity, and . . . it is important to find and live out one's own, as against surrendering to conformity with a model imposed on us from outside, by society, or the previous generation, or religious or political authority' (ibid.).

Studies of postmillennial teenagers and young adults in Euro-American societies have described authenticity as a particular moral imperative for younger generations, requiring them to 'discover, express, and live out "who you are"' as part of a process of self-realization (Katz et al. 2021: 76; Catto 2014; Gärtner and Hennig 2022). As digital technologies increase opportunities to express different presentations of self, they also enable hyperbole, manipulation and distortion. Thus, this broader cultural valuing of authenticity that appears intensified amongst younger generations who have grown up as digital natives, is perhaps, as Katz and colleagues argue (2021: 78ff.), bound up with a moral desire for honesty and believability as young people learn to live in a digital world. But 'authenticity' is not only significant for the young in Europe and North America. Working with young men in rural Egypt and Cairo, for instance, Schielke demonstrates the moral significance of ideas of individual self-realization in their lives, which for them, are often experienced as in tension with dominant religious community- and family-oriented values (2009: 172).

Given this pervasive cultural imperative of authenticity, it was not surprising that children in our study articulated this as they spoke about religion and belief. When asked what was important in her life, Hailey from St Peter's commented, 'my beliefs are important to me because they are my opinion. I don't really want to copy anybody . . . I actually want to speak true of what I think. Say things that are true, and just believe what I think is real. . . . Not just . . . what other people believe in, [but] about me too.' Hailey was critical of those who weren't, in her eyes, authentic in expressing themselves:

> Some people try to impress people and I just find that weird. I just think people should be themselves, because some people just don't act themselves. . . . Some people just copy people, and is that actually you? Is that actually what you want, or are you just doing it because your best friend [is]?

She further emphasized, 'Sometimes, if people just want to be someone else, I just think, "You don't have to be like them, you can just be who you are, and do what you like . . . Just do the things that you love doing."' When asked whether there were any figures she found inspiring, she mentioned a popular tennis player who 'just inspires me to go for anything. Sometimes they say on TV, "Just go for what you want to do", like beliefs, "Go for what you believe". People who say that just inspire me to be myself. They've inspired themselves to be themselves.' Further articulating the value she placed on self-expression, Hailey said that although sometimes she found RE boring, at times she liked it 'because we can just express our feelings and express our beliefs about how we're feeling, to show us who we are and who we believe. Not just about other people, actually about you as well, which I find quite special.' Theo from St Peter's expressed a sense that who you are is shaped by your individual thoughts and tastes, and how these differ from those of others: 'Everyone likes different things. Everyone thinks differently. Everyone has a different life, so that's what makes you you.'

Expanding on these ideas of choice and authenticity in relation to religion, Hailey spoke about her Irish and Jewish heritage, and mentioned that her mother had been christened, but clarified, 'it's only because my nanny and granddad wanted to get her christened'. Hailey contrasted her mother's religious identity having being determined by her grandparents with the freedom her mother had afforded her, commenting that her mother had said to her, 'You can believe whatever you want to believe.' Children used this vocabulary of choice to speak not only about religion but also other categories of difference. Fran from Waterside said her father had told her she could make her own decisions about belief in God and she compared this with 'choice' in relation to sexual orientation, saying, 'like, it's your choice if you want to be gay or not, it's your choice of everything, isn't it?' She expanded on this, commenting that some parents might say to a daughter that when they're older they should marry a man, 'but you should be able to make your own decisions. My dad didn't say, "God doesn't exist", and he didn't say, "God does exist", he said, "you decide". Your parents can't make all your decisions, can they? You've got to make some yourself.'

These children exemplify a classic expressive individualist sensibility as they articulate a strong sense that they—and others—should be free to choose their beliefs and also be free to 'be themselves', as Hailey put it. These moral grammars were also clear in the parents' emphasis that their children should be free to choose their own beliefs and religious identity, as we explored in chapter 2, echoing other studies emphasizing the imperative of personal worldview choice amongst both religious and non-religious parents in the US (Manning 2015; Smith et al. 2020; Smith and Adamczyk 2021). Megan, for instance, a Sunnybank parent, described herself as both non-religious and Church of England, and was unsure whether she believed in God. She emphasized that although her children had been baptised as infants, their choice was still paramount, describing her approach as:

> very much choice-based, however they want to perceive it, then they can do. That's entirely up to them. They both know that . . . they're christened Church of England. . . . However they grow up choosing to believe is entirely up to them. Or what they decide to practise is entirely up to them.

Religion as Anti-Autonomy

Reflecting on their children's 'choice', several parents described how they had experienced religion as anti-autonomy in their own upbringings and how this had intensified their desire for their children's autonomy. Neera, who we met in chapter 2, had grown up in a Muslim household and had moved away from her Muslim faith while at university. Talking about her desire for her children's autonomy, she contrasted this with religion:

> the thing with religion is, when you have that whole collective mentality. It's always about, 'What do people think of me? . . . How am I viewed by God?' . . . It's always trying to get affirmation from lots of different sources, because you're constantly looking for that, aren't you? I just want the children to think, 'Yes, actually, I'm okay. I made a choice', and just the freedom to make choices. I think, sometimes, religious beliefs can restrict that freedom.

Neera said that having had a religious upbringing had undermined her self-confidence: 'you were never good enough, in terms of that religious stuff', and said that 'undermines you as a human'. Julian, her husband, similarly saw his Catholic upbringing as undermining his sense of self, stating, 'I don't want to pass that on, because I think it's hindered me. Certainly, in terms of self-doubt and confidence and things like that.' He said he hoped to instil in his children a sense of 'self-belief, self-value, self-worth', while Neera said she wanted them 'to have faith and belief in themselves, so they can feel confident that the choices that they're making are the right choices. Not to be overly bothered about what people think about them.' Mary from St Peter's, who was raised in a mixed Protestant and Catholic household in Northern Ireland during the Troubles, likewise emphasized that she wanted to enable her children's capacities for authenticity and autonomy, commenting, 'I guess it comes back to self again. . . . It's all about them . . . being who they are, being true to themselves, and going out and finding out about the world, and making their own decisions based on that, really.'

Laura, a Sunnybank parent, positioned her strong valorization of autonomy as a reaction against her Christian upbringing, in relation to a broader tension between religion and autonomy:

> Essentially, I don't want to be told what to do and what to think. I want to think for myself, I want to decide for myself. There is a tension, isn't there, with following a particular faith and being told how to think about the world? I don't think that all religions necessarily do that in the same way. I think that there is the subtlety of how far you're allowed to have your own beliefs within that.

She described how having gone to a Church of England school had shaped her sense of religion as opposed to autonomy and as 'very patriarchal. The idea of biblical narratives, and women's role in biblical narratives, really worries me. That's something that I've always felt doesn't fit with how I think about the world.' She noted an incident at a church youth group as a teenager when they were being taught about AIDS and she had disagreed with the youth leader's teachings and had challenged him. That incident had stuck with her in terms of feeling that the church's 'particular attitudes weren't conducive to my attitude . . . I didn't feel like I belonged, maybe. . . . The way I felt that my beliefs were different than his.' Like Neera, Laura identified her own moral reaction against the religion of her upbringing as playing an important part in subsequently shaping the ethics of authenticity she was encouraging in her children, which she described in terms of 'wanting to have the freedom to be able to choose your own path, and to give that freedom to our children to say, "You choose your own path", and question if somebody says to you, "This is the truth".'

Several parents said that they had turned away from religion because it was, in their eyes, hypocritical, which we would situate as also interwoven with the value of authenticity, since authenticity can be 'a synonym for honesty' and integrity (Katz et al. 2021: 194). Faye, a Waterside parent, had attended church every Sunday as a child, and said that in her twenties, she started to question how a God could allow suffering in the world. She added, 'there is a lot of hypocrisy in the church and I don't like that. For me, and as a parent, I feel much more strongly that values are important. So kindness, generosity, and being able to look out for yourselves and other people.' She commented that her mum had been actively involved in her church, and had been made 'very unhappy' by 'church politics, and a couple of nasty dominant people that were involved in the church. That's that hypocrisy that I saw then.' She reflected that this hypocrisy made her realise that much more important than petty church politics was 'what you do in life and who you are as a person'. Melissa, the mother of Minnie from Sunnybank, described her perception of Catholicism as 'a very hypocritical religion', elaborating that Catholics

> say they don't believe in divorce, but then they get divorced, and then they go to confession and think it's all right to do bad things and confess it and say, 'Everything's okay now.' They don't believe in abortions, they have abortions. . . . As far as I'm concerned, Catholic is a very hypocritical religion. A bit like the Muslim religion.

A Waterside teacher also said she had been turned off religion by 'the hypocrisy of some people who hold very vocal religious beliefs, who are upheld members of society who say that they're Christian or whatever', and she commented on particular Conservative politicians who were vocal about their faith as exemplifying this in her eyes.

These expressive individualist values were also articulated through grammars of non-conformity. For instance, when asked what were the most important values he was hoping to pass on to his children, Danny from Waterside said:

> Believing in yourself really. Stand for what you believe in, don't be a sheep really. If your opinion is different to your friends' and you go, 'I'll change because they are', just to conform. Stand for what *you* believe in.

Some parents positioned religion as in tension with this non-conformist autonomy, and expressed their sense of ambivalence about belonging to or identifying with a particular community (Blankholm 2022). John, the father of Mason from Sunnybank, said:

> this is the one problem that I do have with religion is where you do see the tribalism, and that's what I'm against . . . It gets in the way of community, it gets in the way of—I like to think we can live in a democracy, a better democracy than we have now. One that's more of a meritocracy. I just think that the tribalism very often gets away of that.

Because of his aversion to 'tribalism', John said that he was 'put off the Humanist thing because it just seems like you're just joining another tribe. It's almost becoming a religion in its own right.' While Mason's mother Natalie said that she would identify as humanist, she nevertheless expressed a similar sensibility, noting that 'non-religious people . . . don't tend to want to join a tribe, generally'.

Several parents also positioned religion as anti-autonomy in terms that drew on an Enlightenment Humanist contrast between heteronomous religious morality and non-religious autonomy. Julie, a Sunnybank parent, expressed an implicit 'othering' of religion as opposed to her own sense of individual autonomy as she spoke about how religious upbringings inculcated a sense of

> 'Thou shalt not do this, that and the other', and that's that, you know? But that's how they've been brought up . . . and it's been instilled. . . . They go to church every Sunday, every whatever night. It's their life, isn't it, really? It forms their life, whereas I've not had that. Actually, I've chosen my own path.

Greg, a parent from St Peter's, positioned this idea of heteronomous religious morality as linked with patriarchy:

> Religion seems to grasp ownership of morality in a way that I think . . . undermines each individual. Religion traditionally, for me, has kind of said, 'No, we'll be your morality and you'll follow that.' I think actually each individual, as a human, through all sorts of social interactions in different communities, they build up their own moral compass. I think it's good in the community to have that kind of healthy debate, but to have it written down on a stone tablet and come down upon you, to me, it links up to the whole male dominance in society and the mess we're in now with sexual harassment. The sooner we can rid ourselves of that father figure dominance . . . the better.

Other parents criticized religion as anti-autonomy in terms which indexed humanist ideals of bodily and sexual autonomy (Brown 2017). Alongside her critique of Catholicism, Melissa perceived Islam and Catholicism as undermining autonomy in relation to intimate relationships, commenting:

> I don't think you should force anyone into marriage or anything like that, I think you should be able to live with somebody without being married, I think you should be able to have same-sex marriages, I think you should be able to have everything; each to their own. Whether religion

comes into it or not. . . . We believe in divorce, if your marriage doesn't work, why should you stay? I've been married twice; I've been divorced, but my church [Church of England] says you can be divorced and you can get remarried in church again, where Catholics can't.

These kinds of negative appraisals of religion as opposed to autonomy and authenticity were relatively common in the parents' accounts, sometimes linked to their own upbringings, and sometimes linked to simplistic—and in a handful of cases Islamophobic or anti-Catholic—stereotypes. And for many of these parents, this moral tension was something that they saw as significant in pushing them away from religious faith, as well as informing their own desire to bring up their children to be autonomous, authentic selves. However, these moral critiques of religion as undermining autonomy or authenticity were largely absent from the children's accounts, even while at the same time they strongly emphasized ideals of individual choice, authenticity and autonomy. This is because, in contrast with their parents' or grandparents' generations, these children had little experience of religion as curtailing their freedom to find or live out their own path. This does not mean that moral critiques of religion or theism were absent in the children's narratives: their most common moral concerns were to do with why a God would allow human or animal suffering. When the children did implicitly draw a binary contrast between religious unfreedom and non-religious freedom, this was most commonly to do with the restrictions that religion might place on their ability to participate in particular festivals or churchgoing limiting their freedom to do what they wanted on a Sunday. Zoe, for instance, as mentioned in chapter 1, described 'no religion' as meaning 'a free way in doing things', and noted that she could celebrate Christmas, whereas 'if you're religious, like Muslim, then you can't celebrate Christmas, which to me would be really, really sad because I really like Christmas'.

The expressive individualist pursuit of authenticity and individual choice has been widely portrayed as undermining commitment to the civic good. Often cited here is Robert Bellah and colleagues' plaintive lament for community in *Habits of the Heart* (1985) and their warning that Americans had become adrift in a self-indulgent 'cult of the self', that they had lost a common moral vision that could justify mutual commitments—in essence, that individualism had triumphed over its uneasy subjects' (Pugh 2009: 215).[8] Organized

---

8. Galen Watts's *The Spiritual Turn* (2022) provides an illuminating discussion of these critiques of expressive individualism, especially in relation to *Habits of the Heart*.

religion, so this argument goes, forms us as subjects who are called to be responsible for others' needs and abide by the order set by a higher authority, whereas 'in personal choice spirituality we are no longer responsible for larger social problems because gender, racial or economic inequality can simply be blamed on the poor choices made by other individuals' (Manning 2015: 151). The religious and spiritual lives of the young are, as noted above, often judged according to these terms. Smith and Denton, for example, depict US teenagers as following a 'moralistic therapeutic deism' which they present as 'colonizing' and 'displacing' 'the old faiths' through a vision of 'divinely underwritten personal happiness' (2005: 171). Yet challenging judgemental critiques of younger generations as self-centred, we argue that interwoven in what the children—and their parents—say about autonomy and choice are commitments to humanist values of respect, equality and care for others, and a concern for others' autonomy. Self-determination is, in other words, not the same as selfishness. Let us turn then to explore how these ideas of equality and respect were being articulated and shaped.

Valuing Equality

Equality and respect are both 'textured concepts' (Beaman 2017a: 15). Both 'incorporate difference' and the ways in which difference is imagined, negotiated, and felt. How, then, were these concepts being situated in relation to religion amongst our participants? Considering the parents first: while many parents expressed positive sentiments about religion—often describing it as fostering community—and they emphasized the importance of respecting religious difference, many also perceived religion as at odds with equality, especially in relation to gender and sexuality. Neera said she found her Muslim upbringing 'massively oppressive . . . I just remember it being really quite stifling. Especially, I think, being from an Asian background, and sometimes the freedom of women within that.' Delphine discussed how her daughter had been learning about the book of Genesis at school, and said: 'I can't bear it. I absolutely can't bear Genesis . . . it feels like it's so antiquated, and the fact that it's still being taught. I feel like some of it's completely sexist.'

This perception of religion as anti-equality was also articulated by religious parents. Lisa, who we met in chapter 2, started attending church to get her children into the local Anglican secondary school, and spoke about how she had not been attracted initially to Christianity because of 'the liberal values I hold', as she put it. She described how her belief in equality in relation to LGBTQ+ rights was important to her, and that she had found a church that aligned with this ethic. Portraying her humanist form of life as the orienting framework within which she had found a place for her faith, she said, 'at the end of the day, the Christian faith means that you don't judge anyone, whether or not they are this, that, or the other. That's what I hold true in myself and I always have, and I like how our church holds that as well.' She added:

> I mean, I am quite unsure about my faith, but yes, those are the values that I hold dear to me. This church, I enjoy going there because they hold those beliefs too. We probably wouldn't be going if the values were very different to what we believed in, regardless of whether or not we're doing this for the kids to get into a school, you know.

Other parents also expressed critiques of theistic beliefs on the grounds of social inequalities. Helena, a former schoolteacher, spoke about she had moved away from the Christian faith of her childhood because she found it hard to square a belief 'in a god that loved everybody' with the deprivation she saw amongst families she worked with. As she articulated her critique, she noted, 'as you get older and you meet a wider variety of people, certain aspects of Christianity come to seem quite intolerant. Not everybody, but certain parts of it didn't really square with real life.'

This perception of religion as intolerant—at odds with a humanist ethic of accepting difference—was expressed by several parents. Alice and Rich spoke about how they sought to foster in their children an ethic of 'tolerance' for other people's ways of life:

> ALICE: I try very hard to introduce into conversations issues around homosexuality, disability, ethnicity, and all those kinds of things, but an intolerance for . . . I think we're quite intolerant of—
> RICH: Intolerance.

Expanding on this, Alice described 'religion' as feeding into intolerance:

> People often put religion in with homosexuality, ethnicity and gender, whereas I would move religion more into the other camp. To me, religion is something you've chosen. It's not something that you are. You've chosen a religion, and I think you can judge people based on that. If someone has chosen a religion that advocates intolerance, then I reserve the right to judge them on that.

Occasionally parents described religion as an instrument of social control which perpetuated global inequalities. Alastair from St Peter's said that he saw religion as a hierarchical, undemocratic tool used 'to control people' and as a significant instrument of colonialism.

The children did not express this moral critique of religion as anti-equality. Yet their expressions of their belief in equality resonated with their parents' views. When asked what she believed in, Fran said she believed 'you can make your own decisions, as I said. I believe that, you know in the olden days when the women didn't have rights? I believe that they should have had the rights, like men did. . . . Yes, that's mostly what I believe in.' As well as parents being significant sources for these moral convictions, Fran commented that her moral ideas were being resourced through TV programmes. She noted how *Horrible Histories* had 'songs about women's rights' and through learning about historic forms of gender inequality, 'it just tells you that women should have had the same rights as men'. These comments are revealing of how children were choosing to engage with forms of culture that further strengthened the moral convictions they were coming to hold. This was also exemplified by posters stating this belief in equality which one child had put up in their bedroom (see Figures 5.1 and 5.2).

As well as valuing gender equality, the children often spoke—more frequently than their parents did—about equality in relation to other categories, especially race, ethnicity, religion, disability, and sexual orientation. Rosie from St Peter's said that she liked Sikhism because it emphasizes equality, and commented that she had learnt that if someone was unable to sit on the floor at a gurdwara due to disability, everyone would then 'have to sit on a chair, so that they would be the same level as the person who is disabled'. As well as TV programmes, the children's comments also revealed how books encouraged this ethic. For instance, discussing the book *Wonder*, which his class at St Peter's were reading together, Connor commented on how people could be mean to people who looked different or had a disability, and he compared this to 'racism' and 'judg[ing] people on their religion'. The children were also making links between different forms of difference in their reflections on their own everyday interactions. When asked whether she thought you could be friends with people from different religions, Pearl replied:

You don't even have to bring it [religious difference] up in conversation or anything, it's completely fine. For example, if you're friends with someone from a different country, let's say, I would still be friends with them because it doesn't really matter what race or language you speak, it's about if they're nice or not. Yes, because I would be friends with, let's say, Milan is half Indian, I'm still friends with him . . . and everyone is. I think that's really good, because it doesn't matter what skin colour you have, country you're from or if you have a disability, everyone should be friends.

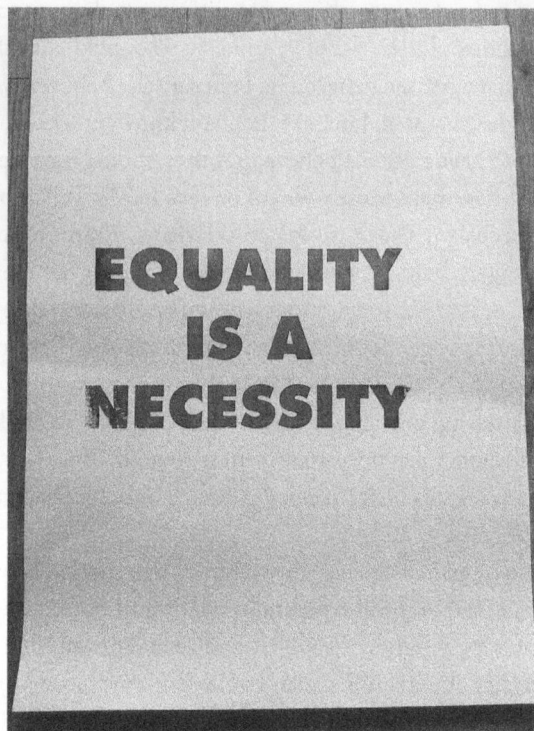

FIGURE 5.1. Child's poster

This largely taken-for-granted ethic of equality and respecting difference was widely expressed by the children, in contrast with those parents who saw religion as an intolerant, anti-egalitarian force in the world—which meant they had little desire to pass it on to their children.

Parents' perceptions of religion as violating equality tended to be most strongly expressed in relation to issues of gender and sexual orientation. This can be understood in relation to wider historical trajectories which are helpful for situating the children and their parents in terms of the intergenerational expansion of humanism. Discussing the 1960s generation of atheists in the UK, US, and Canada, Brown notes that in relation to homosexuality, the main opponents of decriminalization and same-sex marriage were conservative Christians and churches, who were generally more numerous than the liberal Christians who supported these changes (2017: 169). This public clash between churches and equality campaigners helped stoke the perception of religion as anti-equality, while at the same time, lived feminist perspectives led women to

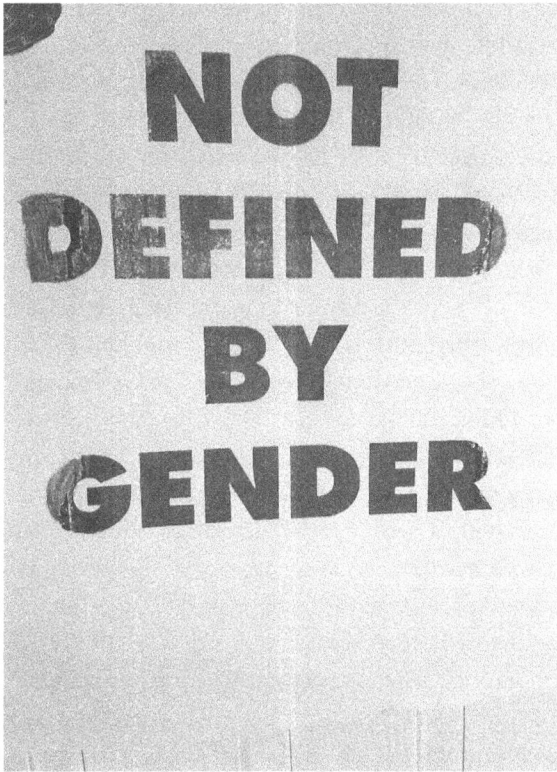

FIGURE 5.2. Child's poster

defy 'cultural constraints and religious discourses to craft a new female self' (2017: 183). These men and women of the long sixties generation 'were the first en masse to confront religion' as they challenged dominant Christian norms, and were the first en masse 'to find ways of losing [religion]' (ibid.). The parents we worked with are broadly the generation of Brown's participants' children and inherited from their parents' generation equality as central to their moral cosmos, and also the sense of tension between religion and equality, with many also experiencing this tension through their own youthful participation in religion. Rather than a narcissistic self-centredness, their valuing of choice and freedom has therefore been formed through a fundamentally *moral* concern for the rights and freedoms of those who were—and in many instances still are—oppressed by a historically hegemonic Christian culture.

This changing social, cultural, and political landscape Brown evokes—in which 'wave after wave of the previously more marginalized have come to have more voice and choice in the course of the twentieth century' (Woodhead 2017: 257)—was described by cultural theorist Raymond Williams as 'the long democratic revolution' (1961). As Williams analysed, the roots of this revolution can be traced through a range of social and cultural changes within schooling and the growth of higher education, struggles for diverse forms of representation, changing media and publics, new modes of cultural consumption, and human rights legislation (Williams 1961, 1983). While this egalitarian revolution is unfinished, Linda Woodhead describes how it 'has involved more social categories of people being able to acknowledge, express and act upon their own desires' (2017: 258). When thinking about how the children in our study were growing up humanist, it is important to underscore that this long democratic revolution also includes children. Changing practices of childrearing and education have increasingly provided children with their own freedoms and rights to lives of their own—a process described as 'a democratization of the family' (Beck 1997; Giddens 1998). This democratization, we suggest, plays an important role in shaping the children's humanist valorization of respect and egalitarian forms of relationality. Before examining this further, it's worth briefly contextualizing this 'democratization of the family'.

In contemporary England, ideas of 'gentle' and 'respectful' parenting are typically seen as the best ways of ensuring a child's development. At the start of the twentieth century, this was not the case: prevailing wisdom was that adults should impose regimental discipline on their children from earliest infancy.[9] In the early twentieth century, child-centred approaches began to challenge this orthodoxy and gained further prominence in the first half of the twentieth century through Maria Montessori and the growing nursery school movement, as well as Jean Piaget's developmental psychology, influencing philosophies of both education and parenting in Europe and the US (Jones 2023). In the post-war years, child-centred approaches became widespread throughout North America and western Europe, exemplified, as Susan Ridgely describes, in the figure of Dr Benjamin Spock, who advised parents to engage with their children in a respectful manner and nurture each child's individuality (Ridgely 2017: 9). In a post-war context marked by anxieties about fascism and totalitarianism, Spock and other parenting experts 'used their child-rearing manuals to argue that individuality was the key to a vibrant American democracy' (ibid.). Spock argued that authoritarian parenting was opposed to

---

9. This was exemplified in the methods used by Frederick Truby King.

democratic principles, and those who followed Spock's approach saw it as 'providing a more "democratic" domestic life for the post-war era' (Jenkins, cited in Ridgely 2017: 9). There were of course—and continue to be—reactions against this philosophy.[10] However, these child-centred, 'respectful' ways of engaging with children have increasingly become the cultural default in homes and schools in England, with children growing up involved in decision-making and learning to achieve their goals through communication and cooperation.

These more horizontal modes of adult–child relationship—interwoven with values of equality, autonomy, respect, and mutual rights—can be seen in several parent–child interactions described in chapter 2 and permeated how our participants spoke about adult–child relationships.[11] Laura, for instance, said she wanted to encourage her children to question the world as it was presented to them 'and to question adults. Adults are not always right. It makes life more difficult as a parent. I imagine their teenage years are going to be fabulously exciting as they challenge us.' Children's comments also revealed their sense that they could challenge adults and their strong sense of their right to self-determination. Discussing the fact that he was christened as an infant, Joe from Waterside said:

> JOE: I used to say to my mum when I was in Year 2 and Year 1 . . . I said, 'Mum, why did you ever christen me? Why didn't you let me choose what I wanted to do with my life, and things like that?'
> RACHAEL: What did she say?
> JOE: She said, 'Because I want you to believe in God. If you don't, that's fine . . .' Well, why didn't you wait until I could choose? I might have chosen Christian. I might have chosen to get christened, but I just don't like being told what to do really.

These comments illustrate not only how this ethic of the child's right of self-determination was shared across generations, but also how it could intensify:

10. See, for instance, Susan Ridgely's study (2017) of how and why US families drew on James Dobson's *Focus on the Family* resources, and Strhan's study (2019) of how British conservative evangelicals position their hierarchical forms of family relationship as countercultural.

11. This democratization in relation to family relationships does not mean that children necessarily have an increased voice in the public sphere. Noting how children have become 'larger than ever' in the domestic sphere in the USA, in the public, 'children's role has shrunk to the size of tiny glass figurines, brittle, silent, and unable to command significant public support, attention, or presence' (Pugh 2009: 19).

Joe's mother valued his ability to choose, but Joe thought she could have further opened up his capacity to choose. Further evidencing this democratization, several parents said their children were the primary decision-makers in the household in relation to religion and spirituality, and several children— such as Steve and Marisa—also situated themselves as the primary decision-makers in their families on these matters.

The children's strong sense of their own and others' autonomy in relation to religion is unsurprising given that this affordance of autonomy and decision-making through negotiation pervaded family life. Describing family meal times, Izzy from Waterside said that her mother negotiated with her about what she ate:

> I get to make decisions of what I eat and stuff. I always tell my mum what I like and don't like. But then, she always says, 'You haven't tried it in ages, so can you try it again?' So, other examples for me, I wear what I want, and I do most stuff that I want.

Other children spoke, for instance, about how their preferences had shaped their family decisions about where to go on holiday.

These more horizontal modes of adult–child relationship were also being reinforced in the schools, shaped by a broader educational ethos which privileges child- and student-centred approaches to learning, giving children freedom to express their views and to choose to follow their own interests. Describing the ethos of 'respect' at St Peter's, Ms Aspin, the deputy head, spoke about how this was embodied in how 'the children relate to each other; it's the way the staff relate to each other, and it's also the way all members of staff speak to the children. . . . You know, it's like a two-way street, isn't it, you know? Is there respect both ways? Is there compassion both ways?' Mr Horton from St Peter's said that it was 'just common, day-to-day practice whereby we treat all the children as equals. At the same time, they're all individuals, they all have a voice, and you respect their voices regardless.' Parents also valued this child-centred ethos in the schools. Debbie, a Waterside parent, commented,

> people . . . talk about child-centred education and stuff like that. . . . And I think some elements of it are pretty much the normal [approach] of schooling now, what's considered to be good . . . educational practice. But [Waterside] is very good in that it . . . it sees a child as being at the centre of their education, you know, what makes them tick, how can they expand on a particular topic to meet their interests.

Overall, the 'long democratic revolution' thus means, we suggest, that the children were growing up with a strong sense of their own and others' autonomy and freedom—including their freedom to cultivate their own beliefs and (non)religious identities—nurtured within both family and school environments. The term 'respect' reverberated repeatedly as a way of articulating what this sensibility meant in terms of living in relation to 'difference'. How, then, was this being expressed?

An Ethic of Respect

At each school, 'respect' was one of the core school values. This reflects wider educational frameworks. In England, all schools have since 2014 been required to actively promote 'mutual respect and tolerance of different faiths and beliefs' as a 'fundamental British value' (Department for Education 2014). 'Respect' also features prominently in the provision for pupils' spiritual, moral, social and cultural development that all schools in England are required to provide, according to which, schools should 'enable students to acquire . . . an appreciation and respect for their own and other cultures; respect for other people; and encourage respect for democracy and support for participation in the democratic processes' (Department for Education 2014: 5). Encouraging 'respect' was central to how the teachers at each school described the aims of schooling, and especially how they spoke about RE. Mrs Hampson from Waterside positioned developing respect for others' faiths as a core aim when she described a lesson in which she had sought to encourage the children to think about belief and non-belief in God:

> We talked about people who believe in God, people who don't believe in God at all and people who believe in different gods. So we weren't saying, 'Christian', 'Islam'—it was more 'believe in God', 'don't believe in God', and we looked at the reasons for why some people believe in lots of gods. . . . It just comes back to that respect of—it doesn't matter, everybody is entitled to believe but let's try and understand it and gain some knowledge and just respect it, in general, and why people believe things.

Miss Kitson from St Peter's said that she felt that teaching RE was especially important in global contexts of rising Islamophobia—which she saw reflected in Donald Trump's anti-Muslim rhetoric—and she spoke about the importance of enabling the children to be:

knowledgeable about other people's beliefs, but also respectful, asking questions . . . I just think we're giving them that understanding, and the knowledge of what actually these religions are, and about respecting other people, and that just because you're a Muslim you're not a terrorist.

Mrs Reid at Sunnybank positioned 'respect' as an implicitly spiritual value and core to what they were trying to instil in the children, commenting, 'I think the spiritual side of things like, we [the school] are always talking about children being responsible for their own actions and to be proud of themselves. And I think that easily links into probably all religions, you know, to respect yourself and to respect others.'

The parents also positioned 'respect' alongside equality as a guiding value in their lives and in how they were raising their children. Neera described her values as 'just about fairness in terms of belief, equality, just our rights to be happy, be kind to each other, live, co-exist, you know, the kind of harmony that a lot of religions do preach . . . and the freedoms that we have, the freedoms to make choices and decisions'. She emphasized that in her parenting, she hoped that she was 'teaching Ben to be a respectful young man, and be kind, helpful and compassionate, thinking about other people and thinking about his actions'. Discussing the most important values she wanted to pass on to her children, Laura listed 'respect' alongside ideas associated with authenticity:

Integrity. Honesty. The idea of being able to have freedom of expression. Encourage them to be independent. Think for themselves. Question the world for themselves. But have respect for other people. Actually, that's something which is really nice to hear as a parent, when other parents and teachers say that our children—they have noticed—do respect other children, and are able to talk with lots of different people, and not necessarily make those judgments about other children. When we do hear that it does make us really happy.

Laura explicitly positioned 'respect' as a humanist value. Criticizing the idea that 'respect' is a 'Fundamental British Value' as it is positioned in English education law,[12] she said, 'you don't have to be British to have those values'. She described these values—including 'respect'—as 'common values, humanity, being a human. . . . The idea of humanism. We share these values to get on

12. See Vincent (2019) for discussion of the Fundamental British Values policy in English schools.

with each other. You might be of a particular faith. You might be from a particular country. It doesn't matter. They're things that help humans get on with
each other, aren't they?' Laura's comments exemplify how individual autonomy and authenticity are not in tension with an ethic directed towards a wider
collective good. Furthermore, Laura's comments challenged the perception of
authenticity as atomized (Taylor 1991), as she reflected on the fact that she
liked the idea of 'being intellectually engaged with the world without having
to follow a particular structure. Something like the idea that we are not just
individuals, isolated in our own little worlds, but also that we do connect with
other people in a wider sense that's not necessarily just religious.'

Alongside these grammars of respect, several parents and teachers used the
language of tolerance or accommodation—terms which imply a sense of privilege and power as resting with religious and cultural majorities (Beaman
2017a). Mr Wilson from Waterside spoke about the aim of RE as about 'ensuring acceptance of other people and tolerance'. Amanda, a Waterside parent,
emphasized both tolerance and respect for religious difference as values she
was seeking to instil in her children. She commented that she spoke to them
'about how it's important to learn about other religions, because I think that's
where half the problems in the world stem from, people not being accepting
of other people's beliefs'. She went on, 'I want both of my children to be tolerant and accepting of other people's beliefs, being respectful and understanding
that we're not all the same, and we don't all believe the same things, and actually, that's fine.' Nancy, the mother of Lewis, positioned respect along with
accommodating others more broadly as key values she was seeking to instil,
listing these as: 'respect is a big one for us. Valuing yourself. Just the kindness
to others. Recognising other people's ways, and that you have to accommodate
other people's wishes.' Anthony, a Waterside parent, also used idioms of accommodation, commenting that he hoped that his children would be 'able to
make their own decisions, but try to be rational about it' and noting that—
although for him 'rational from my perspective is quite a scientific no God
perspective'—he would emphasize that it was important 'also to be accommodating in your views, lots of people have different views, especially at the
moment with so much anti-Muslim and anti-Semitism in the news. . . . So
while they [his children] can form specific views, it should not be to the detri-
ment of other people or to think any less of other people's views.'

Like their parents and teachers, the children expressed a strong ethos of
respect. Yet they did not use the language of tolerance or accommodation.
In many ways, they saw respect as taken for granted. Rosie and Molly from

St Peter's commented that 'respect' was one of the school's core values, and when asked whether it was important that it was listed as one of the values, they suggested that it was so ingrained that it didn't need to be explicitly listed. Molly said: 'We're used to acting that way and everyone's used to acting that way. I've been in this school pretty much all my life, education-wise, since nursery and you just grow with it. Without thinking you just do it and you can't really change that.' The importance of respect often came up in how the children spoke about RE: although the children did not necessarily like the subject, they felt that it was important in terms of learning respect for different faiths. Reflecting on whether they spent too much curriculum time on RE, Tim from Waterside spoke about respect for religious difference in terms that made clear both how this value was interwoven with ideas of human equality as members of the same species and, at the same time, could be articulated alongside an implicit othering of religious 'them' as distinct from a (white) non-religious 'us'. He said, 'We just have to respect them as how they are. Why do we need to learn so much about them? They're still human, even if they're another skin colour, they're still human, they're no different to us.' Minnie from Sunnybank expressed a similar ethic of respect, which was also interwoven with an implicit white normativity as she commented that she is friends with a girl who is Muslim and 'brown' but noted that this 'doesn't matter', and 'you're supposed to treat everybody the same way no matter what the colour or religion they are'.

Occasionally children were sensitive to the fact that expressing their boredom with RE might be interpreted as disrespectful to the religion that they were learning about. Gracie and Joni from St Peter's commented:

GRACIE: . . . sometimes I think that RE's a little bit boring, but then I realise—
JONI: I feel like I'm being offensive to religion.
RACHAEL: If you think it's boring?
JONI: Yes, I feel that's offensive to the religion we're learning about.

In contrast with Sam's comments discussed earlier in the chapter, Pearl from Waterside, felt that talking about her non-belief in God in RE might risk offending believers, saying, 'I really don't want to offend anyone. . . . There are two people in our class, I think they're strong believers in [God], and I don't want to say that [I don't believe] in front of anyone because I have to be careful.'

Other children articulated ideas of respect for religious difference in other ways. Henry from Waterside spoke about his own non-religiosity in terms which revealed both his own liberal ethic and how he would not like someone who did not demonstrate respect for other faiths. He commented, 'I don't mind it [religion]. I don't care if anybody else is this religion. They can be it . . . I've just decided not to because I just don't have that idea', and he commented that if someone was 'being rude about Christians, I wouldn't like them'. As noted in chapter 3, when asked about collective worship, a number of the children said that they sat with eyes closed and heads bowed out of respect. Coco from St Peter's said 'I just want to be respectful and thankful that people believe in these things'. Rebecca and Clay from St Peter's also expressed a sense that they didn't like RE because it violated this egalitarian ethic of respect by marginalizing minoritized groups:

> RACHAEL: You were saying that you don't like RE, Rebecca. What do you not like about RE?
> REBECCA: I feel for Imran, because he's a—is he a Muslim?
> CLAY: No, he's a Christian, I think . . . or a Hindu, I don't know . . .
> REBECCA: He's one of those, and he doesn't like RE because it isn't about his religion . . . I just feel for him in my heart.

Pearl mentioned that in one RE lesson at Waterside they had been learning about Muslim pilgrimage and one of the children [who was Christian] had said, 'That isn't true'. She commented, 'I don't think he should've said that. That isn't really nice to say, even if there was a Muslim in the room or not. It just isn't nice to say it, because people believe in lots of different things. . . . We all have different beliefs, don't we, so it isn't nice to say, "That isn't real", because it can offend a lot of people.' While in one sense, Pearl's comments show the importance to her of respect, in another, they also reveal a paradox beneath the surface. This ethic of respect extends to those with a religiosity that also embraces this ethic, but appears much more ambivalent about outlooks—such as particular Christian stances—that don't. In other words, this ethic of respect doesn't necessarily, for all children, extend to the idea that some people's worldviews might be less pluralistic than their own.

When asked whether they thought you could be friends with people from different religions, the children all affirmed that they could. Claudia from Waterside said:

> I'm friends with people like Benjy and Jack. They're Jehovah's Witnesses and it doesn't really affect anything for them because they're friends with everyone in the class and everyone in class is probably different types of religions. . . . Some people in the world might think that we can't be friends

if we're not in the same religion, but they're wrong. Because it's like saying boys can't be friends with girls.

At the same time, several children noted that their conversations with their friends and peers tended to focus on what they have in common rather than what sets them apart. While in one sense, the children were skilfully practising conviviality (Neal et al. 2017), in actually working this conviviality out in practice, many children commented that they did not speak much about religion with each other in school. Ryan from Sunnybank said 'I wouldn't really feel comfortable talking about religion and stuff with my friends', and his interview partner Hayden concurred, commenting that one of his closest friends was Muslim and 'it might, like, disturb him if I talk about not believing in God'. This suggests that one strategy that the children were employing as a mode of conviviality was excluding religion by locating it beyond the school gates. Jonathan from Waterside said:

> you shouldn't think, 'I'm not going to play with them because they're a different religion'. Because you don't think about religion in school, because religion is outside of school. Going to church and stuff. So you don't think about it.

Similarly, Katie from Waterside, said, 'one person could be like a different religion to you, but you can still play, you could still like the same things. . . . It doesn't really matter because I wouldn't really discuss it [religion] much anyway, because we'd be playing or talking about different things.' While our study did not focus on them, these comments raise questions about how religious children experience these everyday interactions. Would they, for instance, experience these modes of conviviality as upholding a normative secularity which situates 'religion' as something properly located in the home or within specific faith community settings, and thus concealed in schools?

As well as respect for religious difference, the children's egalitarian ethics also at times extended to animals, and the language of fairness and unfairness they used to describe the treatment of animals challenged the human exceptionalism associated with traditional Humanism. Pearl said, 'I just love animals. I'm just upset that people still put puppies in puppy mills . . . I think that all animals should have a better life, because some are . . . not getting treated fairly.' Some children also expressed a moral critique of theism focused on their concern about animals suffering. Annie from Waterside connected her atheism to instances such as a story that she had seen on the news in which floods had swept away animals. She said, 'I'm really into animals . . . it's just cruel what things happen to animals. So I just don't believe in [God].'

When asked to list things that mattered most to them in their life, many of the children talked about their pets, and many talked about caring for animals and the environment, and their worries about ecological destruction and species extinction. Coco described animals as one of the most important things to her in her life: 'I love helping in any way I can with animals. Animal charities, anything like that', and she also spoke about how she 'love[s] to work with . . . stuff like eco things. Every time I see rubbish on the floor, I pick it up, and I put it in the bin. Even if animals, if they try and eat it, and like, plastic bags, if they get stuck in their throat, they could die, and I don't like seeing animals die.' Several other children expressed their concerns about animals and nature being harmed through humans' actions. Lewis said, 'I think it's really mean to kill all the wildlife, because . . . there isn't as much as there was', to which Dan added, 'Bees have started to become extinct.' Addressing environmental challenges affecting both humans and animals was an important moral concern for the children, and this was being reinforced in their schools, through activities and clubs focusing on 'protecting the planet', as well as being resourced through the media they engaged with, as we explored in the previous chapter.

Several parents also spoke about their sense of relatedness to animals and the non-human world with an attitude of reverence that extended beyond standard expressions of Humanism. Coco's mother Stephanie, for example, described how she became more aware of the interrelatedness of all things following her father's funeral:

> There would be a fly buzzing and I'd be really conscious of it or there'd be an ant crawling and I'd be really aware of it . . . I went for a walk with a friend and I was trying to explain this concept to her and we were walking through this really rustling field and I could hear the rustling through the leaves and grasses, and I said, 'Look, that's dad, he's there, he's everywhere.' That is what makes sense to me. It's really given me some solace and it's given me some peace, but it's like, 'Of course.' It was like an epiphany moment, a religious moment if that makes sense. If I had a religion, that is probably it: look after this planet because ultimately we are all linked into it. The energy that we have as a human race goes back into the earth. It's all there. We are linked in with these animals. We are linked into the roots of these trees.

These articulations of human interrelatedness with animals and the non-human world are revealing of how the humanist worldview that the children and their parents expressed—centring principles of autonomy, equality, and respect—at the same time allowed for and was expressed together with much more inclusive orientations towards the non-human than historic Humanisms. Indeed, they gesture towards the kind of 'emerging worldview' that Lori Beaman identifies in her study of the sea turtle rescue volunteers which is 'more inclusive and recognizes interdependence, based on both scientific evidence and an ethic of respect that invokes a reformulated understanding of equality' (Beaman 2017b: 25–6).

These shifts towards more horizontal forms of interrelationality might, as Beaman and Strumos suggest, further 'flatten the pervasive hierarchical framework within which humans and the world around them live' (2023: 13). Victor Seidler (2022) draws on Rachel Carson's work to challenge Humanist traditions predicated on notions of the control or domination of nature. He cites Carson's writing as articulating this alternative, more expansive humanism—which others might term 'posthumanism'—that recognizes humans' fundamental interrelatedness with the non-human world, resonating with the sensibilities Stephanie was articulating:

> I believe this affinity of the human spirit for the earth and its beauties is deeply and logically rooted. As human beings we are part of the whole stream of life. . . . Our origins are of the earth. And so there is in us a deeply seated response to the natural universe, which is part of our humanity (Carson 1954, cited in Seidler 2022: 258).

These modes of human and non-human interrelationality were not something that we explored with the children at length. However, their comments gesture towards the importance, as Beaman and Strumos (2023) highlight, of further exploring how particular engagements with (non)religion influence these exchanges with animals and the non-human world.

The Ambivalences of Conviviality

Alongside this expansive ethic of respect, there were also ambivalences towards particular forms of difference interwoven in the children's conviviality (Neal et al. 2017; Neal et al. 2023). As we have seen, the children often emphasized their commitment to equality and respecting difference in relation to religion, ethnicity, race, gender, sexual orientation, and disability. In the schools, 'religion' and 'race' often became particular vectors for celebrating 'difference' through, for example, festivals such as Eid and Diwali and celebrating Black History Month, and the ways in which the children talked about religion, race and other categories of identity broadly constructed these forms of difference as a 'non-event' (Beaman 2017a). When the children were explicitly critical of religion, it was mostly a general articulation of the implausibility of theistic beliefs, or a particular aspect of Christian culture or practice. However, there were a small number of children who expressed negative sentiments about minority faiths. One eight-year-old girl at Sunnybank, for instance, when asked what 'no religion' meant to her, replied,

> I just think some religions are quite offensive, or something like that. Back in the olden days religion wasn't very nice. We've been learning about Henry VIII. When we were learning about it he wanted to destroy the religions and things like that. I just don't agree with quite a lot of the religions.

When asked for an example of a religion that was offensive, the girl replied 'Hinduism', and then spoke about the importance of her standing up against racism. Rachael asked how this linked to Hinduism, and the girl replied that she found Hinduism 'offensive because I just don't agree with how they pray. Some people say bad things when they pray.' When asked what she meant by 'bad things', she replied that 'they want to get rid of good things that happen to other people. There was somebody that used to be here in the olden days. They tried to get rid of love . . . so you couldn't have love or you couldn't have happiness. I know that some people didn't want anybody to dance or have fresh clothes.' Rachael asked where she had learnt this from, and the child replied:

> My granddad—he is Christian. He once went to pray with [his partner] goes to a temple to pray to . . . Ganash or is it Ganeesh? It's somebody like that: the important gods. He was hearing someone next to him who was praying to a different god and saying bad things about it . . . [and] they got chucked out because it wasn't very nice to say bad things about the god.

We have seen in previous chapters that children might criticize church as boring, or position (Christian) theistic beliefs as implausible. However, this kind of *explicitly* negative appraisal of a minority faith was very rare in the children's accounts: the vast majority of the children and their parents articulated a strong emphasis on respecting religious difference, especially in relation to minoritized groups. Yet alongside this articulation of respect, there was at times an 'othering' interwoven in how parents spoke about religious difference. Delphine, for instance, commented that there were:

> a lot of Muslim families at school, so the ones who I talk to and stuff, obviously I can tell there's a difference. And because I feel like they come from quite a different world, and a lot of them quite literally do, because they

come from different countries as well. But it's not an issue, but I'm just aware of difference going on.

This sense of difference that Delphine expressed contrasts with her daughter Rosie's comfortable intimacy in her friendship with Molly—as we saw in chapter 1—who was of Muslim heritage.

Comments from school staff indicated that parents' feelings of (non)religious difference could also be bound up with difference-avoidance and stereotyping. Mrs Jarvis, a teaching assistant at St Peter's, commented that she had been speaking with the mother of a Year 3 child when 'one of the Muslim mums walked past us', and the mother had said about the Muslim mum, 'Do you know what, she's one of the nicest people, but I don't feel like I can be her friend.' Mrs Jarvis said she asked why she felt like that, and the mother replied,

> 'well, she's not allowed, is she, because her husband tells her what to do. So I don't know how I would go about trying to make friends with her.' I said, 'Why don't you ask her daughter round to play? . . . Then mum will come, and you can have a conversation going.' She was so fearful of the rejection that she wouldn't do it, and I think that's a real shame, that there's a possibility for real cross-cultural friendships, and the parents are too scared to go for it.

As well as difference-avoidance in relation to religion, marginalization was also bound up with social class. When considering the significance of class here, it is worth noting that while the schools explicitly articulated the importance of equality in relation to religion and race within the curriculum, there was little explicit acknowledgement of class difference, and social class inequalities at each school were reflected in particular children and families being marginalized. At St Peter's, inequalities in social class and income amongst different families were especially pronounced. Mrs Jarvis commented that 'in the Clarkhill flats, they're the top 1 per cent of the poorest people in the UK, and we're catering for them. Some of those kids go home and don't eat a meal in the evening. . . . Then you've got people bringing in avocado and feta sandwiches and a whole brie.' When asked whether she thought the children were aware of these differences, she said that they were, and gave an example:

> I had an incident . . . where one of the children came over and went, 'so and so is really smelly'. They're very aware of other children and how they're different, and that child just hadn't had a bath because the hot water had been turned off, so they couldn't get them clean. Mum was doing her best, but they couldn't get clean. So, I think it was really difficult for children. . . .

When I first started here, they didn't have a uniform and the [social class] difference was really obvious then. I think that's closed a bit since the uniform's been introduced. . . . You'd have to be really in your own world to not notice the difference, wouldn't you, between the kids? It's heart-breaking.

Mrs Jarvis described how a kind of 'sunset segregation' operated in terms of class, where the children might be friends across class difference in school, but have little contact beyond the school gates: 'it's the Tadley Green kids stick to the Tadley Green kids, and the Clarkhill flats kids stick to the Clarkhill flats kids'. While St Peter's was mixed in terms of social class, race and religion, at Waterside, which was predominantly middle-class, although class was rarely mentioned explicitly, it still worked to marginalize some families. Danny, Sophia's father, described himself as 'a council-estate kid', and expressed a sense that the middle-class parents avoided social contact with him because of class difference. 'I've only ever spoken to two parents who are in Sophia's class', he said, 'other than that, I've never spoken to any others. They don't go out of their way to speak to you. Some of the looks you get sometimes.'

While the children didn't explicitly talk about class, they did at times express ideas that challenged economic inequality. Coco, for example, talked about a basic axiom of equality, and considered this in relation to wealth: 'Everyone's got a bit of good inside them. If you steal, you've still got a good bit inside you. . . . If everyone didn't have any money, only one person had money but that person doesn't want to share its money, the world would just be . . . really really bad.' Some children initiated particular actions to address the consequences of poverty they saw in their communities. Mrs Jarvis described how two middle-class children had set up an initiative in the school to collect donations for a local foodbank, and said, 'That's amazing, that's real compassion shown by two fairly young children.' In terms of the parents, she commented that 'most of our parents are really compassionate towards other people, but that's probably quite easy when you've got a four-bed semi-detached house . . . , isn't it? Quite easy to sit there with your heating on.'

Some parents—including those who articulated pro-diversity attitudes—employed strategies of difference-avoidance in ways that connected lines of disadvantage in relation to religion, race, and class. It is worth noting here the racialization of Muslim identities intersects with sharp inequalities of wealth, income and employment rates, all of which are lower for Muslims compared with other religious groups and those with no religion in Britain (Ipsos MORI 2018). In our study, this was also reflected in forms of residential segregation.

Julian, Ben's father, commented that 'if Ben has friends who come round to play, they're nearly all white . . . They might be white–foreign, you know. . . . We haven't had any Somali kids round.' Reflecting on this, he added,

> I think a lot of that is based on where the kids live . . . I think, to be fair, people will stick to their own social groups. So here, it wasn't twenty years ago, but now it's quite a middle-class area. So the kids in this area are going to hang out together, because they live in this area. Their parents are of a similar background. Whereas, I would imagine that if people lived over in Clarkhill in the flats over there, they're more likely to hang out with the kids because of their location. Chances are they're more likely to be an immigrant population, because that's where most of them end up being housed.

While almost all the parents spoke about how they were happy for their children to be friends with children of different faiths and positioned themselves as anti-racist, Paul and Helena, Waterside parents, revealed how their actions could be at odds with the pro-diversity values they articulated. Paul described how when they had lived in London, they chose a school for their daughter Annie that was 'very mixed and very diverse', but not as 'predominantly Muslim' as their local school was, and commented,

> I think the reason there, being totally honest about it, was that we felt that she was not represented in the same way through the school. When you say that, I understand that that sounds very strange in the context of the other things that we've said. . . . So in my head, I like the idea of being able to do something to break down those barriers, but I suppose then you end up using your children's lives as a political tool to effect some wider change. That was quite a big decision to take.

Paul talked about how important he and Helena felt it was for Annie to be able to make friends at school, implying class was a key factor in school choice:

PAUL: You always felt there was a cultural difference [at the school they did not send Annie to]. Some of the girls who were going to the school were either refugees or asylum seekers.

HELENA: It wasn't really a priority, like, 'Would she like to come for tea after school and play?' because that's not really what they do with their own kids. Then, it's hard to make friends if you're from a family where you might— . . . Here [at Waterside], say, four days a week, somebody will come for tea and a play. Certain groups just didn't really do that . . .

PAUL: Although Rainbow [Annie's school in London] was still diverse
and that interaction was fairly easy, but maybe that was a class thing.
HELENA: Maybe.
PAUL: It's so difficult. You get into snobbery, don't you?

Despite Paul and Helena's pro-equality attitudes, the ways they spoke about
cultural difference demonstrate how race, religion, and class intersect, feeding
into middle-class non-religious parents potentially avoiding schools where
they feel their children would be in a minority. Thus, although children were
growing up with an ethic of equality and respect for religious and other kinds
of difference, their engagements were constrained by how religion was entangled with race and class as often unspoken lines of social division. And it is
worth underscoring that these avoidances and ambivalences interwoven in
their conviviality (Wise and Noble 2016; Neal et al. 2023)[13] were located
in local and national contexts in which Islamophobic and other racist 'othering' and violence were—and continue to be—a live threat. Our fieldwork took
place in the period after the Brexit referendum, which saw a significant rise in
hate crimes (Home Office 2020). Ms Aspin from St Peter's noted that although
the city had voted to remain in the EU, there were still instances of violence
affecting local families: 'they have quite a hard time, quite a lot of our Muslim
parents. They have things like, they have trollies pushed into them, and they've
had lighted cigarettes thrown through their letterbox, and things.' Thus, as the
children were figuring out for themselves how to live well together, this process
of 'figuring out' was taking place in the wider contexts of racialized, postcolonial landscapes marked by the persistent threat of dehumanization.

Conclusion

This chapter has explored the interconnections between authenticity,
autonomy, equality, and respect in the lives of non-religious children and their
parents and how these values are interwoven in their stances towards religion.
Echoing previous studies of religious and non-religious youth, expressive
individualism was a pervasive ethic in the children's lives. However, their

13. Neal et al. (2023) note that there has been relatively little attention to the significance of
religion in the rich and burgeoning literature on conviviality, and highlight the need for further
research examining the role of different stances in relation to religion—and how these are interwoven with other forms of difference—in opening up further the possibilities and limits of
conviviality.

concern with choice, freedom, and self-expression was not self-centred, but mediated social relations that are respectful and seek to treat others with dignity. Theirs was a liberal moral stance of 'live and let live', emphasizing the rights and freedoms of others 'provided they also consider the rights and needs of others' (Madge et al. 2014: 8; Woodhead 2017). Although religious freedom has often been politicized as a 'cipher for those who support the "right" of religious groups to exempt themselves from certain discrimination laws', this was not the freedom that these children believed in (Singleton et al. 2021: 180). Resonating with Andrew Singleton and his colleagues' study of Australian teenagers' worldviews, 'freedom' meant 'the right to be who you are and not to fear prejudice or discrimination at school or in the community, based on religion, sexuality, gender or any other part of one's identity' (ibid.). This ethos, we would suggest, is neatly encapsulated by the slogan 'Be True to Yourself' that circulates on merchandise from the Disney blockbuster *Frozen*. Rather than focusing on myself, this is an invitation expressed to (all) others, to be true to yourself, to find and live out *your* own humanity.

While this shift towards expressive individualist values can be traced back at least to these children's grandparents' generation, our findings indicate that there are subtle generational shifts. The parents' moral critique of religion as perpetuating inequality and hypocrisy and inhibiting freedom was not something the children expressed, and the children were often keen to underscore the importance of respecting religious plurality. Moreover, they did not use the language of 'tolerance' that many of their parents and teachers used: the ways in which the children spoke about and enacted respect suggested a more pluralist ethos that seeks to challenge inequalities.

This sensibility is formed, we would argue, through the shifting social worlds that the children inhabit compared with their parents' generation. Miles, a St Peter's parent, articulated how his daughter was growing up in a very different world to his own childhood in terms of encountering different kinds of difference: 'it's a much more expanded world, which is exciting. I guess it can also create difficulties around formulation of identity and ideas, and what are someone's beliefs, when everything seems so much more up for grabs.' Mary similarly commented that while her daughter might notice difference in relation to race, ethnicity, or religion, 'it's so normal, that it's almost as if she's not even necessarily learning, "I need to respect people of different colour". It's more a case of, "why wouldn't I?"'

The children's strong sense of their own and others' freedoms was also, we have suggested, shaped in part by cultural shifts towards child-centred approaches to parenting and education, interwoven with norms of mutual respect and more horizontal forms of relationality. Moreover, we would argue that school curricula also play an important role through shaping the children's consciousness of others' rights and shared humanity as they learn about instances when these have been denied and fought for. For instance, as we noted in the previous chapter, the examples the children encounter through Black History Month resource their moral imagination with individuals who have stood up to challenge racism. These kinds of exemplars also reverberate through the media and books the children engage with, celebrating contemporary activists such as Malala Yousafzai and Greta Thunberg, as well as historical examples such as Civil Rights activists and suffragettes, which many of the children mentioned to us. These figures also stand alongside popular fictional characters such as Disney's *Moana*, who challenges the perceived wisdom of her elders to save her island from ecological destruction. These cultural and educational materials are shaping children with a sense that it is a moral duty to 'call out' and work to overcome injustice when they see it. Challenging wider stereotypes that are often held about the non-religious as lacking a moral compass, the children's non-religion was in fact interwoven with an ethic of equality, care and respect for the 'other'. And although our study did not focus on them, these values were also most likely shared by the majority of their religious classmates, as other studies focusing on the values of religious and non-religious teenagers and young adults have found.[14]

In her rich examination of 'deep equality', Lori Beaman reflects on how her participants underscored the significance of respect: '"respect" is a concept that recurs over and over again. Across the data, respect is the dominant theme articulated in relation to both how people articulate the core of their beliefs about how to treat others who are "different" and in terms of the stories people told that illustrate deep equality' (2017a: 92). In elaborating this concept, Beaman draws on William Connolly's (2005) concept of 'agonistic respect', which is found in 'the in-between space of uncertainty' (Beaman 2017a: 93). This respect, as Connolly puts it,

> grows out of mutual appreciation for the ubiquity of faith and the inability of contending parties, to date, to demonstrate the truth of one faith over other live candidates. It grows out of reciprocal appreciation for the element

14. See, for example, Madge et al. (2014); Katz et al. (2021); Singleton et al. (2021); Nynäs et al. (2022).

of contestability in these domains. The relation is agonistic in two senses: you *absorb the agony of* having elements of your own faith called into question by others, and you *fold agonistic contestation* of others into the respect that you convey toward them (Connolly 2005: 123–4, cited in Beaman 2017a: 93).

For Connolly, this ethos is a necessary condition to work towards deeper equality under conditions he describes as 'the minoritization of the world', by which he means 'the more rapid introduction of minorities of multiple types—including religious, spiritual, ethnic, racial, gender practice, and sensual disposition—on the same territorial space' (2011: 60).[15]

This process of 'minoritization' conveys the world the children are growing up in, within which they are sensitive to the marginalization experienced by different forms of 'minority' whom they encounter not only in everyday school interactions, but also through school curricula and the media and culture they consume, in which the representation of different kinds of 'difference' is a given. While the children sometimes expressed stances that were at odds with agonistic respect, they were also growing up understanding their own (non)religious positions as one possibility alongside others. At times, they acknowledged this contestability of their own beliefs. For instance, Hailey, when discussing her non-belief with her friend Connor, expressed an ethic of openness to the possibility of other perspectives being true:

> CONNOR: With God and the Big Bang theory, at the moment, there isn't a right or wrong answer. No one's proved at all that gods were real. No one has finished proving that the Big Bang theory was real.
> HAILEY: Who knows? They might both exist. There might just be a really good reason which isn't the Big Bang theory or God. There might be something else . . .
> CONNOR: Again, it's different people, maybe, from different countries. Like, maybe someone from India might actually . . . Indian people might have a totally different thing from the Big Bang theory and God.

These comments also demonstrate how despite the pervasiveness of humanism, it could at times be held together with more agnostic stances of uncertainty.

---

15. Connolly warns that this awareness of religious plurality alongside the declining significance of formerly dominant religious constituencies does not necessarily foster respect: such conditions can lead some to develop 'a spirituality of resentment . . . against vulnerable constituencies whose very existence poses a threat to your self-confidence and self-assurance', as we see happening with anti-democratic authoritarian movements in many places around the world (2011: 61).

Other children also reflected on how moral values were contingent on people's circumstances. Joni from St Peter's commented:

> when people say, 'I'm on the good side', you don't know if you're on the good side or not, because in another person's eye you may be on the bad side. In the terrorists' eyes they might be doing some good because their parents are sick, or their child is, and they're doing it to get money, so they can look after [them].

Aware of the cultural contingency of their beliefs and identities, these children expressed sentiments akin to agonistic respect, even if, as we have seen above, these were also held alongside unease about worldviews that did not share the same pluralist ethic. And yet there seemed to be little sense of 'agony' or struggle about acknowledging the contingency of their beliefs. Rather these children expressed, for the most part, a comfortable acceptance of the 'minoritizing' world they inhabit. Instead of 'agonistic respect', we would therefore describe this as an expression of 'ordinary' equality. We use 'ordinary' here in the sense of ordinary language philosophy[16] and the ways the idea of 'the ordinary' has been taken up by anthropologists[17] to locate the ethical within the realm of 'ordinary' practice and action, denoting the everyday, the low, the close-at-hand, which is 'the world of importance, of what matters' (Laugier 2021: 31). This idea acknowledges that the everyday is not a given: it is rather, as Cavell puts it, 'an exceptional achievement. Call it the achievement of the human' (1979: 463). Yet this achievement of the everyday is fragile, defined 'by the permanent threat of the denial of the human, of dehumanization or devitalization' (Laugier 2021: 40).

Interwoven in this conception of the ordinary are ethics of care and compassion, which were articulated in many comments the parents and children made about the importance of kindness as an overarching value, such as Neera's comment that she hoped she was encouraging Ben to be 'respectful . . . kind, helpful and compassionate' or Gordon's comments in chapter 2 about how the kindness of an ambulance driver learning Urdu expressed what 'humanism' meant to him. But they were also often expressed through the children's interactions with each other, as they responded with kindness and

---

16. We draw here especially on Wittgenstein's later work and how it was taken up by J. L. Austin, Stanley Cavell and Sandra Laugier.

17. See, for example, Lambek (2010, 2015a, 2015b); Das (2015).

care to each other in the interviews and at play and lunch times, or worried about Muslim classmates feeling excluded in RE.

The sensitivity that the children demonstrated to how the equality of others might be denied through the content of the curriculum or through people being excluded from friendship groups on the grounds of religion or race evokes this sense that the art of living together is always interwoven with the risk of dehumanization. In this sense, we suggest that an ordinary equality is being expressed as these children make their way in the world, even while at the same time, their interactions or comments may also perpetuate inequality. Just as the children's sense of responsibility towards animals challenges the human exceptionalism associated with historic Humanism, so this ordinary equality also challenges the racism and colonialism with which Humanism has been entangled, resonating instead with Paul Gilroy's concept of 'planetary humanism'. This 'planetary humanism'[18] emerges from opposition to 'the race-thinking with which the language of humanity and species life has been entangled, at least since the dawn of Europe's enlightenment', and seeks to project a conception of humanity which might confront how easily people can be expelled 'from the fragile, precious category of the human' and to work towards 'humanism's re-enchantment' (Gilroy 2019).

Gilroy's articulation of a more expansive, 're-enchanted' humanism is also reflected in contemporary shifts in 'official' Humanism. Sarah Bakewell notes that the most recent Humanists International Manifesto, issued in 2022, included 'greater recognition of humanity's connection and duties to the rest of life on Earth—"to all sentient beings"', and 'reject[s] all forms of racism and prejudice and the injustices that arise from them' (2023: 346). Bakewell notes that this 'evolving manifesto reflects changes in how humanists see themselves, as well as broader changes in the world: it provides more subtlety and respect for difference; there is no triumphalism when it talks of humanity . . . this is a manifesto for something deeper: a joyful and positive set of human values' (2023: 346–7). These changes in organized 'upper-case' Humanism are also, we suggest, mirrored in the intergenerational shifts in the 'lower-case' humanism we have explored in this chapter. Bakewell urges the importance of further challenging the dominance of European thinkers in Humanist discourses and draws on Cambodian film-maker Rithy Panh's

18. In developing this concept, Gilroy draws on humanist ideas in the work of W.E.B. Du Bois, Primo Levi, Toni Morrison, Sylvia Wynter, and Frantz Fanon (Gilroy 2000, 2005, 2015, 2019).

reflections on an 'everydayness of good' in developing richer humanist philosophies. Panh writes:

> Evil's nothing new; nor is good, but as I've written, there's also . . . an everydayness of good.
>
> As for the good part of that former world—my childhood, my sisters' laughter, my father's silence, the tireless play of my little nephew and niece, my mother's courage and kindness, this country of stone faces, the ideas of justice, of liberty, of equality, the taste for knowledge, education—that part can't be erased. It's not a bygone world, it's an effort and a work in progress; it's the human world (Panh, cited in Bakewell 2023: 331).

This evocative idea of the human world in its everydayness, we would suggest, resonates with the children's lived humanism and the laughter, play, kindness, and vivid colours of freedom and equality—which are a work in progress—interwoven within it.

Conclusion

WHEN ASKED what she believed in, Joni, a pupil at St Peter's, replied, 'I believe in the Big Bang and evolution, but then I kind of believe in Adam and Eve, because that means everybody's related to each other and I like that fact. . . . There's a different religion, I think it's Muslim, when everybody's your cousin or brother and sister and stuff—I like that idea that everybody's related.' Her friend Gracie commented that she thought 'a lot of the stories in the Bible are not *actually* true, but they're just teaching a lesson, telling you how to be nice to each other'. Asked why she liked this idea of everybody being related, Joni replied, 'Because I feel like the world should be a better place, if we're like a family we can all work together, even though we may have fights sometimes, me and my brother, we all love each other, and we can all work out our problems. . . . If we all work together, we can stop pollution and stuff like that.'

Rachael commented that both of them had said that they didn't believe in God, and asked if they could talk more about that. Gracie replied, 'I don't really believe in God, because where is he?' She elaborated, 'basically, I don't really want to believe in God because when people say—I find this really annoying, when you've made a picture, they say, "God made this picture because he provided everything for you." No. *I* made this picture, because I made it.' Joni then said:

> JONI: A lot of people say, 'What's important to you?' They say, 'God and religion.' If somebody says, 'What's Christmas about to you?' People say, 'God and religion', but . . . if somebody asks me, 'What's Christmas to you?' I just say, 'Presents, Santa, Christmassy decorations and things. Not Mary, Joseph, Jesus.'
>
> GRACIE: I like the joy of Christmas and happiness.

Discussing whether they would identify as 'no religion' or 'Christian', Gracie commented on how for her, faith was located in her friends and family rather than a religion, while Joni articulated her sense of the equality of all faiths:

GRACIE: I would probably choose—well, I would definitely choose no religion, because I like being myself. I have other things that I feel a part of.

RACHAEL: Such as?

GRACIE: Basically my family and my friends, I feel like they're kind of a religion to me, if you know what I mean.

RACHAEL: Because that's where you belong?

GRACIE: Yes, I feel like I don't really belong in— . . . if somebody could tell me, 'You have to be Christian', I'd probably say, 'Fine then.' . . . but if I did, I probably wouldn't really feel like that's where I belong.

JONI: I kind of feel like I belong to all of them, because I know what they're all about, I don't actually know how to speak in the language or something, but I do feel they're all the same amount of importance as I am, my Christianity . . .

These girls' words express several of the brightest threads interwoven in the humanist form of life we have explored in this book and demonstrate how this humanism infuses the children's non-religiosity and non-belief. While they don't believe in God—because the absence of evidence is at odds with their empiricist sensibilities, and theism jars with their sense of their own agency— they locate their beliefs in the this-worldly realm of science, and relationships with friends and family. They also express the importance of joy and happiness, as well as their valuing of authenticity—'I like being myself', as Gracie puts it. Also interwoven is a moral axiom of equality, as Joni comments that she feels all religions have the same importance as her own. This humanism encompasses positive sentiments about religions—here both Islam and Christianity—and also faith in a vision of humans' relatedness and connectedness as motivating people to work *together* to make the world a better place, including addressing environmental crises. While this is an individualistic ethos in many ways, it is also directed towards a wider collective, planetary good.

This book has sought to add the voices of children—often marginalized in debates about religion's place in society—to the burgeoning literature on non-religion, secularity, and non-belief, and in doing so, to advance our understanding of how non-religion and non-belief are formed and interwoven in everyday life. We have found it deeply encouraging to listen to what children have to say on these issues, and to hear how reflective, thoughtful, and sensitive they were about the significance of faith and religion in their own and others' lives, as well as their school worlds and wider social landscapes. We began this project setting out to explore how and why children are growing up non-religious and non-believing, and to understand what this means to them. As 'no religion' replaces 'Christianity' as the 'new normal' in England, we asked: what are the beliefs, concerns, and values of this new generation of non-religious children? And how are these formed across the different spaces children inhabit, including their home and school worlds? In what follows, we summarize our answers to these questions, and the implications these have for future research.

From Religious Decline to Humanist Becoming

Overall, this book has revealed that non-believing children in England are, in a sense, incidentally atheist. The children we worked with are atheist because they are becoming humanist, and this humanism is being formed in both home and school contexts (Strhan et al. 2024). Their atheism—and its distinctive textures—is thus shaped by two types of factors: not only those that push them (and most of their parents) *away* from religion but also those that draw them *towards* humanism, and these two types of factors are often intertwined (ibid.). While the absence of active religious socialization (a push factor) was clearly important, much more significant to the children in their own narratives of their non-belief were their humanist sensibilities (ibid.). These narratives were mostly expressed in terms of their humanist faith in science, empiricism and rationalism, or their sense that they had no need for religion or theologies of the Beyond because they experienced their present lives—oriented towards this-worldly frames of significance—as *full*. Moreover, expressions of humanism often undergirded their non-religious identification—that is, representing themselves as other-than-religious. While many features of their humanism would be shared by those who identify as religious and/or hold theist beliefs, they are *especially* significant for understanding the formation of non-religious and non-believing stances, since these are how the children made sense of and gave an account of what it means to them to be non-religious and non-believing.

The parents' humanism—centring principles of human equality and freedom—was something that they often saw as at odds with religion. Indeed, parents often positioned their move away from religion as primarily linked to these moral sensibilities, which then shaped the fact that most had little desire to pass on any religiosity from their own upbringing to their children. However, they *did* want to pass on their humanism, and especially the values of respect, autonomy, and authenticity—and this included parents who were religiously identifying and practising. This humanism was also being fostered in the children's schools, and the values of autonomy, equality and respect for others' rights and freedoms which were promoted there intertwined with the humanist values and epistemologies the children were encountering at home. Moreover, the prioritizing of science and maths in the school curriculum helped shape the children's view of humanist epistemologies as non-negotiable and having priority over religious and theist ways of knowing and believing, which were presented to the children as one option amongst others. At the same time, the subtle equation of 'non-religion' and 'science' and ideas of religion and science as in conflict in the RE curriculum, alongside the positioning of non-religious perspectives as requiring no understanding or explanation, fed into the children coming to figure out for themselves that non-religious forms of life were 'normal', as several put it (Strhan et al. 2024). Although some children *were* engaging in regular religious practices, such as attending church, they engaged in relatively little everyday discussion of religion with their parents. This fact, combined with their strong sense of their own individual freedom in relation to religion, fed into the formation of their non-belief. Furthermore, the 'normality' of non-religion amongst their peers meant it felt a live option for them: they do not feel they have to be religious 'to fit in' with classmates, school culture, or family expectations, as Rosie and Molly's comments in chapter 3 illustrate. For those children who received no active religious socialization at home, it was mostly their experience of encountering religion at school that prompted them to reflect on and articulate their own (non)religious identities and beliefs.

Previous studies of the rise of non-religious identification and non-belief in God have tended to distinguish between the roles played by parents and by education in this process. This book has demonstrated that these are harder to distinguish in children's lived experience than they are in theory. Rather they are mutually reinforcing and interrelated, with the positioning of religion as an option rather than a duty, along with principles of individual autonomy, equality, and respect for religious difference encouraged in both. The pervasiveness of this humanism within the children's homes, schools, peer interactions, media and culture supports the suggestion by Jörg Stolz and his colleagues that the most important factor determining declining religiosity across generations is not any specific attribute or type of family context but rather 'the dominant worldview and the perceived social significance of religion in a given country' in which socialization takes place (2023: 18). Furthermore, our study provides insight into *how* the dominant humanism we found was being practically formed, lived and expressed. While this humanism could be held together with religious forms of life—for instance, in Lisa's Anglican humanism—it was overall secularizing in the sense of orienting ways of knowing, valuing, and mattering in the realm of this-worldly, human affairs.

Our portrait fits with standard secularization accounts in terms of showing the declining significance of religion across our three contrasting fieldsites, with many parents having experienced some form of normative Christianity in their upbringing which was then largely absent in how they were raising their children. Moreover, while religion was something that many parents criticized on moral grounds and had moved away from themselves, the children saw their own non-religiosity as taken-for-granted and 'normal'. Yet our analysis highlights also the need to move beyond religion-centred narratives of religious decline—which are still dominant in secularization accounts—to explore the substantive *other-than-religious* forms of life that children are increasingly growing up into and shaping, which are implicated in shifting the place and significance of religion at individual, institutional, and societal levels (Lee 2015; Watts 2022; Strhan et al. 2024). In this sense, we suggest that rather than thinking of secularization as a process of *un*becoming, as in narratives of 'decline' and 'loss', we might instead think of secularization as a process of becoming. Which, for the children we worked with, meant becoming humanist.

In *The Secular Revolution*, Christian Smith argues that secularization in the United States is an intentional process perpetuated by 'an identifiable network' of secularist insurgents who 'intentionally and largely successfully struggled to displace' established religion and 'significantly transformed the cultural and institutional structures that governed the public life of the nation'—including public schools and higher education (2003: 4). In approaching secularization as a process of becoming, our study does show that primary schools in England are making a secular form of life available to children. However, this is not taking place through any *intentional* secularist insurgence, but rather through the long-term diffusion of humanist values and beliefs and their becoming 'official' in documents such as professional ethics codes, international treaties, and institutional values statements. Indeed, this humanist form of life—centring empiricism, rationality, science, and the humanities as ways of knowing the world, and the values of equality and respect—is the water we swim in as scholars working in universities.

This pervasiveness makes humanism a somewhat slippery object, as its taken-for-grantedness means that it often does not need to be made explicit and—unlike many religious discursive traditions—its contradictions aren't necessarily felt as issues that need resolving. In this context, exploring humanism in the lives of children helps to sharpen our focus on this object and makes visible what is practically implicated in its formation. As children talk about what they do and don't believe in and what matters to them, they make explicit how they are learning to situate themselves in relation to religion and belief across different times and spaces. At the same time, looking at their experiences alongside those of their parents and their school contexts also crystallizes how humanism is always co-constructed by and through multiple relations with others.

Children's Lower-Case 'Humanism'

When we began this research, we did not expect to end up writing about humanism. We expected to find a variety of possible worldviews interwoven in the children's non-religion and non-belief, such as the humanist, agnostic, or anti-existential worldviews Lee (2015) identified in her study of the non-religious in south-east England (Strhan et al. 2024), or the indifferent or spiritual-but-not-religious worldviews that Singleton and colleagues (2021) identified amongst non-religious teenagers in Australia. However, as we explored how the children spoke about what it meant to them to be non-religious and non-believing, it was clear that for most of them, their non-religion and non-belief were bound up with a pervasive humanism. This humanism is not a fixed category or tradition but rather a more implicit 'practice of existence' (McKay 2018)[1] threaded through with particular values, practices, moral sensibilities, affective registers, and ways of knowing the world. Moreover, unlike many religious traditions or organized Humanism, it is not expressed in terms of developed propositions or creeds, but rather emerges in fragments and accounts of everyday encounters, and can be held alongside other religious and non-religious worldviews, without any felt sense of contradiction (Lee 2015: 172). Thus, while the children's narratives foregrounded humanism as the way

---

1. McKay (2018) uses this phrasing to refer to 'forms of life' rather than humanism.

they made sense of their non-belief, they also articulated aspects of indifference to religion—such as Lewis's statement that he was 'not too bothered' about whether or not he believed in God—while parents sometimes expressed 'spiritual-but-not-religious' or 'posthumanist' stances alongside the humanism they were also making available for their children. Andrew, Rosie's father, for instance, described himself as drawn towards object-oriented ontology.

While humanism is most often associated with Humanist intellectuals, books, and secular Humanist organizations, we have used the term more broadly to describe a form of life that centres the agency and significance of humans and their equality as members of the same species, and largely rejects the idea of supernatural or divine influences in this world in favour of a this-worldly orientation, and valorizes empiricism and rationalism as ways of knowing the world (Lee 2015). We drew a distinction between an upper-case 'Humanism'—associated with explicit Humanist discourses and identification with Humanist histories, organizations and traditions—and lower-case 'humanism', which identifies a form of life that does not necessarily entail explicit association or identification with these organizations or histories (Strhan et al. 2024). The children were lower-case humanists, mostly not explicitly identifying as humanist—in part, because they were not being resourced with vocabularies to do so. Yet, as noted in chapter 1, they were often not entirely happy with being defined by an absence of religion or belief, and several expressed a clear desire to be defined by who they are rather than what they are not. In responding to that desire, we see humanism as the name that most resonates with what matters to these children and expresses the textures of their (non)belief. Moreover, when some of the children did have the opportunity to learn about humanism at Sunnybank, they tended to be 'happy' to identify as humanist—as Ryan commented.

Distinguishing between lower- and upper-case humanism allows us to observe how this lower-case, more expansive humanism may be expressed in registers that do not neatly correspond with established Humanist discourses in a number of ways. First, while secular Humanist discourses have typically rejected the supernatural, the children's expression of their subjunctive *as-if* modes of belief—in unicorns, dragons, Santa, ghosts, and life after death—gesture towards other enchanted, 'magical humanisms' (Blencowe 2016). These subjunctive modes of belief, along with the children's sense of their lives as full of meaning, depth, and significance challenge narratives which have associated the loss of religion with disenchantment. Moreover, while secular Humanist discourses typically position Humanism against religion (Engelke 2015a) and often express a teleological faith that humanity will—or *should*—ultimately progress beyond religion, superstition, and belief in the supernatural, the children did not express any teleological narrative of advancing beyond religion or the supernatural. For them, religious diversity was just a given.

Second, as discussed in chapter 5, the children's ethic of equality in relation to race, ethnicity and religion challenges the racism and ethnocentric bias entangled in Humanist histories. This resonates with shifts in official Humanism, such as the recent expansion of the Humanists International Manifesto to state that Humanists 'reject all forms of racism and prejudice and the injustices that arise from them. We seek instead to promote the flourishing and fellowship of humanity in all its diversity and individuality' (Humanists International 2022). Furthermore, the connections the children were making between different forms of (in)equality across different spheres of their lives and wider societies, across times and places, resonates with Edward Said's conception of humanism as involving the ability to make transitions from 'one area of human experience to another' (Said 2004: 80). As Said writes, humanism is 'about the practice of identities other than those given by the flag or the national war of the moment. The deployment of an alternative identity is what we do when we read and we connect parts of the text to other parts and when we go on to expand the area of attention to include widening circles of pertinence' (ibid., discussed in Gilroy 2019). Finally, the children's care and concern for animals and planetary flourishing suggests that rather than the historic anthropocentrism associated with Humanism, their humanism has an anthropofugal[2] quality, as the ideas of equality they articulate in relation to humans flow towards non-human life-forms.

Taking Humanism Seriously

Within sociology, anthropology, social theory, and other disciplines, the end of Humanism has been often declared. As Rosi Braidotti expresses it, 'I am none too fond of Humanism or the idea of the human which it implicitly upholds. Anti-humanism is so much part of my intellectual and personal genealogy, as well as family background, that for me the crisis of Humanism is almost

---

2. Here we borrow from Robert McKay's (2018) conception of 'forms of life' as 'anthropofugal'. Our use of the term is intended to convey an understanding of humanism—in contrast with historic exclusionary anthropocentrisms—with a flowing movement outwards *from* the human *towards* other life-forms.

a banality' (2013: 16). Having been a driving force in European thought, from the ancient Greek maxim to 'know thyself' through Enlightenment and existentialism, in late twentieth-century philosophy and critical theory, humanism became portrayed as unable to survive the vanishing of 'the human' (Wentzer and Mattingly 2018: 14; Fassin 2019). This stance was exemplified in famous conjectures by Foucault (1994) and Derrida (1982) that the human was at—or at least nearing—its end (Wentzer and Mattingly 2018: 14; Fassin 2019: 31). Seeking to move beyond the arrogant Eurocentric and anthropocentric impulses seen as inextricably entangled within humanism, we are now, this narrative goes, living—at least in an analytical sense—in the age of the posthuman, the anti-human, or the more-than-human.

Yet perhaps predictions of humanism's analytical demise are premature. As well as Gilroy's articulation of a 'planetary humanism' discussed in the previous chapter, in recent years we have seen growing acknowledgement that humanism may remain important on moral, political, and theoretical grounds (Wentzer and Mattingly 2018; Ingold 2018; Seidler 2022). One of the theorists usually seen as pioneering posthumanist perspectives, Bruno Latour, argued in *After Lockdown* that abandoning humanism runs the risk of ignoring the consequences of human action on our planet, as well as on our own species, at precisely the moment when we are beginning to acknowledge the enormity of our responsibility to other life-forms (2021: 105). As he puts it:

> Should we frankly abandon all pretension to humanism? That's very tempting now that lifeforms are running in the same direction. And yet, what an evasion it would be. . . . People may well be right to criticise 'Anthropocene' as a term, but it tags the goal we need to attain once we see that embracing anti-humanism would be going from bad to worse, another way for Atlas to abandon the mission he recklessly took on. He can't get rid of this crushing burden by shrugging his shoulders. . . . If the myth of Atlas still means anything, it's more about lifting the weight that certain people have put on others (Latour 2021: 105–6).

In anthropology, there has also been a growing sense amongst some scholars that despite the colonial violence and anthropocentrism deeply implicated in Humanist histories, it might be time for 'a new humanism' precisely *because* of 'the complex questions raised by the human influence on our own species and, beyond that, on our entire planet' (Wentzer and Mattingley 2018: 147). Perhaps, then, humanism is not as closed a chapter in intellectual history as is sometimes supposed. And listening to the children we worked with express emerging new humanisms that challenge the racist and ecological violence associated with Humanist histories leads us to question whether future analytical debates about post/humanisms might be enriched through attending to these kinds of voices and perspectives.

Yet whether or not humanism remains *analytically* significant, our study demonstrates that humanism remains an important *empirical* phenomenon, and we propose that better understanding of how humanism is lived and shaped stands to advance understanding of how and why individuals and societies in many global settings are becoming increasingly non-religious (Strhan et al. 2024). Brown argues that a 'humanist condition' has come to dominate western societies and cultures (2017: 169), while Singleton and his colleagues (2021) note that a 'this-worldly' worldview—which resonates strongly with the humanism we identified—was the most common worldview amongst Australian teenagers in their national study. As a qualitative study, we make no claims about wider generalizability to populations. Yet the pervasiveness of the humanism we found amongst our participants does invite further exploration of the wider prevalence of humanism, not only amongst children, but also amongst other age groups, and the ways in which it is found in different local, national, and global contexts (Strhan et al. 2024). It also invites comparative attention to whether and how humanism is expressed and shaped in other institutional settings and how religious and non-religious individuals respond to the dominant forms of life they encounter in these.

Our findings also raise questions about whether and how other alternative non-religious forms of life beyond humanism are being resourced in other spaces, including forms of education outside of schools, or other spaces inhabited by children and young people, as well as how the children's forms of life may change as they move into later childhood, adolescence, and adulthood (Strhan et al. 2024). While humanism was ubiquitous among the children in our study, it may be that this is especially associated with 'middle' childhood, with schooling at this stage, for instance, particularly encouraging humanist epistemologies, and the place of religion in English school curricula meaning there is little opportunity for complete indifference to religion. It is possible that as the children move into becoming teenagers and young adults, they will take on other worldviews, such as the 'spiritual-but-not-religious' or 'seeker' worldviews that Singleton and colleagues (2021) identified amongst Australian teenagers. Further comparative and longitudinal research would help to establish whether and how the processes of humanist becoming we identified in middle childhood unfold over the life course.

Future comparative work across different cultural contexts might also draw out the contingent process of how particular strains within humanism become more prominent than others. For instance, while a liberal ethic and expressive individualism were dominant threads within the humanism we observed, there are also other humanisms which emerge from different historical struggles and lineages, as Schielke's study of Egyptian non-believers (2012) suggests, in which liberal individualism is not necessarily a defining feature. In the US, the legacy of Cold War anti-communism afforded little space for collectivist atheisms. This meant that an individualist secular Humanism dominated organized non-believer spaces, and continues to do so at the expense of more collectivist non-religious orientations, such as Marxist materialisms (Gilroy 2005; Blankholm 2022). But while an individualist strain was pervasive within the humanism we observed, we do not see this as an *intrinsic* feature of humanism, but rather a texture that emerges from a certain set of historical premises, the permutations of which continue to evolve and shift.

As well as these comparative questions about prevalence and formation, our findings also raise questions about the contours of humanism and other non-traditional 'existentialities' (Lee 2019b). Our approach to humanism as a diffuse, decentralized form of life is broader than the approach taken in studies of organized and self-identifying Humanist groups, individuals, and practices,[3] and other scholars have also sought to categorize different humanist worldviews into narrower types.[4] Our broad approach reflects the emerging and exploratory nature of this field of sociological inquiry (Strhan et al. 2024). We hope that future research will enable better understanding of the nature and consequences of newer, non-traditional existentialities and worldviews, which might perhaps involve unpacking further distinctions between, for instance, magical humanism, planetary humanism or exclusive humanism. Our use of 'humanism' overall reflects the children's lived experiences and aims to expand our theoretical repertoire beyond religious decline and explore the 'substance' of the other-than-religious forms of life that children and young people are growing up into (ibid.; Watts 2022). This language also addresses the need for 'non-binary' methodologies (Lee 2015; Blankholm 2022; Watts 2022), since traditionally religious as well as non-traditional worldview identities, beliefs,

---

3. See, for instance, Engelke (2014, 2015a, 2015b); Cragun et al. (2017); Aston (2019); Rejowska (2021); Blankholm (2022).

4. LeDrew (2015) and van Mulukom et al. (2023) distinguish between humanisms anchored by concerns about social justice and those anchored by rationalist and scientistic outlooks.

and practices were combined in various configurations in our participants' lives, and we hope this 'non-binary' lens might encourage acknowledgement of shared values beyond religion and non-religious binaries (Strhan et al. 2024).

Our approach in this book is situated in the growing literature on 'substantive' non-religion (Lee 2015) which is opening up the alternative 'worldviews' (Taves 2019; Singleton et al. 2021), 'existentialities' (Lee 2019b) and 'imaginaries' (Stacey and Beaman 2021) which may be considered in some ways analogous to religious ones. While these concepts are all helpful and we have used them in this book, our preferred way to conceptualize humanism is as a 'form of life'. Here, we follow Wittgenstein's use of 'form of life' in *Philosophical Investigations* and its subsequent interpretation in the work of philosophers such as Stanley Cavell and Sandra Laugier, as well as anthropological approaches influenced by this lineage.[5] Forms of life signify 'regular ways of living, entrenched practices that are not called into doubt', and different 'educations, interests, concerns, languages, different human relations and relations to nature and the world constitute distinct forms of life' (Hacker 2015: 11, 13). This captures how humanism is a *given* way of living, mostly not called into question, recognized by the presence of particular 'textures or moral patterns' (Laugier 2016: 110). Moreover, the ways in which Wittgenstein uses the idea of 'life' stresses that it 'takes its form in what is done, or can be done; communication and thought are parts of such activity, not external to it' (McKay 2018: 256). As McKay notes, this idea of 'can be done' draws attention to how forms of life are always enabled or constrained by particular material and social conditions, including modes of power and marginalization. Thus a 'form of life . . . is an unbroken field of constraint and possibility that combines, indistinguishably, physical, semiotic and historical being' (ibid.). Interwoven here are also questions of care, concern, and importance: exploring a form of life entails attending to 'what matters, makes differences, in human lives' (Laugier 2016: 120). While Humanism has often been thought of in terms of a constellation of intellectual positions, we suggest that approaching humanism as a form of life shifts our perspective to how it is a way of drawing together distinctive ways of thinking, feeling, communicating, and acting into 'a practice of existence', shaped by particular conditions of possibility (McKay 2018: 255).

In conclusion, just as 'lived religion' scholarship has demonstrated the importance of understanding religion as it is found and practised in everyday life

5. See, for example, Lambek (2010, 2015a, 2015b); Das (2015).

beyond the statements of elite religious actors and institutions, our book suggests the need for further attention to lived humanism, as well as the formation and substance of other other-than-religious forms of life. These are also questions of wider public importance. The growth of non-religious identification across many global contexts means that the impacts of non-religious forms of life will continue to become more significant, raising important questions about what it means to live together in contexts of growing religious and non-religious plurality (Beaman 2017a, 2017b). In relation to education, for instance, while the children expressed an ethic of respect for religious difference, this could be articulated alongside dismissive comments about particular religious beliefs. As we discussed in chapter 3, this arises in part from the fact that for many children in England, non-religious forms of life remained relatively unexamined in the school curriculum compared with religious worldviews, meaning that they occupy a contradictory space of *both* privilege *and* marginalization (Lee 2015: 199). The fact that many children are not afforded opportunities to reflect on humanism or other non-religious worldviews means that they do not tend to think of themselves as having their own forms of 'existential faith', which might sit as a conversation partner with religious perspectives (Connolly 2005). This situation also raises questions about epistemic justice. In her writing on epistemic justice, Miranda Fricker develops the idea of 'hermeneutical injustice' to describe a situation where someone has an unfair disadvantage in their capacity as a knower in terms of 'making sense of their social experiences' due to a lack of 'collective interpretive resources' (2007: 1). This might, as we suggested in chapter 3, apply to non-religious children who were not being offered interpretive resources to make sense of their own forms of life in a way that members of some religious communities currently are within schools.

And yet, better understanding the lived realities of humanism—and other other-than-religious forms of life—is not just a matter of self-understanding for the non-religious. It is also about deepening our *shared* understandings of what matters to each other, what we—whether religious or not—place our belief and faith in, and how these forms of faith emerge out of particular situations, times, and places. As William Connolly writes, 'To be human is to be inhabited by existential faith. There is no vacuum in this domain, though there might very well be ambivalence, uncertainty, and internal plurality. On this reading there is no constituency that is simply faithless' (2005: 26; Hickey-Moody 2023). Acknowledging this, and seeking better understanding of how particular forms of existential faith are lived, shaped, and expressed are important questions to address. As the children spoke about what they have faith in, in which particular textures of and relations to religion, non-religion and belief were imbricated, we hope that older generations will find encouragement in their voices, and share with Joni her faith that we—across generations—might recognize our interconnectedness and work *together* to make the world a better place.

Methodological Notes

IN THE INTRODUCTION, we offered a description of our research process. This appendix provides more detailed information about our methodology and sample for readers who are interested.

Research Methods and Qualitative Data

The preceding chapters draw on qualitative data collected through fieldwork and interviews conducted with children, parents, and teachers in three state-funded primary schools in 2017–2018. Since we wanted to work in primary schools in three contrasting geographical 'micro-climates' of (non)religion (Voas and McAndrew 2012), we used data from the Office for National Statistics 2011 census to identify contrasting areas in terms of high and low non-religious populations, as well as other demographic variations, such as race, ethnicity, class, and religious diversity. Our first fieldsite, St Peter's School, was located in an urban area in southern England, an area we chose because of its diverse demography in terms of race, religion, and ethnicity, and higher than average non-religious population. Our second fieldsite, Waterside Primary Academy, provided a predominantly middle-class suburban setting with high levels of non-religious identification. We chose our final fieldsite, Sunnybank Community Primary School, due to the relatively low levels of non-religious identification in the local area. This was a predominantly rural setting in north-west England, within a broader local area that was divided in terms of race and ethnicity. Further details about the schools, and how religion was located within them, are provided in the Introduction and chapter 3. Institutional ethical approval was obtained, and ethical issues were taken seriously throughout the research.

The fieldwork involved Shillitoe spending six to seven weeks in each school, working with Key Stage 2[1] children, acting as a teaching assistant and observing everyday school life, focusing on Religious Education, Personal Social and Health Education, and collective worship or assemblies, as well as more implicit occasions beyond the formal curriculum, such as play and lunchtimes. The children were sampled using a simple worksheet activity which asked the question 'do you believe in God?' and offered three tickbox responses: 'yes', 'no', and 'I'm not sure'. Because our aim was to examine the nature, formation, and lived experience of children's non-belief, we used purposive sampling, and only children who selected 'no' or 'not sure' in response to the question about belief in God were invited to participate. Before the worksheet activity, Shillitoe had spent a fortnight in each school so that the children could meet her and spend time learning about the project and asking her questions. She also gave a child-friendly presentation explaining the project before the worksheet activity, outlining the project aims and what the outputs would be. This included posing some simple questions and statements exemplifying the kinds of questions they might be asked in the interview, while also handing round the classroom examples of academic books and journal articles containing qualitative data, so children could see what we were aiming to produce through the research, and how interview data would feature in the outputs. These presentations stressed that there were no right or wrong answers to these questions—and this was reiterated in the interviews. To minimise any disappointment about not being selected for the interviews, Shillitoe explained she would not be able to talk to everyone, but would be able to spend time with all children through being in lessons and breaktime over the course of the term. During the presentation, Shillitoe explained that the children could add notes or comments if they felt that the three tick-box options did not express their stance, and some children did annotate their worksheets, and these comments were then explored further during the interviews and fieldwork.

We obtained both parental and child consent for the children's participation in the research. Children who expressed interest in participating were given a parental consent letter to take home explaining the project. As well as providing opt-in consent for their children to participate, these consent forms also asked the parents if they were themselves interested in being interviewed. This method of sending consent letters home with children who wanted to participate meant that the children could act as pseudo-gatekeepers who could

1. Key Stage 2 in England is for children aged 7–11.

provide parents with further information about the research beyond the letter and explain who Shillitoe was and why she was spending time in their class. There were a couple of instances where parents expressed suspicion that, because the project focused on children's beliefs, Shillitoe might be a Christian with a proselytizing agenda. Although Shillitoe had not initially disclosed her non-religious identity to the parents, in these situations, she did so in order to allay these kinds of concerns. In addition to parental consent, informed signed consent from the child participants was also gained before any interview, including addressing potential safeguarding issues and to what extent data would be confidential.[2]

Prior to the child interviews, Shillitoe shared the interview schedule with the teacher for them to gain a sense of the kinds of conversations the children would be having in the interviews. Although the teachers were not present for the child interviews and data would remain confidential unless there were safeguarding concerns, we felt it important for the teachers to be aware of the issues the children might be talking about, since typically such discussions did not simply start and end with the interviews but might end up being touched on during playtime or in lessons. The interviews also asked children questions which would reveal data about themselves and their family (such as religious identity and belief) as well as touching on potentially sensitive issues such as death and dying. Showing the teachers the interview schedule and asking for any comments enabled awareness of any potential issues or circumstances that might impact interviews with particular children, such as recent bereavement. Teachers also helped inform us of any child's particular needs, for instance, if they might need questions phrased differently due to learning needs, or whether some children might be nervous or quiet, or energetic and need additional support to aid focus.

We intended to interview 90 children (i.e., 30 per fieldsite), but ended up interviewing 117 children.[3] This was because more children in the classes we were working with wanted to take part than we anticipated and met our sampling criteria. A couple of the children we interviewed had answered 'no' to the 'do you believe in God?' worksheet sampling question, but then in the interview revealed that they had misunderstood the worksheet question and did believe in God. We did not include these children's interview data in our

2. For adult participants, standard ethical procedures in relation to informed consent, privacy, and confidentiality were also followed.

3. 58 child interviews were conducted in total.

analysis, and the total number of children whose interview data we analysed was therefore 115.[4] The interviews took place during the school day, with timings chosen in consultation with the teachers and children to avoid the children missing important lessons and activities or breaktimes. Apart from two interviews which each involved three children, and one individual interview, the children were all interviewed in pairs. This was to mitigate against power imbalances between researcher and participants, but was also a means of enabling us to observe how the children spoke about religion and belief with each other. Interviews lasted anywhere between forty minutes to over an hour, with some needing to be broken up into two interviews depending on what lessons children were allowed to miss. All interviews were confidential and, barring any potential safeguarding issues or wellbeing concerns, no one (including parents and teachers) had access to raw unanonymized data other than the research team. No safeguarding issues became apparent and it was not necessary to disclose any interview contents to anyone. To ensure confidentiality, interviews took place in quieter, more private areas of the school so the children could feel comfortable discussing their beliefs, thoughts, and opinions, including those which were critical of aspects of the school.

We designed and piloted the interview schedule prior to fieldwork, choosing topics and questions that would enable us to examine what it means to children to be non-believing, how, when, and where they learn to be non-believing, and how their non-beliefs were interrelated with particular worldviews. Our interview questions and methods for conducting interviews were based on our own previous research (Strhan 2019; Shillitoe 2023) as well as interview schedules and methodological approaches from Ridgely Bales (2005), Hemming (2009), Day (2011), Manning (2015), and Lee (2015). During the interviews, paper, crayons, felt tips and Play-Doh were made available to children to help articulate and express the topics and areas being covered during the interview. At the start of the interview, we asked the children to talk about or draw things, objects, and spaces that were important to them, and throughout the interview, they often carried on drawing or used Play-Doh to construct objects which represented things that were important to them. These activities also created a relaxed, informal atmosphere for the interviews.

In addition to the interviews, children were invited to participate in a photography activity where they took pictures of spaces or places which were important to them around the school. This was an opportunity for children to

4. Details about the children in the 'research sample' section refer to these 115 children.

articulate the importance of their material and spatial surroundings and how areas such as the playground and objects such as benches and award cabinets revealed values, beliefs, and opinions which were important to them. For example, some children showed Shillitoe the wooden bench they sat on during playtime, articulating memories of previous years and recollecting their beliefs at that time, or walking past school displays and discussing their views on these. This allowed for material and spatial dimensions of the topics covered in the interview to emerge and for us to gain deeper insight into how the children's beliefs, values, and understandings were resourced by their everyday school environments. They completed this activity in small groups, taking turns taking photos and often discussing together where they should photograph. Overall, the children's enjoyment of participating in the different research activities was clear through their feedback, their desire to be interviewed again, and the thank-you cards and gifts given to Shillitoe from the participating classes and children.

Interviews were conducted with the parents/carers of thirteen to fifteen children in each school, with 55 parents/carers interviewed in total.[5] These took place after the child interview, and typically took place at the family home after school, with some conducted at parents' workplaces or nearby cafés, and one taking place after school in an empty classroom. However, it was more usual for Shillitoe to arrange the interviews after school and meet the parents at the school gates with their child and walk home together. The interviews were typically informal occasions lasting between thirty and ninety minutes, with Shillitoe sitting with one or both parents, sometimes with the child coming and going from the room, offering their insights and thoughts. Sometimes Shillitoe was invited to join the family evening meal or after-school snack, or conducted the interview in the kitchen while the parents were busy preparing dinner or cleaning up, with interviews nestled in the rhythms and routines of family life. Only one carer (a grandparent) was interviewed and the rest were the mother and/or father of each child. Twelve teaching staff were also interviewed (four per school), who were selected for their role and position in the school (e.g. headteacher or RE lead) or who were the class teachers of participating classes. These interviews took place at school (except one conducted over the phone) and lasted between thirty and sixty minutes. Interviews were professionally transcribed, and transcriptions checked for accuracy, and data were then anonymized, with names replaced with pseudonyms.

5. 43 parent interviews were conducted.

Data Analysis

During data collection (2017–2018), we held weekly meetings to discuss ongoing fieldwork and emerging themes, and Strhan listened to all interview recordings at least once during the period of data collection. Recurring patterns were noted and coded, with this phase of analysis especially focusing on the formation of the children's non-religious identities. Following this, we paused undertaking further analysis due to Strhan's maternity leave (2019) and Shillitoe's fixed-term contract as research associate on the project ending in March 2019, as well as the subsequent impact of the Covid pandemic in 2020. We returned to analysis from July 2021, with Strhan leading on reviewing the full dataset in relation to the kinds of socialization the children were experiencing in relation to theism, atheism, religion, and worldviews. This latter phase of analysis was also further developed through grant funding from the 'Explaining Atheism' research programme, with Lois Lee also an investigator in this project and playing an invaluable role in contributing to developing the analytic focus and insights developed during this latter phase of the research, as outlined in the Introduction.

While this latter phase of analysis was guided by our initial research questions about the nature, formation, and meanings of non-religiosity and non-belief, analysis was also inductive, identifying themes that we had not anticipated (e.g., the importance to children of magical and supernatural figures). To examine the interplay of causal processes shaping the formation of children's non-belief, all data relating to fifteen children (five per school)—including child, parent, and teacher interviews—were further analysed to identify where, when, and with whom socialization in relation to religion and worldviews was taking place, and how children's experiences at home and in school related to each other. When this was completed, we compared this with the experiences of other children in the wider sample. This analysis also considered the significance and relation between 'push' factors that encouraged children away from religion or belief in God (e.g. the absence of religious socialization, negative perceptions of religion) and 'pull' factors that drew them towards other-than-religious worldviews.

Research Sample

The following provides further details about the profile of our sample. To protect anonymity, we have not provided demographic profiles for individuals.

Child Participants

AGES

7 years old: 5
8 years old: 39
9 years old: 49
10 years old: 22

GENDER

Girls: 71
Boys: 43
Non-binary: 1

BELIEF IN GOD

The following indicates the breakdown of 'no' and 'not sure' responses recorded in the worksheet sampling activity for our sample of 115 children:

No: 85
Not sure: 30

(NON)RELIGIOUS IDENTITIES

The children (and their parents) often expressed more than one non-religious or religious identity in the interview, or shifted between identities over the course of the interview, as we explored in chapter 1. They might move, for instance, between not sure and no religion, or Christian and no religion, or Christian, humanist, and no religion, and the nuances expressed in these often shifting identifications resist any straightforward categorization. We would note however that amongst the children, the most commonly expressed identification was 'no religion' (53), followed by 'not sure' (24), and then 'Christian' (11), although we would underscore that the children did not necessarily see these as mutually exclusive. It is also worth noting that despite their non-belief in God, relatively few self-identified as 'atheist', and even fewer identified with non-Christian religions (one Buddhist, and one Hindu).

When we asked the parents how they would describe their position in relation to religion, their responses included: no religion, humanist, Christian, rationalist, atheist, secular, Jewish, spiritual-but-not-religious, agnostic, Buddhist, not sure. Of the 55 parents we interviewed, the most commonly expressed identity was 'no religion' (38), but like the children, the parents' often expressed more than one— and sometimes multiple—identities. For instance, one parent identified as Jewish, atheist, and non-religious, another as humanist, rationalist, atheist, and secular, another as Buddhist, Christian, non-religious, and spiritual-but-not-religious.

Parent Occupations

We did not ask participants explicitly about social class or income. We recorded the occupation of most (although not all) parents interviewed to offer insight into socio-economic diversity within our sample. Their occupations/ fields of occupation included: finance/risk and compliance, academic/higher education (2), administrator (3), taxi driver, nurse (3), unemployed, teacher (6), web design, theatre/radio, stay-at-home parent (2), audio producer, teaching assistant (3), social worker, research manager, museum engagement manager, operations director of a private company, cleaner, environmental consultant, carer, pharmacist, civil servant (5), paramedic, domestic abuse support worker, photographer, prison support staff, IT manager, engineer, printer, biomedical scientist, market trader, hairdresser.

Interview Schedules

Many of our interview questions were drawn from previous studies, especially Hemming (2009), Day (2011), Lee (2015), and Manning (2015). We have indicated below which questions were drawn from which original studies. Most questions below were followed up with questions such as 'can you tell me a bit more about that?', 'what did that mean to you?', or 'how do/did you feel about that?' to elicit more detailed descriptions.

Child Interview Schedule

Introduction, names, ages.

    a) Prep activity: please could you draw or write down (on small pieces of paper) ten things or people that are important to you in your life (can be things/objects, ideas/values, or people). Are there any that are more important than others here? Can you tell me a bit about them and why they're important to you?

COMMON MEASURES OF RELIGIOSITY

a) What do you believe in? (Day 2011)
   a. PROMPT: Do you believe in God, for example?
b) Are there things that you don't believe in?
c) Do you have a sense of what is right and wrong? How do you know if
   something is right or wrong? (Day 2011)
   a. PROMPT: In the case of stealing, say?
d) Has there ever been someone you've found inspiring, in real life or
   fictional/made-up? (Day 2011)
e) Are there any books, movies, or TV programmes which are important
   for you and influence you? (Day 2011)
f) How much influence or control do you think you have over your life?
   (Day 2011)
g) What do you believe happens after you die? (Day 2011)

SELF-CLASSIFICATION

a) If you had to fill in a survey and you were asked if you belonged to a
   religion, or to state your religious position, what do you think you
   would say? (Lee 2015)
   a. PROMPT: If you were given the following list, which would you
      choose? (Lee 2015)
   b. LIST: Christian, Muslim, Jewish, Sikh, Hindu, Buddhist, Another
      religion, No religion, Atheist, Humanist, Agnostic, Spiritual-but-
      not-religious, Not sure, Other/Something else
b) What does [CHOSEN TERM] mean to you? (Lee 2015)
c) Have you always thought of yourself as [CHOSEN TERM]? Did you
   ever think about yourself differently?
d) Do you think your parents, and other members of your family such as
   your grandparents would use [CHOSEN TERM] to describe
   themselves?
   a. [IF FAMILY IS RELIGIOUS] What do you do as part of your religion?
e) How interested would you say you are in religion? Is it something that
   comes up in discussions? (Lee 2015)
f) Do you think most of your closest friends would describe themselves
   as [CHOSEN TERM] or would they describe themselves differently?
   (Lee 2015)

g) Have you ever taken part in a religious activity (baptism, wedding, etc./visited a religious building? (Lee 2015)

h) How did you find those experiences? (Lee 2015)

SCHOOL LIFE AND ETHOS

a) What do you think are the main values in the school? Values are ideas about how we should treat each other and how we should behave.
   a. Are they important to you personally?
   b. Are there other values that are particularly important to you?

b) What is your favourite subject and why? What is your least favourite subject and why? (Hemming 2009)

c) What do you like and dislike about RE? (Hemming 2009)

d) Are your own beliefs or practices ever discussed in RE? (Hemming 2009) (If not: how do you feel about that?)

e) Can you tell me about assemblies/collective worship and what you do during collective worship? (Hemming 2009)
   a. Can you tell me about whether you like them or don't like them? (Hemming 2009)
   b. How do you feel when you are singing songs in the hall? (Hemming 2009)
   c. What do you think about during prayer or moments of reflection?

Is there anything else you would like to mention that I did not ask you about?

Parent Interview Schedule

Introduction, name(s), age(s), occupation(s).

SELF-CLASSIFICATION

a) If you were completing a survey, like a census, how would you describe your religious position? (Lee 2015)
   a. PROMPT: If you were given this list, would you choose any of these? (Lee 2015)
   b. LIST: Christian, Muslim, Jewish, Sikh, Hindu, Buddhist, Another religion, No religion, Atheist, Humanist, Agnostic, Spiritual-but-not-religious, Not sure, Other/Something else

b) What does [CHOSEN TERM] mean to you? (Lee 2015)

c) Would you use [CHOSEN TERM] to describe yourself to other people? (Lee 2015)

d) When did you start using [CHOSEN TERM] to think about yourself? Did you ever think about yourself differently? (Lee 2015)

e) Do any of these classifications appeal to you? (Lee 2015)
   a. LIST: Not religious, no religion, areligious, secular, spiritual-but-not-religious, atheist, agnostic, humanist, rationalist, free thinker (Lee 2015)

e) How would you describe your child's position in terms of religious or non-religious identity?

f) Were you raised in a religious faith? If yes, did this involve participation in organized religion? What was that like? Or—Can you tell me about your own childhood and upbringing? Were you raised in a religious faith? Or was it nonreligious? (Manning 2015)

COMMON MEASURES OF RELIGIOSITY

a) Can you tell me about your beliefs?

b) Do you believe in God or a higher power?

c) What do you believe happens to you after you die? (Day 2011)

d) Do you have a sense of what is right and wrong? How do you know if something is right or wrong? (Day 2011)

e) If you had a problem or a worry or you were faced with a situation and you didn't know what to do, who or what would you turn to for advice?
   a. Depending on selection—where do you think these people learn their morals from?

RAISING CHILDREN

a) Do you intentionally incorporate religion, spirituality, or a particular secular worldview into your child's upbringing? (Manning 2015)

b) When your child was born, did you have any sort of ceremony or event?

c) Do you celebrate holidays (e.g., Christmas) with your children in the home? How do you celebrate them? (Manning 2015)

d) Are you providing any kind of education about religion or other worldviews to your children? If no: why not? If yes: how and what do you teach them? (Manning 2015)

e) Would you say that you talk about religion much as a family? Is it something that comes up in discussion?

f) Would you say that in your family there's a primary decision-maker when it comes to things to do with religion or spirituality? Has there ever been disagreement in your family about this? (Manning 2015)

g) Has being [CHOSEN TERM] ever made you feel different from other parents? (Manning 2015)

h) As you think about the question of spirituality, religion, or some other worldview in your child's life, what is it that you want to give to him/her? (Manning 2015)

i) How has becoming a parent impacted your own worldview? Has it changed or stayed the same? (Manning 2015)

j) What would you say are the most important values for you in how you are raising your child?

k) Would you say it is more important for your child to be well behaved or considerate?

l) Would you mind if anyone assumed you were religious? Would you mind if anyone assumed you were not religious? (Lee 2015)

RELATIONSHIP WITH SCHOOL

a) Can you tell me about the school your child/children attend? What are your thoughts on it?

b) Did you have a choice whether your child went to this school? Why did you decide to send your child to the school? How does it compare with other schools in the area? (Hemming 2009) Did you consider other schools?

   a. How do you think it would compare to the local church/community school? (Hemming 2009) Was that something you considered?

c) Do you think the school gets particular values across to the children? Does it help them to understand what is important in life and encourage them to do or not to do certain things? (Hemming 2009)

d) Would you say that you agree with the values of the school?

e) How do you think the school approaches matters of religion and spirituality in everyday school life?

f) How well do you feel the school prepares children for life in a multicultural and multi-faith society? (Hemming 2009)

g) Are you aware of any tensions or bullying between different (non) religious or ethnic groups in the school or outside of school? (Hemming 2009)

h) Have you ever been to a school assembly? Is there any religious or spiritual aspect to the assembly? What do you think about this? (Hemming 2009)

i) Do you think the school is effective in helping your child to understand their own beliefs more in the classroom? How about other religions or beliefs? (Hemming 2009)

Is there anything else you would like to mention that I did not ask you about?

Teacher Interview Schedule

Introductions, role in the school, ages.

SELF-CLASSIFICATION

a) If you were completing a survey, like a census, how would you describe your religious position? (Lee 2015)
   a. PROMPT: If you were given this list, would you choose any of these? (Lee 2015)
   b. LIST: Christian, Muslim, Jewish, Sikh, Hindu, Buddhist, Another religion, No religion, Atheist, Humanist, Agnostic, Spiritual-but-not-religious, Not sure, Other/Something else

b) What does [CHOSEN TERM] mean to you? (Lee 2015)

c) Did you ever think about yourself differently? (Lee 2015)

e) Do any of these classifications appeal to you? (Lee 2015)
   a. LIST: Not religious, no religion, areligious, secular, spiritual-but-not-religious, atheist, agnostic, humanist, rationalist, free thinker (Lee 2015)

SCHOOL ETHOS

a) Thinking about [SCHOOL NAME], does the school have a distinctive ethos? How can it be described? How was this decided on? (Hemming 2009)

b) What values are promoted in school? Why these? How does this work in practice around school? (Hemming 2009)

c) Are any elements of this ethos linked to religion and spirituality? How does this work in practice? (Hemming 2009)

d) Would you say that your own religious beliefs or values are integral to this? (Hemming 2009)

RELIGION IN THE SCHOOL

e) How would you describe RE in the school? Is it educational or confessional? (Hemming 2009) What are the aims of RE?

f) What is the purpose of assemblies/collective worship in school? What role does religion and spirituality have? (Hemming 2009)

g) Do pupils have the chance to pray, or reflect? Is music part of assembly? (Hemming 2009)

h) Are these activities compulsory? What happens if a pupil doesn't want to take part? (Hemming 2009)

i) How do staff who are not religious negotiate these aspects of assemblies? (Hemming 2009)

j) How does the school cater for non-religious pupils?

k) How do you cater for religious difference in assemblies? Are pupils ever withdrawn? (Hemming 2009)

l) Are you aware of any tensions about the children's beliefs, or their religious or non-religious identities? How were these resolved? (Hemming 2009)

m) In what ways does the school prepare pupils for life in a multicultural society and a religiously plural society? (Hemming 2009)

Is there anything else you would like to mention that I did not ask you about?

BIBLIOGRAPHY

Altglas, Véronique. 2014. '"Bricolage": Reclaiming a Conceptual Tool'. *Culture and Religion: An Interdisciplinary Journal* 15(4): 474–93.

Ammerman, Nancy T. 2021. *Studying Lived Religion: Contexts and Practices.* New York: New York University Press.

Archer, Margaret S. 2007. *Making our Way through the World: Human Reflexivity and Social Mobility.* Cambridge: Cambridge University Press.

———— 2012. *The Reflexive Imperative in Late Modernity.* Cambridge: Cambridge University Press.

Asad, Talal. 1993. *Genealogies of Religion: Discipline and Reasons of Power in Christianity and Islam.* Baltimore, MD: The John Hopkins University Press.

———— 2003. *Formations of the Secular: Christianity, Islam, Modernity.* Stanford, CA: Stanford University Press.

———— 2015. 'Reflections on Violence, Law, and Humanitarianism'. *Critical Inquiry* 41: 390–427.

Aston, Katie. 2019. 'Formations of a Secular Wedding'. In *Secular Bodies, Affects, and Emotions*, edited by Monique Scheer, Nadia Fadil, and Johansen Schepelern Johansen, 77–92, London: Bloomsbury.

Baker, Joseph O. and Buster G. Smith. 2015. *American Secularism: Cultural Contours of Nonreligious Belief Systems.* New York: New York University Press.

Bakewell, Sarah. 2023. *Humanly Possible: Seven Hundred Years of Humanist Freethinking, Enquiry and Hope.* London: Chatto & Windus.

Ball, Stephen J. 2017. *The Education Debate*, 3rd edn. Bristol: Policy Press.

Beaman, Lori G. 2017a. *Deep Equality in an Era of Religious Diversity.* Oxford: Oxford University Press.

———— 2017b. 'Living Well Together in a (Non)Religious Future: Contributions from the Sociology of Religion'. *Sociology of Religion* 78(1): 9–32.

———— 2022. 'Nonreligion, Changing Religious Landscapes and Living Well Together'. In *Nonreligion in Late Modern Societies*, edited by Anne-Laure Zwilling and Helge Årsheim, 15–32, Cham: Springer.

Beaman, Lori G. and Timothy J. Stacey. Eds. 2021. *Nonreligious Imaginaries of World Repairing.* https://doi.org/10.1007/978-3-030-72881-6.

Beaman, Lori G. and Lauren Strumos. 2023. 'Toward Equality: Including Non-Human Animals in Studies of Lived Religion and Non-Religion'. *Social Compass.* https://doi.org/10.1177/00377686231170993.

Beck, Ulrich. 1997. 'Democratization of the Family'. *Childhood* 4(2): 151–68.

Beider, Nadia. 2022. 'Religious Residue: The Impact of Childhood Religious Socialization on the Religiosity of Nones in France, Germany, Great Britain, and Sweden'. *British Journal of Sociology* 74(1): 50–69.

Bellah, Robert N., Richard Madsen, William M. Sullivan, Ann Swidler, and Steven M. Tipton. 1985. *Habits of the Heart: Individualism and Commitment in American Life.* Berkeley: University of California Press.

Bengtson, Vern, Casey E. Copen, Norella M. Putney and Merril Silverstein. 2009. 'A Longitudinal Study of the Intergenerational Transmission of Religion'. *International Sociology* 24(3): 325–45.

Bengtson, Vern, Norella M. Putney and Susan Harris. 2013. *Families and Faith: How Religion is Passed Down Across Generations.* New York: Oxford University Press.

Bengtson, Vern, R. David Hayward, Phil Zuckerman and Merril Silverstein. 2018. 'Bringing Up Nones: Intergenerational Influences and Cohort Trends'. *Journal for the Scientific Study of Religion* 57(2): 258–75.

Bennett, Jane. 2001. *The Enchantment of Modern Life: Attachments, Crossings, and Ethics.* Princeton, NJ: Princeton University Press.

Benoit, Céline. 2021. '"I'm just British—Normal British": Exploring Teachers' and Pupils' Conceptualisations of Religion(s) and Religious Belonging'. *Journal of Contemporary Religion* 36(2): 311–28.

Berger, Peter L. 1967. *The Sacred Canopy: Elements of a Sociological Theory of Religion.* New York: Doubleday.

Bialecki, Jon. 2011. 'No Caller ID for the Soul: Demonization, Charisms and the Unstable Subject of Protestant Language Ideology'. *Anthropological Quarterly* 84(3): 679–704.

Biesta, Gert J. J. 2016. *The Beautiful Risk of Education.* Abingdon: Routledge.

Billig, Michael. 1995. *Banal Nationalism.* London: SAGE.

Binder, Stefan. 2016. 'Let us Become Human Through Beef and Pork: Atheist Humanism and the Aesthetics of Caste'. *South Asia Chronicle* 6: 205–27.

Blackham, Harold J. 1968. *Humanism.* Harmondsworth: Pelican.

Blanes, Ruy Llera and Galina Oustina-Stjepanovic. 2017. *Being Godless: Ethnographies of Atheism and Non-Religion.* New York: Berghahn.

Blankholm, Joseph. 2017. 'Secularism, Humanism, and Secular Humanism: Terms and Institutions'. In *The Oxford Handbook of Secularism*, edited by Phil Zuckerman and John R. Shook, 689–705, New York: Oxford University Press.

――― 2022. *The Secular Paradox: On the Religiosity of the Not Religious.* New York: New York University Press.

Blencowe, Claire. 2016. 'Ecological Attunement in a Theological Key: Adventures in Antifascist Aesthetics'. *GeoHumanities* 2(1): 24–41.

Bond Stockton, Kathryn. 2009. *The Queer Child, or Growing Sideways in the Twentieth Century.* Durham, NC: Duke University Press.

Braidotti, Rosi. 2013. *The Posthuman.* Cambridge: Polity Press.

Brown, Callum G. 2017. *Becoming Atheist: Humanism and the Secular West.* London: Bloomsbury.

Brown, Callum G., David Nash and Charlie Lynch. 2023. *The Humanist Movement in Modern Britain: A History of Ethicists, Rationalists and Humanists.* London: Bloomsbury.

Budd, Susan. 1977. *Varieties of Unbelief: Atheists and Agnostics in English Society 1850–1960*. London: Heinemann.

Bullivant, Stephen. 2022. *Nonverts: The Making of Ex-Christian America*. New York: Oxford University Press.

Bullivant, Stephen and Lois Lee. 2016. *The Oxford Dictionary of Atheism*. https://doi.org/10.1093/acref/9780191816819.001.0001.

Carson, Rachel. 1954. 'Exceeding Beauty of the Earth'. Speech to the Sorority of Women Journalists, Theta Sigma Phi, 21 April 1954. https://awpc.cattcenter.iastate.edu/2018/01/09/exceeding-beauty-of-the-earth-april-21-1954/ (accessed 8 November 2023).

Catto, Rebecca. 2014. 'What Can We Say about Today's British Religious Young Person? Findings from the AHRC/ESRC Religion and Society Programme'. *Religion* 44(1): 1–26.

Catto, Rebecca and Janet Eccles. 2013. '(Dis)Believing and Belonging: Investigating the Narratives of Young British Atheists'. *Temenos—Nordic Journal for Study of Religion* 49(1). https://doi.org/10.33356/temenos.8616.

Cavell, Stanley. 1979. *The Claim of Reason: Wittgenstein, Skepticism, Morality, and Tragedy*. New York: Oxford University Press.

Chalfant, Eric. 2022. 'Intimate Deconversions: Digital Atheist Counterpublics on Reddit'. In *Global Sceptical Publics: From Non-Religious Print Media to 'Digital Atheism'*, edited by Jacob Copeman and Mascha Schulz, 244–68, London: UCL Press.

Clark, Charles and Linda Woodhead. 2015. *A New Settlement: Religion and Belief in Schools*. The Westminster Faith Debates.

Connolly, William E. 2005. *Pluralism*. Durham, NC: Duke University Press.

——— 2011. *A World of Becoming*. Durham, NC: Duke University Press.

Copeman, Jacob and Johannes Quack. 2017. 'Godless People and Dead Bodies: Materiality and the Morality of Atheist Materialism'. In *Being Godless: Ethnographies of Atheism and Non-religion*, edited by Ruy Llera Blanes and Galina Oustinova-Stjepanovic, 40–61, Oxford: Berghahn.

Copeman, Jacob and Mascha Schulz. 2022. 'Introduction: Non-Religion, Atheism and Sceptical Publicity'. In *Global Sceptical Publics: From Non-Religious Print Media to 'Digital atheism'*, edited by Jacob Copeman and Mascha Schulz, 1–36, London: UCL Press.

Copson, Andrew. 2015. 'What is Humanism?'. In *The Wiley-Blackwell Handbook of Humanism*, edited by Andrew Copson and A.C. Grayling, 1–33, Chichester: Wiley-Blackwell.

Copson, Andrew, Luke Donnellan and Richard Norman. 2023. *Understanding Humanism*. Abingdon: Routledge.

CoRE (Commission on Religious Education). 2018. *Religion and Worldviews: The Way Forward. A National Plan for RE*. September 2018. https://religiouseducationcouncil.org.uk/rec/wp-content/uploads/2017/05/Final-Report-of-the-Commission-on-RE.pdf (accessed 5 September 2024).

Cragun, Ryan T., Christel Manning and Lori L. Fazzino. Eds. 2017. *Organized Secularism in the United States: New Directions in Research*. Berlin: De Gruyter.

Crockett, Alasdair and David Voas. 2006. 'Generations of Decline: Religious Change in 20th-century Britain'. *Journal for the Scientific Study of Religion* 45(4): 567–84.

Das, Veena. 2015. 'What Does Ordinary Ethics Look Like?' In Michael Lambek, Veena Das, Didier Fassin, and Webb Keane, *Four Lectures on Ethics: Anthropological Perspectives*, 52–126, Chicago: HAU Books.

Davies, Bronwyn. 2014. *Listening to Children: Being and Becoming*. London: Routledge.

Davis, Robert A. 2014. 'Religion, Education and the Post-Secular Child'. *Critical Studies in Education* 55(1): 18–31.

Day, Abby. 2009. 'Believing in Belonging: An Ethnography of Young People's Constructions of Belief', *Culture and Religion* 10(3): 263–78.

——— 2011. *Believing in Belonging: Belief and Social Identity in the Modern World*. Oxford: Oxford University Press.

——— 2022. *Why Baby Boomers Turned from Religion: Shaping Belief and Belonging, 1945–2021*. Oxford: Oxford University Press.

Department for Education. 2014. 'Promoting Fundamental British Values as Part of SMSC in Schools: Departmental Advice for Maintained Schools'. https://assets.publishing.service .gov.uk/government/uploads/system/uploads/attachment_data/file/380595/SMSC _Guidance_Maintained_Schools.pdf (accessed 17 July 2023).

Derrida, Jacques. 1982. *Margins of Philosophy*. Translated by Alan Bass. Brighton: Harvester.

——— 2012. 'Avowing—The Impossible: "Returns", Repentance, and Reconciliation'. In *Living Together: Jacques Derrida's Communities of Violence and Peace*, edited by Elisabeth Weber, 18–41, New York: Fordham University Press.

Dinham, Adam and Robert Jackson. 2012. 'Religion, Welfare and Education'. In *Religion and Change in Modern Britain*, edited by Linda Woodhead and Rebecca Catto, 272–94, London: Routledge.

Edgell, Penny, Douglas Hartmann, Evan Stewart and Joseph Gerteis. 2016. 'Atheist and Other Cultural Outsiders'. *Social Forces* 95(2): 607–38.

Eccles, Janet and Rebecca Catto. 2017. 'The Significance of Sacred Secular Space in the Formation of British Atheist Identities'. In *Materiality and the Study of Religion: The Stuff of the Sacred*, edited by Tim Hutchings and Joanne McKenzie, 151–66, London: Routledge.

Engelke, Matthew. 2014. 'Christianity and the Anthropology of Secular Humanism'. *Current Anthropology* 55. https://doi.org/10.1086/677738.

——— 2015a. '"Good without God": Happiness and Pleasure among the Humanists'. *HAU: Journal of Ethnographic Theory* 5(3): 69–91.

——— 2015b. 'The Coffin Question: Death and Materiality in Humanist Funerals', *Material Religion* 11(1): 26–48.

——— 2017. 'Afterword: On Atheism and Non-Religion'. In *Being Godless: Ethnographies of Atheism and Non-Religion*, edited by Ruy Llera Blanes and Galina Oustina-Stjepanovic, 135–14, New York: Berghahn.

——— 2019. 'Afterword: Getting Hold of the Secular'. In *Secular Bodies, Affects and Emotions: European Configurations*, edited by Monique Scheer, Nadia Fadil, and Birgitte Schepelern Johansen, 199–207, London: Bloomsbury.

Erdozain, Dominic. 2016. *The Soul of Doubt: The Religious Roots of Unbelief from Luther to Marx*. Oxford: Oxford University Press.

Fader, Ayala. 2009. *Mitzvah Girls: Bringing Up the Next Generation of Hasidic Jews in Brooklyn*. Princeton, NJ: Princeton University Press.

Fassin, Didier. 2015. 'Troubled Waters: At the Confluence of Ethics and Politics'. In Michael Lambek, Veena Das, Didier Fassin and Webb Keane, *Four Lectures on Ethics: Anthropological Perspectives*, 175–210, Chicago: HAU Books.

———— 2019. 'Humanism: A Critical Reappraisal'. *Critical Times* 2(1): 29–38.

Ferber, Abby. 2012. 'The Culture of Privilege: Color-Blindness, Postfeminism, and Christonormativity'. *Journal of Social Issues* 68(1): 63–77.

Foucault, Michel. 1994. *The Order of Things: An Archaeology of the Human Sciences*. New York: Vintage Books.

Fricker, Miranda. 2007. *Epistemic Injustice: Power and the Ethics of Knowing*. Oxford: Oxford University Press.

Frost, Jacqui. 2019. 'Certainty, Uncertainty, or Indifference? Examining Variation in the Identity Narratives of Nonreligious Americans'. *American Sociological Review* 84(5): 828–50.

Gärtner, Christel. 2022. 'Secularity as a Point of Reference: Specific Features of a Non-Religious and Secularized Worldview in a Family across Three Generations'. *Religions* 13. https://doi .org/10.3390/rel13060477.

Gärtner, Christel and Linda Hennig. 2022. 'Faith, Authenticity, and Pro-Social Values in the Lives of Young People in Germany'. *Religions* 13. https://doi.org/10.3390/rel13100962.

Gervais, Will. 2014. 'Everything is Permitted? People Intuitively Judge Immorality as Representative of Atheists'. *PLoS ONE* 9(4). https://doi.org/10.1371/journal.pone.0092302.

Giddens, Anthony. 1998. *The Third Way: The Renewal of Social Democracy*. Cambridge: Polity Press.

Gilroy, Paul. 2000. *Against Race: Imagining Political Culture beyond the Color Line*. Cambridge, MA: Belknap Press of Harvard University Press.

———— 2005. *Postcolonial Melancholia*. New York: Columbia University Press.

———— 2015. 'Offshore Humanism'. Antipode RGS-IBG Annual Lecture. https://antipodeonline .org/2015/12/10/paul-gilroy-offshore-humanism/ (accessed 19 June 2023).

———— 2019. The Holberg Prize Acceptance Speech. https://holbergprize.org/en/news /holberg-prize/holberg-laureate-paul-gilroys-acceptance-speech (accessed 18 September 2023).

Guest, Mathew, Sonya Sharma, Kristin Aune, and Rob Warner. 2013. 'Challenging "Belief" and the Evangelical Bias: Student Christianity in English Universities'. *Journal of Contemporary Religion* 28(2): 207–23.

Guhin, Jeffrey. 2021. *Agents of God: Boundaries and Authority in Muslim and Christian Schools*. New York: Oxford University Press.

Hacker, Peter. 2015. 'Forms of Life'. *Nordic Wittgenstein Review*. https://doi.org/10.15845/nwr .v4i0.3320.

Hall, Alexander. 2019. 'A Humanist Blockbuster: Jacob Bronowski and The Ascent of Man'. In *Rethinking History, Science, and Religion: An Exploration of Conflict and the Complexity Principle*, edited by Bernard Lightman, 145–59, Pittsburgh: University of Pittsburgh Press.

Hemming, Peter J. 2009. 'Religion & Spirituality in the Spaces of the Primary School: Social & Political Explorations'. PhD Thesis, University of Leeds.

———— 2015. *Religion in the Primary School: Ethos, Diversity, Citizenship*. Abingdon: Routledge.

Hemming, Peter J. and Nicola Madge. 2017. 'Young People, Non-Religion and Citizenship: Insights from the Youth on Religion Study'. *Young* 26(3): 197–214.

Hemming, Peter J. and Elena Hailwood. 2018. 'Religious Citizenship in Schools in England and Wales'. In *The Palgrave Handbook of Citizenship and Education*, edited by Andrew Peterson,

Garth Stahl, and Hannah Soong, 259–73, Cham: Palgrave Macmillan. https://doi.org/10
.1007/978-3-319-67905-1_44-1.

Henig, David and Anna Strhan. 2022. 'Introduction: The Good Between Social Theory and
Philosophy'. In *Where is the Good in the World? Ethical Life between Social Theory and Philosophy*, edited by David Henig, Anna Strhan and Joel Robbins, 1–32, New York: Berghahn.

Henry, Sean. 2022. 'Dissenting from Heteronormativity: Growing Sideways in Religious Education'. *Journal of Religious Education* 70: 299–309.

Hervieu-Léger, Danièle. 2000. *Religion as a Chain of Memory*. Translated by Simon Lee. Oxford:
Polity Press.

Hickey-Moody, Anna. 2013. 'Deleuze's Children'. *Educational Philosophy and Theory* 45(3):
272–86.

——— 2023. *Faith Stories: Sustaining Meaning and Community in Troubling Times*. Manchester:
Manchester University Press.

Hirschkind, Charles. 2011. 'Is there a Secular Body?' *Cultural Anthropology* 26: 633–47.

Home Office. 2020. Hate Crime, England and Wales 2019/20.
https://www.gov.uk/government/statistics/hate-crime-england-and-wales-2019-to-2020/hate
-crime-england-and-wales-2019-to-2020 (accessed 18 September 2023).

Humanists International. 2022. 'Amsterdam Declaration 2022'. https://humanists.international
/what-is-humanism/the-amsterdam-declaration/ (accessed 26 September 2023).

Hutchings, Tim, Céline Benoit and Rachael Shillitoe. 2022. 'Religion and Worldviews: The Way
Forward?' *Journal of the British Association for the Study of Religion* 23(1): 8–28.

Inglehart, Ronald E. 2021. *Religion's Sudden Decline: What's Causing it, and What Comes Next?*
New York: Oxford University Press.

Ingold, Tim. 2018. 'One World Anthropology'. *HAU Journal of Ethnographic Theory* 8(1/2):
158–71.

Ipsos MORI. 2018. 'A Review of Survey Research on Muslims in Britain'. London: Ipsos MORI
Social Research Institute.

Irvine, Richard D. G., Barbara Bodenhorn, Elsa Lee, and D. Amarbayasgalan. 2019. 'Learning to
See Climate Change: Children's Perceptions of Environmental Transformation in Mongolia,
Arctic Alaska, and the United Kingdom'. *Current Anthropology* 60(6). https://doi.org/10
.1086/706606.

James, David, Diane Reay, Gill Crozier, Phoebe Beedell, Sumi Hollingworth, Fiona Jamieson
and Katya Williams. 2010. 'Neoliberal Policy and the Meaning of Counterintuitive Middle-
Class School Choices'. *Current Sociology* 58(4): 623–41.

Jones, Lucy. 2023. *Matrescence: On the Metamorphosis of Pregnancy, Childbirth and Motherhood*.
London: Penguin.

Josephson-Storm, Jason A. 2017. *The Myth of Disenchantment: Magic, Modernity, and the Birth of
the Human Sciences*. Chicago: University of Chicago Press.

Katz, Roberta, Sarah Ogilvie, Jane Shaw and Linda Woodhead. 2021. *Gen Z, Explained: The Art
of Living in a Digital Age*. Chicago: University of Chicago Press.

Kasselstrand, Isabella, Phil Zuckerman and Ryan T. Cragun. 2023. *Beyond Doubt: The Secularization of Society*. New York: New York University Press.

Keane, Webb. 2007. *Christian Moderns: Freedom and Fetish in the Mission Encounter*. Berkeley:
University of California Press.

———— 2010. 'Minds, Surfaces, and Reasons in the Anthropology of Ethics'. In *Ordinary Ethics: Anthropology, Language, and Action*, edited by Michael Lambek, 64–83, New York: Fordham University Press.

———— 2013. 'Secularism as a Moral Narrative of Modernity', *Transit: Europäische Revue* 43: 159–70.

Kitching, Karl. 2020. *Childhood, Religion and School Injustice*. Cork: Cork University Press.

Klingenberg, Maria and Sofia Sjö. 2019. 'Theorizing Religious Socialization: A Critical Assessment'. *Religion* 49: 163–78.

Lambek, Michael. Ed. 2010. *Ordinary Ethics: Anthropology, Language, and Action*. New York: Fordham University Press.

Lambek, Michael. 2015a. 'Living As If It Mattered'. In Michael Lambek, Veena Das, Didier Fassin, and Webb Keane, *Four Lectures on Ethics: Anthropological Perspectives*, 5–51, Chicago: HAU Books.

———— 2015b. *The Ethical Condition: Essays on Action, Person and Value*. Chicago: University of Chicago Press.

Lamont, Michèle. 1992. *Money, Morals, and Manners: The Culture of the French and the American Upper-Middle Class*. Chicago: University of Chicago Press.

Lanman, Jonathan A. and Michael D. Buhrmester. 2017. 'Religious Actions Speak Louder Than Words: Exposure To Credibility-Enhancing Displays Predicts Theism'. *Religion, Brain & Behavior* 7(1): 3–16.

Latour, Bruno. 1993. *We Have Never Been Modern*. Translated by Catherine Porter. Cambridge, MA: Harvard University Press.

———— 2021. *After Lockdown: A Metamorphosis*. Translated by Julie Rose. Cambridge: Polity Press.

Laugier, Sandra. 2016. 'Care, the Ordinary, Forms of Life'. *Iride* 29(77): 109–21.

———— 2021. 'Concepts of the Ordinary'. In *Living with Concepts: Anthropology in the Grip of Reality*, edited by Andrew Brandel and Marco Motta, 29–49, New York: Fordham University Press.

Lauwers, A. Sophie. 2022. 'Religion, Secularity, Culture? Investigating Christian Privilege in Western Europe' *Ethnicities*. https://doi.org/10.1177/14687968221106185.

LeDrew, Stephen. 2015. *The Evolution of Atheism: The Politics of a Modern Movement*. New York: Oxford University Press.

Lee, Lois. 2015. *Recognizing the Non-Religious: Reimagining the Secular*. Oxford: Oxford University Press.

———— 2019a. 'Observing the Atheist at Worship: Ways of Seeing the Secular Body'. In *Secular Bodies, Affects and Emotions: European Configurations*, edited by Monique Scheer, Nadia Fadil, and Birgitte Schepelern Johansen, 43–59, London: Bloomsbury.

———— 2019b. 'Feeling Rational: Affinity and Affinity Narratives in British Science–Non-Religion Relations'. In *Science, Belief and Society: International Perspectives on Religion, Non-Religion and the Public Understanding of Science,* edited by Stephen Howard Jones, Rebecca Catto and Tom Kaden, 173–95, Bristol: Bristol University Press.

Lee, Lois, Stephen Bullivant, Miguel Farias and Jonathan Lanman. 2017. 'Understanding Unbelief: Background'. https://research.kent.ac.uk/understandingunbelief/about/background/ (accessed 23 October 2023).

Lee, Lois, Anna Strhan and Rachael Shillitoe. 2023. 'Christmas as Humanist Rite? Ritual Practice and Identity in New Existential Movements'. Paper presented at the British Sociological Association Sociology of Religion Study Group Annual Conference, July 2023, University of Bristol.

Lenz Taguchi, Hillevi. 2010. *Going Beyond the Theory/Practice Divide in Early Childhood Education: Introducing an Intra-Active Pedagogy*. London: Routledge.

Lévi-Strauss, Claude. 1966. *The Savage Mind*. London: Weidenfeld & Nicolson.

Levine, George. Ed. 2011. *The Joy of Secularism: 11 Essays for How We Live Now*. Princeton, NJ: Princeton University Press.

Long, Robert and Shadi Danechi. 2019. Faith Schools in England: FAQs. House of Commons Library Briefing Paper. https://commonslibrary.parliament.uk/research-briefings/sn06972/ (accessed 17 May 2023).

Long, Robert, Philip Loft and Shadi Danechi. 2019. Religious Education in Schools (England). House of Commons Library Briefing Paper. https://researchbriefings.files.parliament.uk /documents/CBP-7167/CBP-7167.pdf (accessed 5 September 2024).

McDannell, Colleen. 1995. *Material Christianity: Religion and Popular Culture in America*. New Haven: Yale University Press.

McGowan, Dale. Ed. 2007. *Parenting Beyond Belief: On Raising Ethical, Caring Kids without Religion*. New York: Amacom.

McGuire, Meredith. 2002. 'New–Old Directions in the Social Scientific Study of Religion: Ethnography, Phenomenology, and the Human Body'. In *Personal Knowledge and Beyond: Reshaping the Ethnography of Religion*, edited by James V. Spickard, Shawn Landres, and Meredith McGuire, 195–211, New York: New York University Press.

McKay, Robert. 2018. 'A Vegan Form of Life'. In *Thinking Veganism in Literature and Culture*, edited by E. Quinn and B. Westwood, 249–71, Basingstoke, Palgrave.

Madge, Nicola, Peter J. Hemming and Kevin Stenson. 2014. *Youth on Religion: The Development, Negotiation and Impact of Faith and Non-Faith Identity*. Hove: Routledge.

Mahmood, Saba. 2018. 'Humanism'. *HAU: Journal of Ethnographic Theory* 8: 1–5.

Malkki, Liisa H. 2015. *The Need to Help: The Domestic Arts of International Humanitarianism*. Durham, NC: Duke University Press.

Malone, Joanna. 2021. 'Lived Non-Belief: Non-Religion, Religion and Relationality in Older Adults' Worldviews and Identities'. PhD Thesis, University of Kent, Canterbury.

Malone, Joanna, Anna Strhan, Peter Hemming and Sarah Neal. 2024. 'Institutionalising Nonreligion? Locating (Non)religion in a Welsh Primary School'. Paper presented at the Association for the Sociology of Religion Annual Meeting, August 2024, Montreal.

Manning, Christel. 2015. *Losing Our Religion: How Unaffiliated Parents are Raising their Children*. New York: New York University Press.

Mauss, Marcel. 2007. *The Manual of Ethnography*. Oxford: Berghahn.

Meyer, Birgit. 2012. 'Religious Sensations: Media, Aesthetics, and the Study of Contemporary Religion'. In *Religion, Media and Culture: A Reader*, edited by Gordon Lynch, Jolyon Mitchell and Anna Strhan, 159–70, Abingdon: Routledge.

Mills, Sarah. 2021. *Mapping the Moral Geographies of Education: Character, Citizenship and Values*. London: Routledge.

Mocan, Naci and Luiza Pogorelova. 2014. 'Compulsory Schooling Laws and Formation of Beliefs: Education, Religion and Superstition'. *Journal of Economic Behavior & Organization* 142: 509–39.

Müller, Olaf and Chiara Porada. 2022. 'Towards a Society of Stable Nones: Lifelong Non-Demoninationalism as the Prevailing Pattern in East Germany'. *Religions* 13. https://doi.org/10.3390/rel13111024

Myers, Scott M. 1996. 'An Interactive Model of Religious Inheritance: The Importance of Family Context'. *American Sociological Review* 61(5): 858–66.

Neal, Sarah, Katy Bennett, Allan Cochrane and Giles Mohan. 2017. *The Lived Experience of Multiculture: The New Social and Spatial Relations of Diversity*. Abingdon: Routledge.

Neal, Sarah, Anna Strhan, Joanna Malone and Peter Hemming. 2023. 'Conviviality and Children's Citizenship in Superdiverse, Multifaith Primary School Worlds'. Paper presented at the Conviviality in Motion Conference, June 2023, University of Basel.

Needham, Rodney. 1972. *Belief, Language and Experience*. Chicago: University of Chicago Press.

Nynäs, Peter, Ariela Keysar, Janne Kontala, Ben-Willie Kwaku Golo, Mika T. Lassander, Marah Shterin, Sofia Sjö and Paul Stenner. Eds. 2022. *The Diversity of Worldviews among Young Adults: Contemporary (Non)Religiosity Through The Lens of an International Mixed Method Study*. Cham: Brill.

Oliphant, Elayne. 2021. *The Privilege of Being Banal: Art, Secularism, and Catholicism in Paris*. Chicago: University of Chicago Press.

Orsi, Robert A. 2005. *Between Heaven and Earth: The Religious Worlds People Make and the Scholars Who Study Them*. Princeton, NJ: Princeton University Press.

Oswell, David. 2013. *The Agency of Children: From Family to Global Human Rights*. Cambridge: Cambridge University Press.

Partridge, Christopher. 2005. *The Re-Enchantment of the West, Vol. II: Alternative Spiritualities, Sacralization, Popular Culture, and Occulture*. London: T&T Clark.

Pearce, Lisa D. and Melinda Lundquist Denton. 2011. *A Faith of their Own: Stability and Change in the Religiosity of America's Adolescents*. New York: Oxford University Press.

Petts, Richard. 2009. 'Trajectories of Religious Participation from Adolescence to Young Adulthood'. *Journal for the Scientific Study of Religion* 48: 552–71.

Pimlott-Wilson, Helena and Janine Coates. 2019. 'Rethinking Learning? Challenging and Accommodating Neoliberal Educational Agenda in the Integration of Forest School into Mainstream Educational Settings'. *The Geographical Journal* 185: 268–78.

Pinn, Anthony B. 2015. *Humanism: Essays on Race, Religion, and Cultural Production*. London: Bloomsbury.

Prout, Alan and Allison James. 1997. 'A New Paradigm for the Sociology of Childhood'. In *Constructing and Reconstructing Childhood: Contemporary Issues in the Sociological Study of Childhood*, 2nd edn, edited by Allison James and Alan Prout, 7–33, London: Falmer.

Pugh, Allison J. 2009. *Longing and Belonging: Parents, Children, and Consumer Culture*. Berkeley: University of California Press.

Qvortrup, Jens, Marjatta Bardy, Giovanni Sgritta, and Helmut Wintersberger. Eds. 1994. *Childhood Matters*. Aldershot: Avebury Press.

Rejowska, Agata. 2021. 'Humanist Weddings in Poland: The Various Motivations of Couples'. *Sociology of Religion* 82(3): 281–304.

Ridgely Bales, Susan. 2005. *When I was a Child: Children's Interpretations of First Communion*. Chapel Hill, NC: University of North Carolina Press.

Ridgely, Susan B. 2017. *Practicing What the Doctor Preached: At Home with Focus on the Family*. New York: Oxford University Press.

Robbins, Joel. 2007. 'Continuity Thinking and the Problem of Christian Culture: Belief, Time and the Anthropology of Christianity'. *Current Anthropology* 48(1): 5–38.

Rose, Gillian. 1997. *Love's Work*. London: Vintage.

Ruel, Malcolm. 1997. *Belief, Ritual and the Securing of Life*. Leiden: Brill.

Ryrie, Alec. 2019. *Unbelievers: An Emotional History of Doubt*. London: William Collins.

Said, Edward. 2004. *Humanism and Democratic Criticism*. New York: Columbia University Press.

Savage, Sara, Sylvia Collins-Mayo, Bob Mayo, with Graham Cray. 2006. *Making Sense of Generation Y: The World View of 15- to 25-Year-Olds*. London: Church House Publishing.

Schaefer, Donovan O. 2022. *Wild Experiment: Feeling Science and Secularism after Darwin*. Durham, NC: Duke University Press.

Scheer, Monique, Nadia Fadil, and Birgitte Schepelern Johansen. 2019. *Secular Bodies, Affects and Emotions: European Configurations*. London: Bloomsbury.

Schielke, Samuli. 2009. 'Ambivalent Commitments: Troubles of Morality, Religiosity and Aspiration among Young Egyptians'. *Journal of Religion in Africa* 39: 158–85.

———— 2012. 'Being a Nonbeliever in a Time of Islamic Revival: Trajectories of Doubt and Certainty in Contemporary Egypt'. *International Journal of Middle East Studies* 44(2): 301–20.

Schofield Clark, Lynn. 2003. *From Angels to Aliens: Teenagers, the Media, and the Supernatural*. Oxford: Oxford University Press.

Schutz, Alfred. 1962. *The Problem of Social Reality*, edited by Maurice Natanson. The Hague: Nijhoff.

Scourfield, Jonathan, Chris Taylor, Graham Moore, and Sophie Gilliat-Ray. 2012. 'The Intergenerational Transmission of Islam in England and Wales: Evidence from the Citizenship Survey'. *Sociology* 46(1): 91–108.

Scourfield, Jonathan, Sophie Gilliat-Ray, Asma Khan, and Sameh Otri. 2013. *Muslim Childhood: Religious Nurture in a European Context*. Oxford: Oxford University Press.

Seidler, Victor Jeleniewski. 2022. *Ethical Humans: Life, Love, Labour, Learning and Loss*. London: Routledge.

Seligman, Adam B. Ed. 2014. *Religious Education and the Challenge of Pluralism*. New York: Oxford University Press.

Seligman, Adam B. and Robert P. Weller. 2012. *Rethinking Pluralism: Ritual, Experience, Ambiguity*. New York: Oxford University Press.

Shillitoe, Rachael. 2023. *Negotiating Religion and Non-Religion in Childhood: Experiences of Worship in School*. Basingstoke: Palgrave Macmillan.

Shillitoe, Rachael and Anna Strhan. 2020. '"Just Leave it Blank": Non-Religious Children and their Negotiation of Prayer in School.' *Religion* 50(4): 615–35.

Singh, Jasjit. 2012. 'Keeping the Faith: Reflections on Religious Nurture Among Young British Sikhs', *Journal of Beliefs & Values* 33(3): 369–83.

Singleton, Andrew, Anna Halafoff, Mary Lou Rasmusen and Gary Bouma. 2021. *Freedoms, Faiths, and Futures*. London: Bloomsbury.

Smith, Christian. 2003. 'Introduction: Rethinking the Secularization of American Public Life'. In *The Secular Revolution: Power, Interests and Conflict in the Secularization of American Public Life*, edited by Christian Smith, 1–96, Berkeley: University of California Press.

Smith, Christian and Melinda L. Denton. 2005. *Soul Searching: The Religious and Spiritual Lives of American Teenagers*. New York: Oxford University Press.

Smith, Christian, Bridget Ritz and Michael Rotolo. 2020. *Religious Parenting: Transmitting Faith and Values in Contemporary America*. Princeton, NJ: Princeton University Press.

Smith, Christian and Amy Adamczyk. 2021. *Handing Down the Faith: How Parents Pass Their Religion on to the Next Generation*. New York: Oxford University Press.

Smith, Jesse. 2010. 'Becoming an Atheist in America: Constructing Identity and Meaning from the Rejection of Theism'. *Sociology of Religion* 72: 1–23.

Smith, Jesse and Ryan Cragun. 2019. 'Mapping Religion's Other: A Review of the Study of Nonreligion and Secularity'. *Journal for the Scientific Study of Religion*. https://doi.org/10.1111/jssr.12597.

Smith, Zadie. 2018. *Feel Free: Essays*. London: Penguin.

Spyrou, Spyros, Rachel Rosen, and Daniel Thomas Cook. 2019. 'Introduction: Reimagining Childhood Studies: Connectivities . . . Relationalites . . . Linkages . . .'. In *Reimagining Childhood Studies*, edited by Spyros Spyrou, Rachel Rosen, and Daniel Thomas Cook, 1–20, London: Bloomsbury.

Stolz, Jörg. 2009. 'Explaining Religiosity: Towards a Unified Theoretical Model'. *British Journal of Sociology* 60(2): 345–76.

——— 2020. 'Secularization Theories in the Twenty-First Century: Ideas, Evidence, and Problems'. *Social Compass* 67(2): 282–308.

Stolz, Jörg, Judith Könemann, Mallory Schneuwly Purdie, Thomas Englberger, and Michael Krüggeler. 2016. *(Un)Believing in Modern Society: Religion, Spirituality, and Religious–Secular Competition*. Abingdon: Routledge.

Stolz, Jörg, Oliver Lipps, David Voas and Jean-Philippe Antonietti. 2023. 'Can We Explain the Generation Gap in Churchgoing?'. Lives: Swiss Centre of Expertise in Life Course Research. https://www.centre-lives.ch/sites/default/files/inline-files/Stolz_et_al_generation_gap.pdf (accessed 26 October 2023).

Strhan, Anna. 2010. 'A Religious Education Otherwise? An Examination and Proposed Interruption of Current British Practice'. *Journal of Philosophy of Education* 44(1): 23–44.

——— 2012. *Levinas, Subjectivity, Education: Towards an Ethics of Radical Responsibility*. Chichester: Wiley-Blackwell.

——— 2013. 'Practising the Space Between: Embodying Belief as an Evangelical Anglican Student'. *Journal of Contemporary Religion* 28(2): 225–39.

——— 2015. *Aliens and Strangers? The Struggle for Coherence in the Everyday Lives of Evangelicals*. Oxford: Oxford University Press.

——— 2017. '"I Want There to be no Glass Ceiling": Evangelicals' Engagements with Class, Education, and Urban Childhoods'. *Sociological Research Online*. https://doi.org/10.5153/sro.4259.

——— 2019. *The Figure of the Child in Contemporary Evangelicalism*. Oxford: Oxford University Press.

Strhan, Anna, Stephen G. Parker, and Susan B. Ridgely. 2017. Eds. *The Bloomsbury Reader in Religion and Childhood*. London: Bloomsbury.

Strhan, Anna and Rachael Shillitoe. 2019. 'The Stickiness of Non-Religion? Intergenerational Transmission and the Formation of Non-Religious Identities in Childhood'. *Sociology* 53(6): 1094–110.

Strhan, Anna and Rachael Shillitoe. 2022. 'The Experience of Non-Religious Children in Religious Education'. *Journal of Religious Education* 70: 261–72.

Strhan, Anna, Joanna Malone, Peter Hemming and Sarah Neal. 2023. 'Mapping the Contours of Citizenship, Religion and Education in "Postsecular" Britain'. Paper presented at the American Sociological Association Annual Meeting, August 2023, Philadelphia.

Strhan, Anna, Lois Lee and Rachael Shillitoe. 2024. 'Becoming Humanist: Worldview Formation and the Emergence of Atheist Britain'. *Sociology of Religion*. https://doi.org/10.1093/socrel/srad050.

Taves, Ann. 2019. 'From Religious Studies to Worldview Studies'. *Religion*. https://doi.org/10.1080/0048721X.2019.1681124.

Taylor, Charles. 1989. *Sources of the Self: The Making of Modern Identity*. Cambridge: Cambridge University Press.

———— 1991. *The Ethics of Authenticity*. Cambridge, MA: Harvard University Press.

———— 2007. *A Secular Age*. Cambridge, MA: Harvard University Press.

———— 2011. 'Western Secularity'. In *Rethinking Secularism*, edited by Craig Calhoun, Mark Juergensmeyer, and Jonathan Van Antwerpen, 31–53. New York: Oxford University Press.

Tervo-Niemelä, Kati. 2021. 'Religious Upbringing and Other Religious Influences Among Young Adults and Changes in Faith in the Transition to Adulthood: a 10-Year Longitudinal Study of Young People in Finland'. *British Journal of Religious Education* 43(4): 443–57.

Thiessen, Joel and Sarah Wilkins-Laflamme. 2017. 'Becoming a Religious None: Irreligious Socialization and Disaffiliation'. *Journal for the Scientific Study of Religion* 56(1): 64–82.

———— 2020. *None of the Above: Nonreligious Identity in the US and Canada*. New York: New York University Press.

Thurfjell, David, Cecilie Rubow, Atko Remmel, and Henrik Ohlsson. 2019. 'The Relocation of Transcendence: Using Schutz to Conceptualize the Nature Experiences of Secular People'. *Nature and Culture* 14(2): 190–214.

Tomkins, Silvan. 1995. *Shame and Its Sisters: A Silvan Tomkins Reader*, edited by Eve Kosofsky Sedgwick and Adam Frank. Durham, NC: Duke University Press.

Toren, Christina. 1993. 'Making History: The Significance of Childhood Cognition for a Comparative Anthropology of Mind'. *Man* 28(3): 461–78.

Turpin, Hugh. 2022. *Unholy Catholic Ireland: Religious Hypocrisy, Secular Morality, and Irish Irreligion*. Stanford, CA: Stanford University Press.

van Mulukom, Valerie, Hugh Turpin, Roosa Haimila, Benjamin Grant Purzycki, Theiss Bendixen, Eva Kundtová Klocová, Dan Řezníček, Thomas J. Coleman III, Kenan Sevinç, Everton Maraldi, Uffe Schjoedt, Bastiaan T. Rutjens, and Miguel Farias. 2023. 'What do Nonreligious Nonbelievers Believe In? Secular Worldviews Around the World'. *Psychology of Religion and Spirituality* 15(1): 143–56.

Vincent, Carol. 2019. *Tea and the Queen? Fundamental British Values, Schools, and Citizenship*. Bristol: Policy Press.

Vincett, Giselle and Sylvia Collins-Mayo. 2010. '(Dis)engagements with Christianity among Young People in England and Scotland'. In *Annual Review of the Sociology of Religion I: Young and Religion*, edited by Giuseppe Gordon, 219–49, Leiden: Brill.

Voas, David. 2007. 'The Continuing Secular Transition'. In *The Role of Religion in Modern Societies*, edited by Detlef Pollack and Daniel Olson, 25–48, New York: Routledge.

Voas, David and Siobhan McAndrew. 2012. 'Three Puzzles of Non-Religion in Britain'. *Journal of Contemporary Religion* 27(1): 29–48.

Voas, David and Ingrid Storm. 2012. 'The Intergenerational Transmission of Churchgoing in England and Australia'. *Review of Religious Research* 53(4): 377–95.

Voas, David and Steve Bruce. 2019. 'Religion: Identity, Behaviour and Belief over Two Decades'. In *British Social Attitudes: The 36th Report*, edited by John Curtice, Elizabeth Clery, Jane Perry, Miranda Phillips, and Nilufer Rahim, 17–44, London: The National Centre for Social Research.

Watts, Galen. 2022. *The Spiritual Turn: The Religion of the Heart and the Making of Romantic Liberal Modernity*. Oxford: Oxford University Press.

Wentzer, Thomas Schwarz and Cheryl Mattingly. 2018. 'Toward a New Humanism: An Approach from Philosophical Anthropology'. *HAU: Journal of Ethnographic Theory* 8: 144–57.

Wigger, J. Bradley. 2019. *Invisible Companions: Encounters with Imaginary Friends, Gods, Ancestors, and Angels*. Stanford, CA: Stanford University Press.

Williams, Raymond. 1961. *The Long Revolution*. London: Chatto & Windus.

——— 1983. *Culture and Society: 1780–1950*. New York: Columbia University Press.

Wise, Amanda and Greg Noble. 2016. 'Convivialities: An Orientation'. *Journal of Intercultural Studies* 5: 423–31.

Woodhead, Linda. 2010. 'Epilogue'. In *Religion and Youth*, edited by Sylvia Collins-Mayo and Ben Dandelion, 239–41, Aldershot: Ashgate.

——— 2016. 'The Rise of "No Religion" in Britain: The Emergence of a New Cultural Majority'. *Journal of the British Academy* 4: 245–61.

——— 2017. 'The Rise of "No Religion": Towards an Explanation'. *Sociology of Religion* 78(3): 247–62.

Wuthnow, Robert. 2007. *After the Baby Boomers: How Twenty- and Thirty-Somethings Are Shaping the Future of American Religion*. Princeton, NJ: Princeton University Press.

Wynter, Sylvia. 1995. 'The Pope Must Have Been Drunk, the King of Castile a Madman: Culture as Actuality, and the Caribbean Rethinking Modernity'. In *The Reordering of Culture: Latin America, the Caribbean and Canada in the Hood*, edited by Alvina Ruprecht and Cecilia Taiana, 17–41, Ottawa: Carleton University Press.

YouGov. 2014. 'YouGov / The Sun Survey Results'. http://cdn.yougov.com/cumulus_uploads /document/otjwvdct9z/SunResults_141027_Ghosts-Website.pdf (accessed 22 February 2023).

Zuckerman, Phil. 2008. *Society without God: What the Least Religious Nations can Tell us about Contentment*. New York: New York University Press.

——— 2011. *Faith No More: Why People Reject Religion*. New York: Oxford University Press.

——— 2014. *Living the Secular Life: New Answers to Old Questions*. New York: Penguin.

——— 2019. *What It Means to Be Moral: Why Religion Is Not Necessary for Living an Ethical Life*. New York: Catapult.

Zuckerman, Phil, Luke W. Galen, and Frank L. Pasquale. 2016. *The Nonreligious: Understanding Secular People and Societies*. New York: Oxford University Press.

INDEX

A NOTE ON THE TYPE

This book has been composed in Arno, an Old-style serif typeface in the
classic Venetian tradition, designed by Robert Slimbach at Adobe.

GPSR Authorized Representative: Easy Access System Europe - Mustamäe tee 50, 10621 Tallinn, Estonia, gpsr.requests@easproject.com